Talking with Television

FEMINIST STUDIES AND MEDIA CULTURE

Series Editor
Andrea Press, University of Illinois at
Urbana-Champaign

Talking with Television

Women, Talk Shows,
and Modern Self-Reflexivity

HELEN WOOD

University of Illinois Press
URBANA AND CHICAGO

1 2 3 4 5 C P 5 4 3 2 1
∞ This book is printed on acid-free paper.

Library of Congress Cataloging-in-Publication Data
Wood, Helen
Talking with television : women, talk shows,
and modern self-reflexivity / Helen Wood.
p.   cm. — (Feminist studies and media culture)
Includes bibliographical references and index.
ISBN 978-0-252-03391-9 (cloth : alk. paper)
ISBN 978-0-252-07602-2 (pbk. : alk. paper)
1. Television talk shows—Great Britain.
2. Television and women.
I. Title.
PN1992.8.T3W66   2008
791.45'60941—dc22   2008027214

For my parents,
Albert and Pauline Wood

Contents

Acknowledgments

This project has involved a long journey and there are numerous people who have guided it and me along the way. I am indebted to Andrew Tolson and Shaun Moores, who gave it life, and thank you Andrew for keeping me on track and patiently leading the way, although of course I own all the limitations. Thanks to those who helped me work and play at Queen Margaret University College, Edinburgh: Debra Bowyer, Richard Butt, Lindsay Dalziel, Kerry Kirk, Anna Malina, Julie Ramage, and Michael Stewart. I owe a great deal to colleagues at the University of Wolverhampton who supported me in writing many of these ideas as a PhD thesis, particularly Pauline Anderson and Karen Boyle, from whose sharpness and wit I hope I have greatly benefited. More recently, thanks to those at the University of Manchester who have helped me to tread the paths of social theory with a good drink, particularly Lisa Adkins, Bridget Byrne, and Nick Thoburn. Thanks to the Ross Priory Broadcast Talk group for their particular blend of media and linguistic analysis that informs this book, and the members of the Midlands Television Research Group, who have offered me a fruitful intellectual environment and let me rehearse these findings. Thank you to Marie Gillespie for invaluable support and for reading the introduction. Thanks to my editor Andrea Press for enabling the book to finally see the light of day. Thanks to Charlotte Brunsdon for seeing merit in the work in the first place and to Ann Gray for being such a wise mentor since my earliest attachments to cultural studies. Thank you to Bev Skeggs for helping me to see where this work might lead and for livening up my thinking and my conversations no end. I must also thank my dear friends Lisa Taylor and Paul Willis, who have read drafts, forced me to be clear, and always kept faith in me and my work. To Rachel

Moseley and Helen Wheatley, who have resuscitated me intellectually and emotionally time and again, I cannot begin to thank them enough.

I owe a great deal to my mother Pauline for everything she did in helping me to arrange the practicalities of the research and to my wonderful family for their unwavering support: Albert, Jane, Robert, Matthew, Sharon, Luke, Emma, Norma, and Sheila. Thank you to Jodie and Phill for giving me a home where I could edit the book. To my fabulous friends for patience, more patience, and humor: Emma, Flis, Julie, Nik, Vanessa. Of course, I owe Phil for constantly showing me that there is so much more to life!

Two of the chapters have appeared elsewhere in earlier forms and I am grateful to the original publishers for giving permission to reprint them here.

Chapter 6 was first published as: "The Mediated Conversational Floor: An Interactive Approach to Reception Analysis," *Media, Culture & Society* 29 (1): 75–103. Sage Publications.

Chapter 7 was first published as: "Texting the Subject: Women, Television, and Modern Subjectivity," *Communication Review* 8 (2): 115–35. Taylor and Francis, http://www.informaworld.com.

Transcription Conventions

Adapted from conventions used in Scannell (1991).

( )	If empty, indicated indecipherable utterance; otherwise best guess at what was said
[Bold]	Verbal description of non-verbal behavior
(2.0)	Latency between or within utterances in seconds
word-	Word is cut off abruptly
(.)	Brief untimed pause within or between utterances
=	Latching together separate parts of a continuous utterance or indicating that B's utterance follows A's with no gaps or overlap
[	Point at which overlap occurs between speakers
word	Stress added to word or syllable
WORD	Extreme stress
Co::lons	Stretching of vowel or consonant sound.
↑	Rising intonation
↓	Falling intonation
'	Brief pause at a syntactically relevant point in the utterance
.hh	Audible inhalation
hh	Audible exhalation
heh	Laugh token
!	Excited intonation

Talking with Television

Introduction

This book is about television and talk. It is concerned with talk *about* television and involves drawing upon a number of popular and academic discussions dealing with issues to do with contemporary television forms, talk
shows and daytime magazine programs, and their associated cultural values.
More specifically the book addresses questions to do with talk *on* television,
not least those concerned with the gender politics of "talking personally" on
daytime talk programs that have been associated with feminine modes of
talk. More unusually, this book sheds light on the phenomenon of talk *with*
television, making visible the commonly rehearsed, if often unacknowledged,
practice of talking back to the television set.

Just as extended television viewing is often derided with negative images
of the couch potato, talking back to television might be associated with social
pathology. Whereas it might seem acceptable for the football fan to shout
instructions to their team as though they are the coach, it is seen as somehow
pathetic for an individual to interact verbally and one way with television
personalities (perhaps they do not have any "real" friends!). These evaluations
lie firmly within the conventional terrain of the classification and assessment
of gendered forms of talk, with their typical divisions between masculine
public discourses such as those pertaining to sports, for instance, and the
more "trivial" and feminine private discourses of personal relationships.
But it is surely time to move beyond these simple divisions and scenarios.
The television set is the centerpiece of most living-room geographies and
is at the heart of domestic social action. Therefore it seems rather obvious
that television should be bound up with our everyday interactions. Indeed,
so acknowledged within the popular imagination and lived practice is the

possibility of pseudo-interaction with television that an American company marketed Styrofoam "TV Bricks" to be lobbed safely at the media figures that enrage us (Caughie, 1986). Yet, despite this commonsense understanding that television is part of our interactive worlds, there has been hardly any attempt to account for how that is relevant to the broader aim within media and cultural studies of understanding the role of media in everyday life.

Therefore this book also has broader implications for the analysis of mediated relationships and mediated identities as they are established through both "old" and "new" media. Empirically, it is about how the television world and the social world of audience members collide in the living room, but it is concerned with how mediated relationships produce a "doubling" of place (Scannell, 1996), asking questions about how the two realms are stitched together and how those links are sustained across the ubiquitous reach and kaleidoscopic forms of broadcasting. Talk is one route through which we might begin to unpick some of those connections, since much of television is basically "talk TV": continuity announcing, news, talk shows, lifestyle programs, game shows, and so on. The staples of broadcasting have sought a voice that is commensurate with the daily chords, routines, and rhythms of the household (Matheson, 1933). However, all of this is not to return us to essentially non-social ideas about how media talk might offer compensation for those with some human deficiency. It is to take seriously the possibility of the formation of mediated social relationships in the case of a medium like television that has traditionally been analyzed as the one-way mode of communication par excellence. In that sense the book begs questions about received assumptions made about television as essentially a "transmission" medium, against theories posed about new media as more interactive, networked, and dialogic. I draw attention to the ways in which theoretical shifts in media studies have posed this apparent distinction, while my empirical work begins to challenge that hypothesis by weighing mediated communication within its broader social and political communicative frame. As Roger Silverstone reminds us, "Any entry into electronic space has always presupposed and required physical space as both its beginning and its end point" (1999:11). This is an important point, and while I am primarily concerned here with the nexus between television talk and everyday talk, there are broader repercussions for grasping the complex set of relations in which *all* mediated communication, including the so-called old as well as the new, take place within the raw as well as the rule-governed orders of daily interaction and exchange. While face-to-face communication has been traditionally observed as the primary mode of communication against which the mass media cannot compare, this book contributes to the understanding of the redefinition of social interaction as it is increasingly mediated.

That television talks to audiences is obvious, but we have rarely applied the same rigor to the analysis of mediated talk that linguists have to face-to-face talk. Yet it is clear that there is much at stake in the analysis of talk. Talk *enacts* power relationships between speakers, as well as having a central role in the distribution of political meanings and the establishing of cultural values. In terms of gender politics, feminist authors have described how women have often occupied the role of servicer in interaction, doing the "shitwork" involved in maintaining conversations (Fishman, 1980). And when feminine styles of talk are dismissed as "tittle-tattle" and thus inconsequential, or "bitchy" and therefore dangerous, these evaluations are revealing of the relationship between talk and gender inequality more generally. What is also notable is that many of the arguments about gender and talk, and their relationship to the hierarchical demarcation of public and private realms, resonate with critiques of television talk shows and arguments that trash television preys on private fears and personal insecurities. In this book I want to suggest that fruitful lines of inquiry are made available by drawing out the parallels between mediated and non-mediated communication and make a wider plea to locate the debates about television discourse within the broader politics of communication per se, offering an alternative route to the analysis of mediated identity that may also have a broader purchase on the analysis of other types of media.

Talking with Television, therefore, takes a multi-disciplinary perspective, drawing on resources from socio-linguistics, conversation analysis, pragmatics, ethnomethodology, and social theory, at the same time as taking its lead from the cultural studies tradition of audience research influenced by feminist researchers accounting for the pleasures involved in women's consumption practices of popular culture (Hobson, 1982; Radway, 1984; Ang, 1985; Press, 1991; Gray, 1992; Moseley, 2002, etc.). When Radway took a step outwards from a literature department into using the tools of anthropology, she described how her particular aggregate of methods began to illuminate the complexity of the Smithton women's reading practices of romance literature. Here too, I want to suggest that a particular combination of cultural studies, social theory, and linguistics might give fresh inflection to understanding the prism of relations between television and audiences. In part returning to simple observations about television as a cultural form might do this. The uniqueness of the medium itself is characterized by its relationship to immediacy and intimacy, created through its special claim to liveness: the ability to represent the world "out there" as though it is "here and now" (Williams, 1974; Ellis, 1982). Television is therefore a dynamic medium that enters into the space of the home, while the home itself of course has its own "here and now." This is a simple set of orientations, obvious to television studies more broadly, but that rarely comes into play in audience research. Therefore, this book considers the dynamic entry of television talk into the socio-communicative sphere of everyday life, but in doing so it demands that we return to some of the boundaries of communications research and to fundamental concerns in media studies over the establishment of meaning.

Media and audience studies have been centrally concerned with deconstructing meaning in media texts and then understanding how that meaning is unravelled by audiences in their own social locations. That premise seems fairly straightforward, but it serves to reify meaning as established at each end of the exchange—first in content and then in context. Such an approach brackets out the texture of the experiences that audiences might have as they engage with television as a medium. Like those language preservationists who worry over media language eroding the spoken English of contemporary youth,[1] this approach assumes that language and meaning can (or should) at points be fixed and stable over time. While that might work for some television genres, particularly factual programming where a secure meaning or ideological position might be found, some genres, like the television talk shows discussed here, prove more elusive in that regard. However, there is a ready acceptance in socio-linguistics that language is a vitally amorphous and dynamic entity in social change, and that one can only capture language as it is *used* in any given situation, place, and time. This book suggests that it is possible to adopt such sentiments to account for the reception of talk television. It suggests that broadcast discourse *dynamically* enters the socio-communicative sphere of the home, establishing particular spatio-temporal conditions and mediating our senses of "here and now" through the union of televised and lived environments. This approach to television discourse combines talk on, talk through, and talk with television to suggest that it is possible to gauge how meaning is established in the communicative *achievements* of broadcast discourse in the life of the home.

As a consequence, I suggest that in some cases it is necessary for television research to throw off its attachment to analyzing television programs as texts. The literary influence over audience studies has secured a tradition in which audiences have been assumed to "read" meaning from television. But the analogy of reading rather flattens the spatial and temporal experience of television as it takes place, *happens,* in the life of the living room. This book tries to think through what it might mean to consider that television programs are alive and in motion in reception contexts. For example, work on early radio in Australia suggests that the *act* of listening was considered the primary mode of pleasure over any specific engagement with content (Johnson, 1988, cited in Bennett, 1996). Focusing on acts as ways to grasp meaningful engagements with media leads to the outlining of an alternative and unique methodology that may invigorate the field of audience research, establishing a focus on the temporality of television through considering *"texts-in-action."* It accounts for how the viewing of talk television pragmatically evolves in the live moments of television reception, re-centering meaning as a dynamic process fought over in the interplay between mediated and non-mediated realities.

Here is one short example from the data made available via this research methodology, which is collected by recording the television program and the viewer responses as they watch, simultaneously. Talk on television and the talk at home is then transcribed in parallel, making visible television viewing as a communicative event. The television program in this extract is from a daytime talk show, screened in the UK in the nineties and hosted by television personality Vanessa Feltz. It is a genre of talk show associated with a "therapy" style, like *Oprah,* which directly addresses women and is mostly concerned with family relationships. This particular show is organized around the topic of jealousy, which has been rather flippantly set up at the beginning by the host asking whether the "green-eyed monster" ever takes hold of "you." As this studio participant (whose talk is transcribed on the left-hand side of the transcript) demonstrates, the topic strays into the very serious business of domestic violence. Just as with many talk shows, the focus on the personal and the private realm often implicates the talk within feminist political issues.

	Studio		Home	
1	Vanessa	Has she ever ended up in	Eve	He ain't jealous he's just mental.
2		hospital?		
3	Participant	Yes I've been arrested on three		
4		different occasions for violence		
5		against her through jealousy		
6		erm the last was three		He wouldn't hit me three times,
7		months ago where I had tried to		one'd be the last!
8		strangle her.		

While the man is talking in the studio, at home, one of the participants in my research, Eve, a married woman in her late fifties, gets enraged. She is clearly concerned that the perpetrator of domestic violence can frame his actions around the condition of jealousy, rather than a more serious pathology, which she describes as "mental." As in all of my recordings of audience members watching talk shows and magazine programs at home, Eve turns to what the discussion means for her. She is adamant that she would stand up to abuse. The point here is not to overplay this response as particularly "resistive" to the power of the text. It is only one moment in the viewing process and Eve is rejecting the way in which the abuser gets to tell his story, rather than the text as such. But it is useful here to highlight the nature of these engagements as acts that register Eve's participation in the program, her ability to "talk back," and the way in which she locates herself within the propositions of the discursive equation. In this sense the communicative act allows the conversational floor to be opened out across broadcasting, and therefore the meaning of the talk show is established through its temporality. Her engagement is based upon how she positions herself as a speaker, another woman, within the topic of domestic violence. The text becomes meaningful as it performs the function of allowing Eve into the dialogue, encouraging her to stake her own position in relation to the discourse. Her viewer responses, therefore, are played out as part of a communicative exchange, rather than as the reader of an already completed text with an established and coherent meaning.

I want to make it clear that this approach to audience research does not register "talking back" in and of itself as oppositional; the business of interaction is always bound up within complex power relations. Rather, it suggests that a focus upon communicative action might offer a different route towards analyzing the role of television within the dynamic business of meaning making and power relations in daily life. This work sets out to think about meaning as not only established in "signs" as they are already encoded within texts, but also as they are pragmatically accomplished through "actions" in communication, following traditions of work on face-to-face interaction. The research thus has some continuities with current shifts in post-structuralist thinking on the way in which identity (and in particular gender identity) might be accomplished over time through action, rather than fixed in time through attachments to particular forms of representation. According to Judith Butler (1990) gender is a "performance" achieved in social temporalities, an account that has rarely been brought to bear upon the temporalities of media reception and its links with identity formation.

This work aims to paint a complete picture of the communicative process of talk television as it comes into contact with a group of women speakers, testing out a unique methodology for audience research along the way. Instead of establishing the final word on the ideological content of talk shows per se, I work out what it is that talk shows *do* in their communicative relationships with their audiences as *processes* of viewing. In the data, the women self-reflexively engage in forms of sociability with the television and are called to perform their gendered identities through forms of talk. I use the metaphor of "mechanics" to help explain this as a communicative process, rather than as a reading strategy, and suggest that the forms of mediated self-reflexivity induced here demand further exploration in terms of contemporary theories of selfhood in post-industrial society. Available theories include abstract observations about the media's role in stretching forms of human contact across time and space, which this book tests through empirical observation and feminist analysis. Recent contemporary theory recognizes a broader neo-liberal political push towards processes of "individualization." Where identity patterns are more uncertain and are constituted by increasing risk, the individual must embark upon a reflexive project of the self in which the media is rather loosely assumed to play a significant part (Giddens, 1991a, 1991b; Beck, 1992). These practices are generally deemed to uproot traditional identity formations, made for example through gender and class, whereas the findings here demonstrate how those "older" identity ties can be multiplied rather than "freed" through a particular form of mediated self-reflexivity and self-government. Thus this work illuminates the site of gendered domesticity as it is mediated in modernity, a position often overlooked in the grander claims of social theory, drawing attention to the mechanics that impel that process. By taking a closer look at viewing practices at work, as "texts-in-action," we might take some small step towards a fuller understanding of the more intricate parts the media play in the "drive belts" of social change.[2]

"It's Good to Talk": Morning Talk Television in Britain

To undertake the study outlined above, I focus on British daytime television and its reception. It is useful in this introduction to outline how this programming has imitated US television production as well as its orientation to talk. The slogan above is the British Telecom advertising slogan that framed the British morning magazine program *This Morning* during the empirical phase of this study. The phrase has also become one of the most popular commonsense truisms of contemporary Western culture. Deborah Cameron's (2000) book of the same title takes issue with the rise of such a tenet's regulatory intervention in many areas of our personal and professional lives whereby "good communication is said to be the key to a better and happier life; improving communication 'would improve everything else'" (2000:1). Cameron locates this phenomenon as part of the reflexive project of the self that is characteristic of modernity (Giddens, 1991b), whereby "communication" has become the latest subject of self-government. The use of this slogan for daytime television talk therefore registers its consequence in the mediation of the contemporary incitement to talk.

On British television for nearly two decades there has been a concentration of talk-based programming between 9:00 a.m. and noon, the mid-morning slot, consisting of magazine programs and audience participation talk shows. This particular period of the day is significant on terrestrial channel schedules as it is marked out for housewife-consumers, despite an increasingly changing demographic of students, retired people, and home-workers.[3] For the duration of the empirical phase of this study the programs that filled this slot were *This Morning* (ITV—independent, commercial television network), *Good Morning* (BBC1), which are morning magazine programs similar in style to *Good Morning America* (ABC) but with a less serious news focus; and talk shows *Kilroy* (BBC1), *The Time . . . The Place* (ITV1), similar to *Donahue*, and *Vanessa* (ITV1), similar to *Oprah*.

This programming has tended to reflect—if with some considerable time lapse—developments in the United States. There, network television discovered the commercial benefits of daytime television, delivering relatively large audiences with low production costs. NBC's pioneering of the *Today Show*, a mixture of news and chat, led to CBS following in 1954 with *The Morning Show*, another news and chat-based program hosted by journalist Charles Collingwood. This was followed by *Home*, a domestically oriented show hosted by duo Arlene Francis and Hugh Downes. In the UK, at least until the mid-1980s, the public service ethos had maintained scheduling in the daytime for children's programming (mostly educational), news, and eventually Open University programs with long periods of the test card. In 1983 the launch of breakfast television broke the mold to experiment with daytime entertainment, and in October 1988 ITV's Daytime Committee came up with the idea of a live ninety-minute morning entertainment magazine program, *This Morning*. The show's success prompted the BBC's rival copycat show *Good Morning*, which was launched in October 1992. Developments in daytime broadcasting were therefore direct reflections of commercial successes across the Atlantic: "The two breakfast shows launched in 1983 accordingly were based on US models, with the name of TV-a.m.'s *Good Morning Britain* signalling its debt to the ABC's *Good Morning* America. Later came the rival shout-ins *Kilroy* and *The Time . . . The Place*, both feeble copies of *Donahue*. Then ITV's *This Morning* (now abjectly mimicked by the BBC), in which husband and wife hosts Richard Madeley and Judy Finnegan are a reasonably convincing simulacrum of the classic American winsome twosome. All that's lacking is a facsimile of *The Oprah Winfrey Show*" (Dugdale and Saynor, 1992).

The content mix of daytime television reflected the estimations of a predominantly female audience share,[4] encompassing cookery programs, soap operas, quiz shows, music, and chat programming, which has a traditionally hetero-normative and conservative appeal to female audiences: "One of the

most profitable daytime programming categories for adult women throughout television history has been the talk show/news magazine . . . all maintain
the objective of informing the audience, while giving them a healthy dose of
entertainment" (Matelski, 1991:13).

These shows talked and debated domestic issues: women's health, relationship advice, issues around the family, and so on. The talk shows on British
television, *Kilroy* (BBC1), *The Time . . . The Place* (ITV), and *Vanessa* (ITV),
provide avenues of participation for the ordinary public. However, the "ordinary" people that populated these first British morning shows were not
"men who say they've had 4,000 lovers," or "women who need to tell her
partners that they're really men"—a style that has been described as "bringing the margins to the center" (Joyner-Priest, 1995). Rather, the "ordinary"
voices on earlier British programs are women who have had operations that
have gone wrong, or women who have undergone IVF treatment, or the
husbands who have left them, or people who are struggling to pay for the
care of their elderly parents—more "everyday" matters for discussion. As one
media commentator describes morning television, "It was a revolutionary
concept in television. It was about the way ordinary people live their lives:
their heartbreaks, their worries and medical problems, their joys, their set-
backs and recoveries; in short, their everydayness" (Stephen, 1996).

The prevalence of women's voices and women's issues raises the debate
about the value of the private sphere in televised discussion. There are con-
flicting positions over whether a talk show can be evocative of a feminist
therapy and connect to a public political agenda, or whether its staging of
personal intimacy is ultimately voyeuristic and exploitative, particularly of
women. However, there is one constant factor—these programs encourage,
facilitate, and broadcast talk, and "talk" more generally has long been at the
center of feminist concerns. In the consciousness-raising groups of the 1970s,
women were encouraged to speak to each other, to speak of the "problem"
that had no name, and at the same time women's talk was often derided and
ridiculed as gossip, prattle, bitching, whining, and so on. We have a similar,
but particularly modern, debate occurring about the *televising* of mundane
talk. To analyze a film or a fictional drama, one would automatically investigate the devices of the narrative and therefore it makes sense to analyze the
talk of "Talk TV." As Dell Hymes points out for research on the ethnography
of communication, "Interpretation that excludes speech falls short, as would
a treatment of painting that excludes paint" (1981:9).

In the chapters that follow, I establish the communicative features of watching talk television and mark their relationship to the politics of feminized
forms of talk. The development of a text-in-action methodology makes visible

the mediation of talk across broadcasting, capturing how women viewers take up the current public incitement that "It's Good to Talk." I use the analysis of talk to establish the mechanics of television at work, here breaking new ground in understanding television's role in instituting contemporary acts of self-reflexivity within the dislocated conditions of modernity.

Chapter Outlines

Chapter 1 summarizes the key debates that exist about talk shows and suggests that some of the critical discussions have paralleled concerns about women's speech and debates about the gendering of talk. There are polarized discussions about talk shows in which a fixed reading of them as ultimately either progressive or regressive has not been secured. Instead, more recent studies have suggested an emphasis not so much on *what* is said on talk shows, but rather on what talk *performs* in terms of testimony, catharsis, therapy, and so on, which helps to anchor a sense of self that is continually disrupted by risk and fear in contemporary society. Therefore, talk shows become meaningful as "ritual" forms of communication, which as well as representing social formations also crucially *perform* key social actions.

Following this claim, chapter 2 addresses the theoretical history that has led media and audience research away from an analysis of ritual communication and speech. Using Volosinov's reading of Saussure, it considers how media studies' derivation of a text-reader model of audience research from Saussurian linguistics ultimately closed off our ability to understand the role of the media in the dynamic business of language-use. Arguing for a focus upon "speech genres" (Bakhtin, 1986) as constituted *in time,* this chapter reflects on how broadcasting embeds itself into the quotidian rhythms of everyday life. This involves consideration of the media in modernity and its physical re-organization of time and space. It offers some insights into how discourse analytic approaches can deconstruct the way in which broadcasting establishes its own field of "here and now" in the home, thereby providing the tools for the analysis of television as a socio-communicative sphere.

Chapter 3 offers a discourse analysis of the programs in question, concentrating on their gendered address. It pulls out the para-social appeals to immediacy and liveness, often through direct address, that serve to locate the viewer as participant in programs that appear unfinished and in progress. By orienting the talk shows' debates as being on "our side," they are also constituted as "for us." These factors contribute to the erosion of traditional notions of spectatorship, as the address induces a social sphere within which female audiences are assumed to share space, time, and cultural competences, thereby implicating them within the action. This formula is explored as a type of mediated "gossip" genre in which intimacy, mutual disclosure, and the everyday become the structuring frames of the talk.

To conduct audience research into this phenomenon as a socio-communicative sphere requires rethinking our traditional methodological approaches. Departing from text-reader models of research entrenched in the binary encoding/decoding model, chapter 4 argues for a research paradigm that can take into account the *temporal* experience of broadcasting. Through a focus upon "moments" of television in order to register the mechanics of the *act* of television viewing, it is possible to stretch the concept of textuality to embrace the physicality of the experience. This leads to a new methodology, "texts-in-action," which envisages the speech of the broadcast and the speech of the audience member simultaneously, capturing the life of the text in the life of the home. A method that focuses upon speech *acts* also allows us to unfix the women's gendered positions and suggests the need to test out how performative acts of gender might also be ritualized *mediated* acts. Drawing on analyses of speech from linguistics completes the theoretical jigsaw that can illuminate audience relationships with television as "communicative events." The chapter then details the background of the women involved in the study and the practical approach to the research design.

The voices of the women who took part in the empirical stages of this study come alive in chapter 5. Here their conversations about daytime television in the interviews and the focus group are explored as they recount, not so much the content of what they understand about the programs, but rather the *feelings* they get about the presenters and the way they sense the address implicates them in the talk. The discussion conjures up the intimate way in which the women are engaged in a type of electronic sociality, which correlates with sociological arguments about the transformation of intimacy across new disembedded social relations (Giddens, 1991a, 1991b). While we see the vernacular of the women as a community of speakers, we also encounter the expressions of their own personal experiences, which mediate their relationship to the television programs.

Chapter 6 details the "texts-in-action," wherein the women's responses to the programs while they are broadcast constitute a "mediated conversational floor." They respond to the para-social invitations in a form of interaction that in some ways approximate forms of everyday conversation: using minimal responses that suggest they are listening, answering questions asked in the studio, finishing turns, formulating responses, and so on. In response to a particular mediated speech genre, they also produce their own accounts of personal experience relevant to the programs' discussion, as they are called to perform speech acts as they accomplish their roles as women through talk. In this way the genre does not become meaningful by its content alone, but meaning is *pragmatically* negotiated across the broadcast medium. Meaning is not fixed at any point, but is constantly negotiated in the flux of the talk, potentially getting us closer to applying Volosinov's account of the "multi-accentuated" nature of the sign.

Two longer extracts of the way in which textuality and subjectivity are intertwined are the focus of the final empirical chapter. It offers a close reading of how personal details and stories are imbricated in and through the broadcast talk. This takes us to precise and determinate moments that shed light on the way in which identity is mediated in contemporary modernity. Rather than assuming that the women in the study produce referential statements about viewing *because* they are women, as previous studies have done, this chapter accounts for how the mediation of the process is in tune with the contemporary push towards the narrativizing of the self in broader processes of individualization.

Finally, the conclusion draws together the implications of this study more broadly for media and cultural studies and feminism. Arguing that the relationship between "mass" communication and interpersonal communication needs deeper consideration, I suggest that other routes to understanding how media become meaningful might be registered in the *mechanics* of the process. This also goes some way towards seeing the continuities between old and new media in forms of connectivity, if we look to account for a broader spectrum of communication. However, that is not to jettison ideas about power, since throughout the book it is clear that all forms of communication are always implicated in, and constitutive of, contexts of power. I suggest instead that a focus upon *mechanics* might help reveal more of the workings of the media's role in contemporary identity formation. In the case of the relationship between women and talk television, these are constituted through a speech genre of gossip that has implications for understanding gender identity in the modern age. If it is the case that the telling of a life is the more significant struggle than dealing directly with the material constraints that surround and condition it, as in the individualization thesis (Giddens, 1991a, 1991b; Beck, 1992), then women should here be ahead of the game. But such daily ritualized acts of self-reflexivity call them to explore and enact their feminized roles, which in effect re-embeds within the quotidian baseline that experience—along with its many oppressions and constraints. Rather than this public space transporting the women from the private domestic sphere, it can serve only to double their only too-well-trodden experiences.

1. Talk Is Not So Cheap

Introduction

Talk on television, particularly varying forms of talk shows, have attracted much popular and academic critique as they have exploded in number and diversified in style. Talk shows provide lucrative exports and cheap national productions now staple to the television economy. They have also been at the center of popular debates about "dumbing down" and the tabloidization of contemporary culture, often being regarded as emblematic of the "cultural rot" infecting Western culture. Public debate on talk shows has been concerned with television's faltering role within "serious" political democratic discourse, igniting discussion about changing relations between private and public culture. This has often led to wildly polarized evaluations of the talk show. Some suggest that talk shows offer the worst kind of cheap voyeuristic spectacle, ideologically repositioning social issues as personal problems. On the other hand, others have lauded them as introducing progressive spaces for exercising (sometimes feminist and anti-racist) electronic democracy.

Here we take a relatively brief look at the main recurring debates, since there are many accounts of the talk show debates now available, and argue that either looking for virtue or demonizing the genre does not provide an understanding of the popularity and centrality of talk on television. The *gendering* of the debate and the specificities of the *form* of talk provide the particular foci that shape the foundation for the subsequent empirical research of this book. Therefore, this chapter draws attention to some of the parallels between debates about talk shows and critiques of gossip as a denigrated (and feminized) form of talk, attempting to home in on the process of communication itself. Here, concentrating on the ritual talk of daytime television, and on what this talk *achieves*, offers a route to further understanding the specificity of the phenomenon of mediated talk in contemporary culture.

Popular Fears and Feminine Pleasures

Popular media debate about talk shows has often generated fierce, barbed criticism. It is resonant of a common topical theme about the increasing tabloidization of culture that has been held "responsible for everything from voter apathy to family breakdown" (Lumby, 1997:117). In popular discourse, on the one hand talk shows are banal, and on the other they are dangerous. For many commentators, talk shows represent the decomposition of the moral fabric of the nation as part of the damaging effect of an increasingly commercial culture. In America, Senator Joseph Lieberman, a Democrat, told a press conference that: "Talk is cheap and too often on these shows it is also demeaning, exploitative, perverted, divisive, and immoral."[1] Lieberman speaks as a member of a group known as "Empower America" that campaigns against the apparent tidal wave of culturally perverse chatter engulfing broadcasting.

This book also takes in a broader account of talk programming that encompasses the UK daytime magazine programs, similar in style to *Good Morning America*, which focus on personalities and chat. In a similar fashion, commentators have described these programs as "stupidvision" or "tepid dishwater soup" that are apparently tame and patronizing: "It is Stupidvision—where most of the presenters look like they have to pretend to be stupid because they think their audience is. In other words, it patronizes. It talks to the vacuum cleaner and the washing machine and the microwave, without much contact with the human brain" (Toynbee, 1996). "Coffee-time TV," as it has been labelled, has even induced criticism from the British production executives responsible for its existence in the UK. The chief executive officer of Carlton TV,[2] Andy Allen, one of the original members of the Daytime Committee that commissioned *This Morning*, likens the daytime chat shows to "a flotation tank where you are able to relax by being robbed of all sensory experience" in a "dull and predictable wasteland."[3]

Such vilification of television that is associated with the private and personal (and thus feminized world) echoes a traditionally gendered demarcation of value. These debates parallel the paternalistic conception of the public sphere that privileges the world of business, economics, medicine, science, and so on, and wants to regulate what is deemed appropriate for valuable consumption. Of course, there is a relatively long history of tracing the mass culture/femininity association as having its particular roots within the tradition of Modernism. Andreas Huyssen describes how, "Time and time again documents from the late nineteenth century ascribe pejorative feminine characteristics to mass culture. . . . It is easy to see how such statements rely on the traditional notion that women's aesthetic and artistic abilities are inferior to those of men" (1986:194–95).

In relation to morning talk programs this issue needs to be thought about carefully. Is programming that has addressed women audiences at home in the daytime mind-numbing and patronizing? Most commentators refer to the programs as valuable only in that they offer a purely soporific quality that lulls a passive audience with its banality. What does this imply about the viewers of these programs? Is it the program makers or the critics who assume women at home to be stupid and dull, conforming to all the worst stereotypes of the domestic housewife? It is the association with the private world of issues about relationships, women's sexuality, and the family that invokes such aggressive rhetoric. But, I would suggest that it is not just the *content* (despite topics such as rape, domestic violence, and police brutality, which are couched within makeovers, finding inner talents, and weight loss) that triggers such caustic disregard, but also the *form* that this talk takes. In opening up talk on television, multiple, rather than solely legitimated, voices are now recognized, the chaos of debate is endorsed, and ordinary experience is validated. These characteristics reflect another traditional realm of cultural distaste—around feminine modes of oral communication often characterized as idle chatter and "gossip," and I want to begin here to think about these two sets of debates as analogous as I work towards a communicative account of the reception of talk television.

Gossip and Oral Culture

There is a relatively long tradition in feminist politics accounting for the relationship between the gendering of speech and the persistence of gender inequality. For instance, Spender (1980) and Daly (1978) drew attention to the fact that the amount of talk women do has often been a contentious issue. Women are often derided as "empty vessels" that talk too much and, at the same time, are encouraged to be silent. When Kramer investigated popular perceptions of the characteristics of women's language, she found that the most frequent responses were that women talk about trivial topics and that they indulge in "gossip and gibberish" (1977:157). While "women chatter, tattle, gab, rabbit, prattle, nag, whine, bitch, men devote themselves to more consequential tasks; they build ships, discover continents, fight wars.

They do not hang about nattering" (Emler, 1994:118). Popular mythology therefore tells us that when *men* talk they debate, philosophize, exchange ideas, conduct business, and engage in politics. The gendering of practices of talk represents the two separate spheres of public and private politics, dividing what is important and inconsequential subject matter for discussion and relegating family matters and personal relationships to the "irrelevant" private world of women. The devaluation of women's talk as "gossip" assists in containing women's voices within the private sphere, since their conversations are not deemed serious enough for rational and critical debate within the public sphere. This draws out interesting parallels for this study between the gendering of talk and the popular critiques of daytime television and talk shows that label the shows as simultaneously inconsequential (too private and banal) and dangerous (infecting public space).

The relationship between the sexes, their different discursive strategies, and thus their proximity to the public sphere, is conceived in terms of women's "relational," versus men's "rational," ethical reasoning. In her study of women's and men's responses to moral dilemmas, Gilligan suggests that their moral judgements significantly differ: "The conventions that shape women's moral judgements differ from those that apply to men. . . . Women's construction of the moral problem as a problem of care and responsibility in relationships rather than as one of rights and rules ties the development of their moral thinking to changes in their understanding of responsibility and relationships, just as the conception of morality and justice ties development to the logic of equality and reciprocity. Thus the logic underlying an ethic of care is a psychological logic of relationship, which contrasts with the formal logic of fairness that informs the justice approach" (1982:73).

Women therefore negotiate their connectedness to one another through a "different voice," which is based upon the ethic of care whereby responsibility is inextricably tied to relationships (Gilligan, 1982). Thus, apparently women generate contextualized relational senses of self as opposed to the masculine (neo-Kantian) tradition that separates the personal from the moral.

Through this emphasis on women's relational connectedness, some feminists have reevaluated gossip as a moral virtue. Some argue that gossiping throughout history has been despised precisely because of the potential it offers women for group solidarity, which has historically been seen as threatening to the social order. Oakley (1975) points out that between the fourteenth and eighteenth centuries gossips endured public shaming, the ducking stool, the stocks, or were even made to wear an iron mask with a spike or wheel that projected into the mouth to stop their tongues. Others suggest that many of the half-million women burned as witches throughout Europe were probably killed for gossiping (Gluckman, 1963; Oakley, 1975; Emler, 1994). According to Spender, this fear of gossip is legitimate since, "When women come together they have the opportunity to 'compare' notes, collectively to 'see' the limitations of patriarchal reality, and what they say—and do—can be subversive of that reality" (1994:108). Thus, gossip can be reevaluated in terms of what it can offer women collectively, including the notion that it poses a threat to the patriarchal status quo.

Therefore, Spacks (1985) suggests that gossip promotes close and emotionally fruitful human associations, reflects intense interest in the personal and, rather than being judged as random and careless, requires the skills of subtle judgement and discrimination. Similarly, Levin and Arluke (1987) state that gossip serves useful psychological functions, such as: enhancing the self-esteem or status of a group; providing information that helps to evaluate ourselves through comparison with others; maintaining social cohesiveness within a group; and helping to define ambiguous and stressful situations. These benefits to group dynamics have a political function since gossip is a key characteristic facilitating cohesion among oppressed groups. Spacks (1985) claims that gossip has always been an outlet for the disadvantaged, for instance: servants talking of their masters, students of their teachers, and mistresses telling secrets of their lovers. Gossip is therefore often defended by feminists for assisting in generating a sense of social cohesion and sisterhood between women. Cassell (1977), for example, describes gossip as having a significant role in the feminist consciousness-raising movements of the 1970s, which campaigned for serious political change.

However, these rather triumphant feminist declarations of the productive role of gossip have offered no real analysis of its form beyond suggesting that its basic content belongs to the private and personal realm. Thus, we need to focus our attention on the centrality of talk and speech to feminist debates and not take the content of women's speech for granted. McRobbie goes on to tease out the double bind of both the historic need for women to find a voice but also of the traditional denigration of women's speech: "This is a political struggle in itself. It amounts to an attempt to break out of the confines of talk, which is a comfortable but ultimately restricting ghetto. It is a form called 'gossip' where women have been located through history. However, it is a particularly contradictory route outwards from the privatised local sphere of feminism to full-scale engagement in the public sphere" (1991:67–8). Therefore, feminists have suggested that the nature of talk between women calls for serious critical attention, since the apparent eagerness of women to talk is a complicated political issue that might be both liberating and simultaneously confining.

There is a critical convergence of relevant feminist issues around gender and talk that may be explored through an analysis of talk television; chapter 3 outlines the formal properties of daytime talk television as a mediated gossip genre. In popular debate, the programs themselves are trivialized and de-valued within the time-honored tradition of disparaging mass culture as feminine. This is compounded by the problematic nature in which women's speech has been traditionally framed as trivial and deficient. Women are encouraged to talk and also derided for their talk, and this double bind resonates in the popular discourses about daytime television. Therefore, it is because daytime talk programming contains both the political issues of the denigration of a "feminine" genre, as well as the scorn of *perceived* feminine modes of speech, that it becomes a topical object for feminist study. This book sets out to bring to the center of media analysis a set of questions about the nature of this programming as *both* oral communication and mediated communication, an approach not currently available in the larger body of literature. This begins to map out my own initial set of interests, but that by no means represents the array of literature that has appeared on the talk show as it has come to occupy a focal space where numerous critiques of contemporary culture have converged[4] and in which reside similar ambiguities over the progressive and regressive nature of "talking personally."

Theorizing Talk Shows

Much of the academic debate about the talk show has been characterized by polarized positions. For some authors the genre offers a new, potentially democratic space affording citizens access to public address normally denied them. This has sometimes been discussed in terms of a feminist project of "consciousness raising" for women, or more recently *Oprah* has been contextualized as containing a diluted black political consciousness (Wilson, 2003). However, the other dominant critique suggests that talk shows offer potentially dangerous pleasures that foreground issues of personal psychology without appropriate support or sociological reasoning. Here the talk show offers a commercial spectacle that dupes participants and viewers, signifying a collapse of critical debate in public culture. Illouz (2003) suggests that these contradictory positions reflect trends in cultural studies whereby a postmodern critique evaluates multi-vocality and fragmentation as offering a positive democratic forum, while a critical theoretical position reminiscent of the Frankfurt School sees only the media's trademark exploitation for profit.

Attempting to chart a description of critical accounts of the talk show phenomenon is problematic due to the explosion of the different forms talk takes on our screens. The talk show almost defies description due to its amorphous nature. Some commentators have ignored the distinctions between talk shows, but more recently academics have seen the distinctions between different formats as crucial to understanding them. Haarman refers to the term "talk show" as a portmanteau term that has been used to describe a range of formats including "conversation between elite peers, round table or group discussions, interviews, debates, topical discussions between experts and ordinary people, and talk between people, normally not peers, with interventions from a studio audience" (1999:1). There are differences between how talk shows have evolved; between the more public-issue oriented (*Donahue, Kilroy* UK), the more spectacular and trashy (*Jerry Springer, The Ricki Lake Show*), and the more therapeutic (*Oprah, Vanessa, Trisha* UK) or the more morally pedagogic (*The Jeremy Kyle Show* UK). *Oprah* has morphed through a range of these styles over time, partly in response to popular attacks of sensationalism. Such variety is not only a response to the economic imperative of cheap popular programming, but as cultural, as well as commercial products, they are part of a contemporary phenomenon around a public incitement to "talk." These issues have induced a number of interpretations of the cultural significance of the talk show.

Democratic Participation and Media Spectacle

At the heart of many critiques is speculation over whether the talk show's format hosts democratic potential or whether that possibility is brutally cancelled out by the spectacle of television. Particularly in the earlier examples, audience participation programs encouraged a constellation of voices, broadening access to discussion for the "ordinary" citizen, as well as providing a space where public figures could be forced to confront the populace. Understanding the talk show on these terms usually stems from making comparisons with the concept of an ideal public sphere where the privileged "right to speak" becomes de-hierarchized. These theories have drawn upon Habermas's historical account of how the conditions born out of the genesis of capitalism allowed the rise of the bourgeois public sphere in seventeenth- and eighteenth-century Europe (Habermas, 1989). He argues that capitalism brought with it a distinction between the modern state and civil society that provided a clear democratic space for a public sphere to emerge. The public sphere here therefore refers to "the emergence of a critical and independent public domain, a space formed between the economy and the state in which public opinion could be formed and thus exert influence over the government" (McLaughlin, 1993:41).[5]

Some accounts of the talk show, both positive and negative, can be understood within this critical framework. The more disparaging media critics discussed earlier see the talk show as emblematic of the demise of the public sphere. There is a real fear about the way the talk show intervenes directly in the (serious) political system, as electoral candidates are encouraged to do the "talk show circuit." Howard Kurtz gives a thorough account of how such processes are deeply embedded in the American political system through a focus on electioneering and punditry. He suggests that politicians grow obsessed with "winning the week" by appearing on talk shows, echoing Habermas's fear that the "spectacle" or staging of debate fundamentally undermines its functional and critical purpose. The talk show here contributes to an increasing commercialization of politics wherein "the political effort to 'sell' an initiative on the talk circuit begins to overshadow the substance of the proposal itself" (Kurtz, 1996:5).

The issue of spectacle/participation is central to media studies and has most often been associated with the presence of television. One cannot ignore what Dahlgren (1995) refers to as television's ultimate "entertainment bias." However, in terms of the talk show, the critical distancing of performance and audience embedded within this bias has been reevaluated. Carpignano et al. suggest that in the mediated culture of the late twentieth century it is "the spectacle itself that is in crisis" (1990:35). They give a series of examples from current media forms whereby the classic distinctions between spectacle and spectator are becoming eroded: for instance, the transparency of production techniques (cues to camera operators, etc.) and the reduction of news reporters to commentators in TV news formats that have become increasingly conversational. Within these broader changes in media and public culture, the talk show becomes *the* prime example of the dissolution of older conventions of spectatorship. Here the boundaries between performer and viewer are blurred in a genre where the studio audience members are also the performers; therefore, for these authors, "the talk show is the most eloquent example of the crisis of theatricality" (1990:49).

These re-assessed circumstances allow an evaluation of the talk show as an exercise in electronic democracy because they suggest the talk show provides a site with seemingly few exclusionary practices, encouraging the participation of the general public in political debate. Perhaps the talk show is democratic because of its tolerance of a diverse number of voices, which arguably opens up a forum that challenges the traditional hierarchical organization of rights to speak resonating more broadly within liberal politics. Many talk shows invite a large studio audience of lay people to take an active role in the discussion of the topic of the day. Ordinary people and representative experts from various institutions and organizations—politicians, doctors, counsellors, police, executives, and so on—take part in the production of live talk. These phenomena help shape a democratic evaluation of the talk show. Here is a space where rank, class, and expert status are subordinated to debate and "authentic" experience. This suggests a site unlike any other, where contact between the state and the populace can potentially be direct and open.

In this most optimistic of critiques, the contributions of lay people, usually through personal narratives, are juxtaposed against the discourses of the institutional representatives. The talk show offers a unique site whereby the traditional polarization of public and private realms is eroded. In Habermasian terms, therefore, the "life-world" (lived experiences of citizens) and the "system" (state representatives) are brought together in such a way that transcends the separation of the two spheres for the common good (Livingstone and Lunt, 1994). In fact, "lay" contributions to the discourse even take priority over those of the experts. Talk shows afford a primacy to common sense over institutionally affected registers. Hosts continually appeal to expert representatives to speak plainly. Again, this accords with a liberal concept of an ideal public sphere. As Durham Peters notes, "Habermas prizes conversation, reading and plain speech as worthy forms of discourse for a democratic culture and is frankly hostile to theatre, courtly forms, ceremony, the visual and rhetoric more generally" (1993:562).

But this is not to suggest that speech between experts and ordinary members of the public evolves naturally where common sense must prevail. Talk show hosts play a significant role in the management of talk as agents of the broadcast network in the interests of good television (Wood, 2001). It is obvious that the most positive reading of the talk show may well hold for the earlier permutations of the genre. For instance, Phil Donahue from the outset was insistent that his talk show debates were influenced by traditions of liberal politics and feminism, taking seriously the challenges posed by lay members of the public to expert/institutional representatives. But frankly, theater has become central to the newer guard of talk shows too (*Springer, Ricki, The Jeremy Kyle Show*) where the experts have been removed entirely and "the people" and their interpersonal dilemmas and crises are the stars ("My boyfriend's secret: he's a girl," "Teenage sex secrets," "I'm just using you," "Transvestites on parade"). The industry itself recognizes a (relatively loose) distinction between the "classy" and the "trashy" production styles of the talk show.[6]

These developments in talk show formats incur a particular ambiguity for any reading of the genre. This is explored in Joshua Gamson's (1998) book *Freaks Talk Back,* in which he discusses how the talk show imperative to give voice offers visibility to previously marginalized groups of different sexual orientations. Indeed, representatives from organized bodies use the talk shows as a platform from which to influence the terms of popular debate around sexuality. While Gamson acknowledges that there has been some success here in re-drawing the lines between the normal and abnormal, this is subsequently straightjacketed by the production methods, which require spectacular "freaks" who are often unfairly manipulated to present a shock to the dominant heterosexual discourse of the program. So Gamson is left in a quandary: "As they open the door, so it is shut" (1998:168). Clearly, these developments in the entertainment drive of the talk show shift the ground of debate from an entirely utopian reading of public discourse, while at the same time they acknowledge the presence of multiple "others" in the public arena. Such ambivalence characterizes similar discussions within feminist arguments, where the main contention is over the value of talk as therapy.

The Talk Show as Feminist Public Sphere

The talk show's privileging of "common sense" and everyday life-world ex-periences has led to a feminist interest in the form as an oppositional public sphere. If the talk show indeed blurs boundaries between an oppressive di-chotomy of private and public spheres, then this obviously has repercussions for gendered practices. As we have seen in relation to gender and talk, the distinction between "private" and "public" as binary opposites has led to the marginalization in mainstream politics of issues central to women's lives. In these terms, the spheres of public and private have traditionally been associ-ated with essential characteristics of masculinity and femininity that usually depend upon "woman" symbolizing nature and "man" symbolizing culture (Landes, 1998). The apparently logical inferiority of nature structures the patriarchal inequality of women.[7]

In terms of roles in the political arena, and in the gendered myths of dis-course as we have seen earlier, men take part in serious, rational, political debate while women are associated with the emotional realm of the domestic, which is ultimately invisible and silenced. Feminism has sought to raise aware-ness of the problems of such a crude division since, obviously, actions in the public realm impact directly upon the private world, not least in areas such as welfare politics (Fraser, 1989; Pateman, 1989). Furthermore, serious political issues of power are embedded within the private sphere. Issues around the family, the body, domestic labor, and sexuality have been central to feminist concerns about the entrenchment of the dominant laws of patriarchy. Such a focus can be found in many of the central feminist texts of the 1970s.[8]

Feminism's attention to politicizing the private domain has to some extent successfully disrupted the firm division between public and private, which is now central to liberal politics. In terms of this discussion, the airing of private and personal issues, such as domestic violence and rape, on talk shows has often been praised for bringing these politics of injustice into mainstream public debate. This has not been a straightforward process, and the correct "terms" of how such debate should take place have been hotly contested. As the talk show evolved, discussion of personal trauma has often been accompanied by therapy, offering victims "self help" to produce a narrative of personal triumph over adversity. The dominance of the therapy style of programming, characterized particularly by *Oprah,* has again received polarized critiques based upon its "value."

The Talk Show as Women's Therapy

The therapeutic turn in the talk show has been recognized as a feminizing of the genre (Shattuc, 1997). Discussion about the feminist possibilities of talk-as-therapy has subsequently echoed the public sphere debates in terms of the appropriateness of private hurt for the purposes of public entertainment. These debates mainly fall along two lines: either the talk show may optimistically represent an alternative feminized public sphere, or more depressingly offer the spectacular transformation of social inequality into personal psychological trauma. Oprah Winfrey has been seen to champion the feminist cause in the "TV-talk-as-therapy-genre" (Masciarotte, 1991; Squire, 1994; Landeman, 1995; Shattuc, 1997), while more cynical readings of the show again see the theater of the event as dominating the discourse, whereby the individual's pain is used as a voyeuristic commercial proposition. In this case, the personal and emotional is understood as an exercise in postmodern mimicry where pain and tears are false gestures to meet televisual requirements (White, 1992; McLaughlin, 1993; Peck, 1995).

The most celebratory interpretation of *Oprah* suggests that cultural critics may fear the talk show because it presents an alternative space for the articulation of identity through the suggestion of a mass subject. For Masciarotte, *The Oprah Winfrey Show* "begins to articulate a significantly different politics of the subject which re-inscribes the 'making of the self' in terms of mass subjectivity" (1991:83). In this case, the collective experience of "telling yourself" in the program resembles the terms of women's consciousness-raising groups of the 1970s, an experience whereby the individual shifts from private citizen to social citizen, thus claiming a voice.

The consciousness-raising groups of the 1970s were always regarded with suspicion by the dominant order but have been undeniably productive within the women's movement and central to feminist action. Interestingly for my argument, Spender's (1994) discussion suggests that it is the *form* that consciousness-raising groups took that was also central to both their success and their vilification. They offered a space where women were taken seriously as speakers and listeners and their authentic experiences were endorsed. In these terms, televisual arenas that support women's talk can be understood as feminized oppositional public spheres where, as in the women's movement, the "personal" is validated. Mellencamp argues, "It's not too far fetched to imagine daytime talk as the electronic syndicated version of consciousness raising groups of the women's movement" (1990:218). Donahue is proud of his program's debt to the liberal American feminist movement of the 1960s (Shattuc, 1997), and Oprah Winfrey has claimed that her show presents an unrivalled space for black woman's perspectives (Squire, 1994).

This view of the talk show as a mediated form of consciousness raising is also reinforced by its claim to offer multi-accentuated discourses—an alternative method of structuring debate to those recognizable in more "masculine" forms of public discussion. The foregrounding of personal narrative testimonies from multiple voices with non-linear discussion directly represents an "interruption in the classical strategies of knowledge construction, information gathering and proof through argumentation" (Masciarotte, 1991:90). Oprah Winfrey, for example, exhibits a good deal of empathy, touching and crying with audiences, which might be regarded as both feminine and feminist in its insistence on personal intimacy.

The talk show's connection with a feminist conscience has been further documented by Shattuc (1997), who suggests that its principal social service is in building women's self esteem, confidence, and identity in a space where advice is shared within the group and not handed down from above. Here, the therapeutic discourse offered by the talk show draws upon Freud's concept of the "talking cure," re-routed within feminist therapy: "Feminist therapy turns the humanist concept of self-actualization around and places it within a critique of social constraint. Feminism named the process 'empowerment,' which has become a central discourse of talk shows. In fact an audience member jumped up during a discussion of bad husbands and announced to Oprah: 'It's about power and empowerment'" (Shattuc, 1997:123).

More generally however, White (1992) sees a trend of therapeutic discourse running through much contemporary American television, from *Oprah Winfrey* to *The Simpsons*. In her analysis, this therapeutic discursive space relies on an overwhelming concentration on the "confession" in modern societies, following Foucault, whereby the confession is a structure of speech that enacts self-identity. Here the primacy of the narrative form of telling becomes part of the therapeutic discourse. Thus the confession of your own experience is not so much part of the process of recovery and empowerment, but a more cynical apparatus of governmentality in which telling and self-work are mechanisms of the dominant neo-liberal political agenda.

Catharsis as Ideology

Despite the optimism in some of these readings, there is also an understanding of these cultural products as part of the capitalist economy. They are after all *televised* commercial products, and any theorization of them must be understood within the institutional context from which they emerge. White cannot extricate the talk show debate from the consumer culture within which it and its viewers operate: "Television offers a double-edged intervention. It is perhaps more crass and thorough in its commodity/consumer operations than prior forms of therapeutic engagement, and apparently more totalizing. All viewers are always already inexorably caught up in the confessional mode and also in the consumer culture that it supports" (White, 1992:183). In her conclusion, the utilization of therapeutic discourse within the structure of television's commodity ethic, what she calls "crass consumerism," means that speaking for oneself is not always what it seems.

Similarly, McLaughlin's (1993) critique of Carpignano et al.'s essay locates their thesis of an oppositional public sphere within a "populist cultural studies" that is naively obsessed with valorizing the genre. She takes issue with their particular celebration of the talk show's elevation of "common sense" as facilitating multiple and diverse discourses because common sense itself is a problematic and politicized concept that usually serves to reinforce dominant ideologies. McLaughlin analyzes the construction of common sense in discourses about sexuality. The talk show's liberal emphasis might allow the presence of marginalized groups—prostitutes, homosexuals, working mothers—but the commonsense discourses produced about them are anything but progressive. Such labels act only as confrontational devices in the talk show's overriding primacy of the "spectacle."[9] Thus, the focus on confrontation, or what Grindstaff (2002) calls "the money shot" within the talk show, might allow alternative voices, but rarely does this produce progressive debate that is meaningful for women. Simply allowing working-class people space to vent "commonsense" opinions does not necessarily create a new forum free of dominant hegemonic practices since, and central to McLaughlin's point, commonsense discourses are contaminated by, and indeed dependant on, "official discourses."

In this way, the talk show simply reinforces traditionally motivated ideologies while presenting a gesture to access and participation. For many feminist authors this represents a serious problem. Peck (1995) sees ideological processes carried out through the broaching of therapeutic discourse. The emphasis on therapy is indebted to the Freudian psychotherapy of the "talking cure," which is not entirely value-free. The therapy industry has often been regarded as a venture in disciplining subjects for the modern capitalist order.[10] This has a particular gendered inflection, as women have been traditionally overrepresented as clients within the therapy industry, as well as being the largest body of consumers of literature on self-help and cognitive development.[11] The particular emphasis on feminine talk, sharing, and consciousness raising emerges here with less of a progressive edge; like the earlier discussions about women's talk it must be registered within the politics of its production. The talk show's reliance on the lay narrative personalizes the discussion in individual psychological terms, ignoring the social conditions from which the experience has emerged. Therapeutic intervention thus placates political problems, ideologically locating the social as personal dilemma and ultimately suppressing personal objections that might otherwise have been channelled into collective activism. Invoking the "personal" is not enough to evoke the political, since personal experience is only ever inscribed in the therapeutic practice of finding catharsis, rather than political action.

Performing Selfhood

We are left with a bewildering set of arguments that oscillate between good and bad judgements. Andrew Tolson argues that the feminist debate on the talk show has reached something of an impasse: "In one argument *Oprah* is progressive because it transcends social structures; on the other hand it is regressive because it fails critically to engage with them" (2001:24). The ambiguous nature of these accounts make a position on the overall "meaning" of the talk show as a genre only more elusive. As Wayne Munson has argued, it has become difficult for us to deconstruct the talk show in media studies' traditional terms of the politics of representation: "Its play with discursive boundaries and identities, with chaos and contingency have made it threatening to critics desperate for clear labels and stable structures—in other words, for a representational 'purity' the talk show will not allow" (Munson, 1993:111).

However, all sides of this debate agree that talk shows rely on "multivocality" and on the right to speak from personal experience. Many of the available critiques attribute the centrality of the style of conversation and dialogue to the success of talk shows, not only in terms of recognizing the oral traditions of feminist consciousness-raising groups, but also in *Oprah's* case, maintaining the importance of dialogue to a black epistemology and history (Illouz, 2003; Wilson, 2003). Wilson cites *Oprah* as a forum for "talking back," employing bell hooks's discussion of how the act of speech offers a liberated voice for oppressed groups.[12] This emphasis upon the process of "giving voice" to personal experience can also be located within broader neo-liberal political and cultural shifts.

Contemporary popular culture is awash with examples of personal testimony: telling the self, working on the self, and potentially transforming the self are common traits of other television formats, like the makeover show and reality television. Such phenomena are recognized as the motifs of social changes in contemporary identity practices. Jon Dovey suggests that "They reflect the changing sense of self that accompanies the rise of neo-liberalism and the breakdown of traditional social arrangements" (2000:154). In this context, talk shows replay our ontological insecurity in (post)modern industrialized societies in which our sense of self has fragmented as older social orders such as religion and class have been uprooted. This condition calls us to constantly narrativize and reflexively re-articulate a sense of self. The ideas of Beck (1992) and Giddens (1991b) represent this current sway in thinking, arguing for an "individualization thesis" whereby contemporary social identity is enacted not through traditional social groups, but through the production of reflexive biographies of the self.

In these terms, Illouz calls for a "moral sociology" wherein Oprah is an ethical force in the generation of cultural meaning. Her conclusion is that Oprah's cleverly conceived multi-media enterprise offers not one "message," but guidance towards, "how to cope with a world that consistently fails us" (2003:4). In a similar vein, Sherryl Wilson (2003) outlines the project of narrating the self in Oprah's TV format, whereby identity is recognized as simultaneously fragmented (in trauma) and recoverable (able to heal).

If the talk show's popularity is about comfortingly coaxing us towards a reconstituted self-identity, then how exactly is that achieved? The crucial point here is that the *way* in which this is done cannot entirely be explained by deconstructing the content of the talk show—the fixing of meaning is eluded by the anarchic wrestling between numerous voices. For example, Illouz makes clear that Oprah violates the norms of the public sphere not because of the problems that she raises on the shows but because of the "mode of speech in which she casts these problems . . . what maintains this boundary in the public sphere is not any given kind of topic, but rather who can raise a problem and through what kind of language" (2003:215). Speech (as well as embodiment) enacts and potentially accomplishes self-identity in talk shows. In her behind-the-scenes ethnography of talk shows, Grindstaff

(2002) describes the way in which participants are coached not so much in the details of their stories, but in the way those stories should be told. It is not the content, but the style that becomes central to how the talk show actually functions in contemporary culture. "Meaning" is therefore generated not only through the more straightforwardly symbolic resources of representation, but also through the speech events that are performative social actions: Oprah establishes trust relationships with her audiences and encourages dialogue, self-help, and solidarity to combat contemporary demons.

This directs us to one of the basic distinctions in communication between *ritual* and *transmission* models of communication (Carey, 1989). Here the transmission model suggests that messages are transferred linearly from a central point to the mass, while the ritual model assumes communication not as acts of imparting information, "but the representation of shared beliefs . . . that draws persons together in fellowship and commonality" (Carey, 1989, cited in Grindstaff, 2002). Illouz points out that the talk on talk television creates the very event on which it reports, wherein saying is also doing in the performative pragmatics of communication.[13] Despite these observations, there is little analysis yet of how the mechanisms of speech in the talk show *do* quite so much work: provide testimony, offer therapy, produce conflict, establish trust, and even enact self-identity. Therefore, arguments about the multi-vocality of the talk show point us to questions about the performative and *pragmatic* functions of the talk. For instance, what do the discourses *enact*? What do they *achieve* on television and how do they establish and maintain these trust *relationships* with audiences? These are questions that are central to the concerns of this book.

There may well be some clues from existing research within feminist audience studies that has pointed to speech communication as a central part of the construction of group cohesion around women's cultural practices. For instance, Brown (1994) discusses the importance of women's gossip networks around soap opera viewing. She describes the way in which soap opera's emphasis upon forms of orality helps to draw women together to produce a "tertiary text" that is fundamental to their experienced subordinate position as women and thus offers a space, in gossip, where forms of struggle and resistance can be articulated. Brown's analysis, while it suggests that talk is important to women's articulation of experience through the strength provided in the women's network, does not actually detail the particularities of how such talk emerges. However, when Dorothy Hobson in "Soap Operas at Work" offered an account of women talking about soap opera in the workplace, she did note some of the operations involved in the group's discussion: "The closeness of the group of women has an effect not only on the free way in which they spoke about the television programmes which they viewed and these programmes' relation to their own lives, but also on the actual mode of discourse in which they operated. They interrupted each other, finished each other's sentences, and presented the same word in unison to respond to something which someone had said. An example was when Gill was talking about *Brookside*. 'There are certain ones in there that get on your nerves . . . ' 'The Corkhills!' she was interrupted in unison by all the women. They were so aware of what they all thought that their responses were simultaneous" (1991:153).

This demonstrates that in audience responses to television the actual formulation of the talk, the *mode* of discourse itself, cannot be separated from the content of the discussion about the soap operas. Talking about soaps fits into the working lives of these women, but also *how* they talk about soaps fits with their competences as speakers. They discuss events in relation to the fictional text and in relation to real-life experiences, but as Hobson suggests, "there is no confusion, only an interweaving" (1991:166). Brown goes on to argue that the way in which women incorporate their discussion of soap operas into their lifestyles is partly related to its textual form: "Soap opera's connection to orality also gives it a unique connection to women's oral culture" (1994:59). In the case of soap opera, the texture and way it is experienced as mediated communication reverberates within the social and ritual exchanges of interpersonal communication. While the interplay between orality and televised texts is registered here, the complexity of the relationship between mediated and non-mediated communication has barely been explored in relation to the study of media audiences, or more surprisingly, even in relation to the study of the reception of talk shows.

Conclusion

This chapter has discussed how talk shows have been the subject of much popular abuse, which can be located within arguments around tabloid (feminized) culture, and has traced some of the similarities between debates about women's orality and critiques of gossip. This inquiry has set up the grounds for the empirical research with women viewers. Various academic positions on the talk show have been outlined, ranging from democratic public sphere, feminist consciousness-raising therapy, spectacular voyeurism, and ideological self-regulation, all of which are focused primarily on evaluating the genre either for or against. Many of these earlier readings of the talk show were preoccupied with pinning down the symbolic *meaning* of the genre, thus leaving a rather unsatisfactory polarity in the debates. More recent critiques are beginning to locate the talk show's emphases upon self-identity as *performative* exercises in assuaging contemporary anxieties within broader shifts towards individualization; this book takes this further.

Talking with Television is not intended to be the last word on talk shows per se. Rather, it sets out to engage with a number of questions about mediated communication that neatly coalesce around the talk show. Simply put, these programs rely on talk, on ordinary people talking in a *televisual* space, through frameworks and discursive strategies that have been traditionally feminized, and yet (with some notable exceptions) few critics draw our attention to the mechanics of how this takes place. They do, however, indicate that this talk seeks to elevate the nature of the audience and implicate the audience at home in the dialogue, registering a relationship between the talk of those at home with those in the studio. This is not the first time that television texts have been conceived of in terms of how they become implicated in the business of daily talk. In the discussion of soap opera and women audiences, the form of the text was experienced as resonating within the discursive practices of how the women talked about the text. In this sense, the "meaning" of a *mediated* text is also generated through its place in the broader communicative framework of everyday *interpersonal* interaction. In thinking about the mediation of talk in relation to its entry into everyday speech genres, this book offers a new methodology for media research. This methodology requires a paradigm shift that includes capturing how meaning is *pragmatically* as well as symbolically established in media texts. In order to do so, we need to think of broadcasting's relationship with its audiences as established through communicative "events." The next chapter takes on some of the entrenched theoretical frameworks to re-center the nature of *ritual* communication in media and cultural studies research.

2. Making Talk *Talk* in Media Studies

Introduction

This book argues for an analysis of talk TV that concentrates on the talk itself in order to offer a more sustained analysis of an example of how meaning is generated performatively in contemporary culture. Chapter 1 began to suggest that this approach might help to open out the sets of relations between mediated and non-mediated communication. Such an inquiry necessitates rethinking speech communication within the field of mass communication, and re-centering mass communication within broader contexts of social communication. This involves drawing from traditions of thinking that have usually evolved as distinct modes of intellectual inquiry. In Lana Rakow's "The Field Reconsidered," she laments the separation of communication studies into different categories of communication: "Scholars specialize in such areas as linguistics, public address, interpersonal communication, marital communication, organizational communication, health communication, public relations, advertising, film studies, journalism, popular culture, technology and mass media. By organizing inquiry as these categories do, from the starting point of contexts, content, means, or practices of communication, rather than from the starting point of humans in their particular historical and cultural locations, much of what is interesting and crucial to human existence and experience is made invisible; the context, content, means, and practices of communication are usually taken as givens; the connections between them often do not get made" (1992:10).

To distinguish the study of mediated communication from all other communicative contexts is to miss the opportunity to comprehend just how media are integrated into the daily experience of social interaction. Given the ubiquitous nature of broadcasting, it is surely worth conceptualizing it in terms of its relationships, consistencies, and inconsistencies with other forms of communication. Therefore, I consider talk television in terms of its communicative function as a televised event that also flows into the daily communicative context of the home. Highlighting communication per se in this way absorbs *both* the sense of the mediation of talk, as well as its interpersonal (feminized) character on daily talk programs. However, the theoretical bedrock informing much media and cultural studies research has so far served to eclipse such an approach, circumventing crucial ways of understanding broadcasting's "reach" into everyday experience. This is because approaches to language analysis in media studies have largely been influenced by a semiotic model in the widely recognized "linguistic turn." This chapter, by tracing some of the language debates in media and cultural studies, accounts for how this has transpired, and calls for resurrecting critical insights into speech to account for the embedding of broadcast communication in the home.

Language Issues in Cultural Studies

Cultural studies has certainly not ignored language issues altogether. The publication of *Culture, Media, Language* (Hall et al., 1980) brings together a number of philosophical themes that the Birmingham Center for Contemporary Cultural Studies (CCCS) had engaged in the 1970s. In accounting for the state of language analysis in cultural studies at the time, there is the recognition that all cultural phenomena require some linguistic component, while the study of language itself was of marginal concern. Weedon, Tolson, and Mort suggest that it was the manner in which early cultural historians Raymond Williams and Richard Hoggart defined culture as "a vital descriptive effort," a "way of seeing . . . things and . . . relationships" that has hindered the development of a "specific theoretical interest in language and signifying practices within cultural studies which would pay attention to the way meaning is constructed and *communicated*" (1980a:178, my emphasis). Understanding language as a descriptive reflection of some external reality or experience meant that language studies were dominated by semiological approaches. These refer to how language comes to "represent" the world as the site where the meanings of any given culture are generated and negotiated. Thus, much of the theoretical labor around language and culture followed the path laid down by structuralism, which conceived of language as no more than an order of signs that are interpretable by the cultural analyst.

The impact of structuralism on the study of language within media and cultural studies is pervasive, beginning with the early influence of the linguist

Ferdinand de Saussure (1988 [1916]). He described the bifurcation of language into *langue* and *parole,* which procured the marginalization of research into *spoken* language. *La langue* refers to language as an abstract system that is made up of arbitrary signs that can be studied and described. *La parole,* on the other hand, represents language as it is spoken, which is, according to Saussure, too unpredictable to investigate. Thus, with this distinction we are forced to accept la langue as the deep structure for all other manifestations of language, including speech. It is precisely here, in the enthusiasm of cultural theorists to engage with language as only an arbitrary structure of signs, that we can observe the way in which language and meaning as generated in interaction was sidestepped in early developments in cultural studies.[1]

British Cultural Studies' willingness to embrace this version of language is understandable given its Marxist commitment to engaging with the media's power over the masses. Influenced by Gramsci's (1971) writings on the role of the cultural sphere in the maintenance of capitalist societies, the CCCS conceptualized the media in terms of hegemony—the penetration of the state into all areas of civil society. One can understand the appeal of a semiotic approach as a method of demystifying the media's messages. Early work concentrated on the ideological meanings of the media's output, where the construction of meaning came to be understood in terms of signs and systems. While Saussure split the linguistic sign into signifier and signified, Roland Barthes developed a "second-order of signification" that allows for the analysis of culture. Barthes' hugely influential *Mythologies* (1973) accounts for the naturalizing effect of ideology by deciphering the structures through which messages are produced, thus exposing their underlying meaning.[2] The uncovering of sign systems as a language, semiotics, provided the basis for research into the politics of representation and continues to be a foundational building block for students of media and cultural studies.

Concepts of power and ideology were therefore central to cultural studies as it attempted to theorize how the dominant classes maintain the status quo through the dissemination of their ruling ideas. Althusser's (1971) understanding of ideology and subjectivity helped to explain how these "ruling ideas" reached the masses through "Ideological State Apparatuses." Residing in his concept of "interpellation"—the moment a subject recognizes the "call" of a text—is the guiding principle that describes how subjects are recruited to the hegemonic discourses of the state. This is easily appropriated to explain media influence, presuming a particular hierarchical and fixed relationship between media texts and their audiences.

Subsequent theoretical insights have not wrestled free of this version of a textually inscribed subjectivity. In the feminist post-structuralist critiques of culture and meaning, French writer Julia Kristeva (1984) did argue for the removal of la langue to consider the true "speaking subject," but this continued to take shape through Althusserian means. French feminism offered a framework for considering the internalization of ideology that accounted for women's negative entry into the masculine symbolic order. Here the dominant theoretical emphasis became Lacanian psychoanalysis, which allowed for the textual analysis of forms such as art and poetry, rather than the "speech" of real women. Toril Moi (1985) outlines the incompatibility of Kristeva's writings with research into language and gender from the "Anglo-American tradition," which is concerned with a social emphasis upon how gender relations are played out in speech in lived contexts. There is a crucial distinction here between feminist writings that focus on the identification of gendered "subject positions" in the realm of the textual (hence its impact upon film theory) and more sociologically centered research into women's lived experiences in their concrete situations.

This point raises another issue central to the history of media and cultural studies in relation to broadcasting. On the whole, products of the media have been described as "texts" as a way of identifying them as critical objects of study in the mold of literary theory. As Paddy Scannell points out: "Media and cultural studies in the UK are still dominated by the encoding-decoding model of communications and a model of language based on Saussure. Mapped onto these is a text-reader theory derived from literary studies of written 'texts' to account for the relationships between the product of radio and television and their audiences" (1991a:10).

This text-reader formulation, when applied to reception, implies that we consume media products by reading them and thus deciphering their messages. In Stuart Hall's (1980) foundational "encoding-decoding" paradigm we are variously interpreting the symbolic "codes" that have been encoded within the (hegemonic) framework of the text depending upon our social and cultural location. Chapter 4 will return to the legacy of Hall's encoding-decoding model by outlining an alternative methodology for audience research, but here I want to question whether broadcasting's relationship with its audiences is textual in exactly the same sense. I want to draw attention rather to the *physicality* of the experience. Is listening to radio or watching television akin to reading? As *acts,* I would suggest they are fundamentally different. Broadcasting's dominant mode of address is through speech (and in the case of television the moving image as well), both of which demand additional affective responses. The reception of broadcasting is surely a different communicative event from that of reading a book, as it is one that can be physically *heard* and *seen*,[3] and therefore experienced as taking place, thus occupying a physical space in the communicative context of the home. This is where a broader conceptual map of communication per se might be useful. Adopting a literary, rather than a more broadly communicative, tradition of language analysis for media and cultural studies has meant that despite the obvious nexus between the production of the cultural sphere and speech, the field has failed to provide a long-standing contribution to theorizing that interrelationship.

The Missing Theorization of Speech

Any objection to the dominance of approaches from structuralism and post-structuralism is based on the premise that langue and parole should be separated out, thus closing the door on the exploration of language in lived (spoken) interaction. This is important, especially given the commitment of ethnographic cultural studies to documenting culture "from below" in everyday experiences and everyday realities. However, it is possible to re-read some of the early cultural studies work of Williams and Hoggart to resurrect the cultural significance of speech. For instance, in *The Uses of Literacy* (1959), Hoggart writes: "We have to try to see beyond the habits to what the habits stand for, to see through the statements to what the statements really mean (which may be the opposite of the statement themselves), to detect differing pressures of emotion behind idiomatic phrases and ritualistic observances."[4]

Interpreting "what statements really mean" also calls for an understanding of "idiomatic phrases and ritualistic observances," which I would suggest is not just dependant upon investigating the structured level of the semantic. Meaning is also located in the "uses" of language, in the "differing pressures of emotion," not only in the expression of content. Thus, Hoggart discussed "the oral tradition" of working-class speech and the relevance of dialect, particular proverbs, sayings, and aphorisms. He saw insights into speech as vital to the understanding of lived culture, claiming that such insights "will indicate a great deal, in particular the host of phrases in common use. Manners of speaking, the use of urban dialects and intonations, could probably indicate even more" (1959:21). Here, Hoggart's references have little in common with a formal structuralist approach to linguistic analysis, and, throughout *The Uses of Literacy,* the centrality of language to the experience of, say, working in a factory or waiting in a queue at the doctor's office were anecdotally recorded.

If Hoggart's suggestions *do* point to a "semiotic" analysis of language, then I would suggest that it was not of the kind descended from Saussure, but rather of the nature proposed by Volosinov and Bakhtin.[5] Volosinov's *Marxism and the Philosophy of the Language* (1973) developed a theory of language in opposition to Saussurian linguistics. Volosinov was critical of two dominant trends he saw in the study of language at that time: individual subjectivism and abstract objectivism. The former referred to the understanding of language as entirely sourced by the individual psyche. In this tradition, language as a system is a ready-made product that becomes active in the psychology of the creative individual. Abstract objectivism, on the other hand, does not recognize the creativity of the individual at all, but rather defines language as a unified system that can be theorized in terms of phonetic, grammatical, and lexical rules. When the study of language is seen as an investigation of these rules it becomes an objective science, the substance of which is formulaic.

Volosinov's basic contention with Saussure's work was in that primary division of language into langue and parole, which in "abstract objectivism" led to the rejection of the significance of the utterance (speech): "Language-speech according to Saussure, cannot be the object of study for linguistics. In and of itself, it lacks inner unity and validity as an autonomous entity; it is a heterogeneous composite. Its composite, contradictory composition make it too difficult to handle" (1973:59).

For Volosinov, however, speech represented the essence of social life. He objected most to the fact that neither of these theoretical positions, "individual subjectivism" and "abstract objectivism," contain the capacity to understand language as it is used by its speakers in society. While "individual subjectivism" draws attention to the uniqueness of the utterance, it can only be discussed in terms of the individual psyche, and "abstract objectivism" sees language as a set of externally appropriated rules, both leading us away completely from the living vitality of language in social life.[6] For, Volosinov, a focus on speech explains the historical dynamism of language as a generative process, and interestingly Raymond Williams *has* actually stressed the organic nature of language in very similar terms. When asked to account for the mutability of language (the way in which terms can come to mean their exact opposite) he replies:

> At the theoretical level, it underlines the fact that language is in continual social production in its most dynamic sense. In other words, not in the sense which is comparable with structuralism—that a central body of meaning is created

and propagated— but in the sense that like any other social production it is in the arena of all sorts of shifts and interests and relations of dominance. Certain crises around certain experiences will occur, which are registered in language in often surprising ways. The result of which is a notion of language as not merely the creation of arbitrary signs which are then reproduced within groups, which is the Structuralist model, but of signs which take on the changeable and often reversed social relations of a given society, so that what enters into them is the contradictory and often conflict-ridden social history of the people who speak the language, including all the variants between signs at any given time. (Williams, 1979:176)

For Volosinov and Williams, language can be theorized as a site where the relations of social production, such as dominance and social change, can be explored. Volosinov advocates a *social* "semiotics" that enables us to interpret the nature of spoken interaction that is not rooted in abstract rules. He suggests that spoken signs are conditioned above all by the social organization of the participants involved and the immediate conditions of their interaction. In this way the sign is *multi-accentual*—subject to the social conditions within which it is produced. This seems rather closer to Hoggart's early references to the particular "oral traditions" of the working class in specific social contexts. According to Volosinov, speech must therefore be at the heart of any Marxist philosophy of language: "The process of understanding any ideological phenomena at all (be it a picture, a piece of music, a ritual, or an act of human contact) cannot operate without the participation of inner speech. All manifestations of ideological creativity—all other non-verbal signs—are bathed by, suspended in, and cannot be entirely segregated or divorced from the element of speech" (1973:15).

To study the workings of ideology and its relationship to the lived subjectivities of people, one must therefore study the social contexts of speech in real, lived, and *social* environments. Given the continual need to engage with the *media's* role in processes of ideology and social change, it makes sense to call for inserting a focus on the dynamism of broadcast communication within social life. My aim is to apply this fundamental idea to an analysis of the relationship of talk television with a female audience, in an attempt to understand the spoken discourse of television as embedded in lived cultural experience, dependent upon the speakers and hearers in the conditions of its environment. This analysis might then inform us more broadly about mediated communicative processes at work in cultural life. To do so, we must consider the specificity of this communicative process, as a particular, mediated speech genre.

Speech Genres: The Significance of the Utterance

Volosinov insists on studying language in connection with its "concrete conditions," stressing the importance of generic conditions of speech styles in their own environment, which is a key insight for the interpretative framework of this book. Different cultural spheres apply their own "speech genres," which correspond to their own specific circumstances, implying that speech styles can actually be studied in context. The concept of the speech genre recognizes that real-life utterances are subject to behavioral genres and the structures of these genres depend upon the specific features of the behavioral situation. These genres are located within the richness and diversity of cultural life and enmeshed within the various organizational structures and regimes of any society: "Village sewing circles, urban carouses, workers' lunch time chats, etc., will all have their own types. Each situation fixed and sustained by social custom, commands a particular repertoire of little behavioural genres. The behavioural genre fits everywhere into the channel of social intercourse assigned to it and functions as an ideological reflection of its type, structure, goal, and social composition. The behavioural genre is a fact of the social milieu: of holiday, leisure time, and of social contact in the parlour, the workshop, etc." (1973:97).

A more precise definition of the characteristics of speech genres emerges from M. M. Bakhtin (1986). In his essay "The Problem of Speech Genres," Bakhtin provides us with an explanation of the importance of the utterance to understanding changes taking place in social life: "Utterances and their types, that is speech genres, are the drive belts from the history of society to the history of language" (1986:65). It is the utterance that gives language its life, yet at the time of writing he claimed that the speech genre had not been given adequate attention in comparison to literary genres, reflecting the wider trend we have seen in media studies.

In Bakhtin's essay, recognizing speech genres means understanding language in terms of *communication,* rather than in terms of traditional linguistic approaches to language structures. For instance, he juxtaposes the sentence as a unit of language as distinct from the utterance as a unit of speech communication. The sentence is a grammatical construct that is complete, whereas the utterance is dependent upon the response of the *addressee* in any dialogue, therefore, "it can determine others' responsive positions under the complex conditions of speech communication in a particular cultural sphere" (1986:76). Each cultural sphere develops its own relatively stable types of utterance that can be studied in terms of genre. These speech genres can be described in terms of their compositional structure, through the conditions and goals of a specific environment. For instance, the way in which we recognize the end of utterances is dependent upon the context, the speaker, and the style of discourse. We learn to master these different genres, which have relatively stable rules of engagement. When hearing other people speak, we identify the nature of the utterance, we predict a certain length, and we foresee the end. These particular stylistic features are dependent upon who is being spoken *to* as well as who is speaking, and enable the distinction of speech genres.

Both Volosinov and Bakhtin stress that there are systematic rules involved in the cultural organization of everyday interaction that determine genres of communication. I am suggesting that we may be able to see broadcasting in parallel terms, as also constitutive of a, or even a range of, speech genre(s). Bakhtin and Volosinov point to the empirical study of language in *action,* but despite discussion of this work at the CCCS in the UK, it is not usually considered as part of the dominant story of cultural studies[7] and to my knowledge has never been taken up to consider the relationships between the media and its audiences. If we return to Bakhtin's assertion that utterances can "determine others' responsive positions," this might well be extremely pertinent for the study of how audiences engage with mediated discourse. Does the speech produced for the audience at home position the viewer's response in a certain way and if so, can we detail this speech as genre-specific? Is it possible to re-conceptualize the reception of television in the home as a grounded, everyday speech genre with its own systematic rules? And, importantly, can this lead us to broader insights into the media's role in daily communicative action and social identity? To begin to answer these questions requires a re-thinking of the ways in which we think of mass communication as only a transmission mode of communication, at the same time that it urges us to re-think interpersonal communication as only face-to-face communication. There have been some interventions in media theory that have an impact upon, and indeed support, my proposition here. These are a set of theoretical proposals that foreground the embedding of the media in everyday life.

Media, Modernity, and Everyday Life

In the outline of the talk show literature in the last chapter, there was discussion of how bringing the audience to the stage breaks down the distinction between spectacle and spectator. This has an important impact on the communicative strategies of broadcasting, especially considering Carpignano et al.'s suggestion that the phenomenon is bringing about "new social relationships of communication embodied in the television medium which have progressively undermined the structural dichotomy between performance and audience" (Carpignano et al., 1990:35). How then can we think of these "new social relationships" built by television's forms? Traditional semiotic tools from media studies, which illuminate symbolic meanings, do not help us here. More useful is a perspective generated by authors such as Joshua Meyrowitz (1985) and John Thompson (1994, 1995), who are concerned with the media's communicative impact on daily life. These authors locate such phenomena as the breach in the divide between audience and performer within wider conceptual themes presented by late modernity. They begin to represent a social theory of the media that reaches beyond traditional schools of thought descended from structuralism and semiotics. Thompson suggests that there is a poverty of resources in thinking about the way in which the media is embedded within the social world and is part of daily communicative action: "One is left with the impression that, for most social theorists, the media are like the air that we breathe: pervasive, taken-for-granted, yet rarely thought about as such" (Thompson, 1994:27). Refusing some of the dominant paradigms that have overly concentrated on the determining effect of the media as a form of social control, he attempts to describe the way in which the media has had an impact on the nature of social interaction in the modern world.

Television has often been thought about as a domestic medium whereby the home, the domestic, and suburbia are embedded within its history and form (Silverstone, 1996), a view that necessitates research into television's place within family relationships (e.g., Morley, 1986; Lull, 1990). In turn, the space of the home as a site of the reconstruction of patriarchal relations has made gender central to thinking about television and the home. Hobson's (1980) pioneering essay, "Housewives and the Mass Media," intervened precisely in this debate when she described the importance of the radio in providing companionship in the lonely space of the home in the daytime, as well as the way in which the scheduling of radio programs helped order the otherwise structureless day-to-day life of the housewife. Notions of *companionship* and the *everyday* are suggestive of a type of familiar and even intimate relationship that women might have with broadcasting that is not directly related to the semiotic encoding of meaning. Is it possible that that relationship is partly experienced or even ratified by a mediated speech genre?

Thompson articulates the everyday within media theory in terms of the modern age, where the media has played a determining role in generating new forms of interaction and new kinds of social relationships between individuals. These have emerged from the changing phenomenological conditions caused by the development of media technologies. Sociologist Anthony

Giddens (1991a) highlights the characteristics of modernity as partly due to the changes that have occurred in the social arrangements of space and time, whereby people inhabiting the pre-modern world would experience time as inextricably bound to a sense of place, whereas the modern era is characterized by "empty time"—an increasingly globalized sense of temporal arrangements. He refers to this as "time-space distanciation," whereby time and space have become increasingly dislocated through the ongoing process of the disembedding of social systems: "By disembedding I mean the 'lifting out' of social relations from local contexts of interaction and their restructuring across indefinite spans of time-space" (1991a:21).

What then does this mean in terms of the media? Put simply, technological mechanisms have "lifted" social relations out of face-to-face contexts and "stretched" them across vast distances. Therefore, we experience events happening at a distance, possibly even at a different moment in time, as though they are "live." In addition, "media events" are increasingly choreographed for the cameras as much as for the co-present spectators (Dayan and Katz, 1992). Social relationships, therefore, are no longer confined to the local. Modern communications systems enable us to engage in interactions with distanced and absent speakers; co-present and co-spatial arrangements are no longer required. While at the same time the consumption of media takes place in locations distant from each other, the moments of reception are simultaneous, a fact that might have a huge impact on human relationships and the shaping of individual and collective identities (Moores, 1997a).

The process of *"re-*embedding" provides a key to understanding the formation of new social relationships through the mediation of experience. Re-embedding is "the reappropriation or recasting of disembedded social relations so as to pin them down . . . to local conditions of time and place" (Giddens, 1991a:79–80). Moores (1995, 2000) articulates the way in which one can take this concept and apply it to televised mediated encounters. For instance, in the modern age we rely upon the trust we place in the institutional representatives of "expert systems," for example, the trust we place in architects as we sit in our homes or in the aircrew as we board a plane. As we, lay individuals, come into contact with representatives of these expert systems, they engage in "facework commitments"[8] wherein we are encouraged to place our trust in them—such as the rehearsed facework of flight attendants as they allay our fears in the air. According to Moores, "Without pushing Giddens's notion of re-embedding too far . . . we can fruitfully extend his notes on trust in co-present encounters so as to take account of the facework commitments made by media figures in their regular interactions with absent viewers and listeners" (2000:112).

In adopting this approach, we are not drawing upon concepts such as "simulacrum" and "hyperreality," as put forward by Baudrillard (1988) and other postmodern theorists, concepts suggestive of a "fake" or "substitute" world in which the media has duped the masses. Rather, we are focusing upon how the media can re-negotiate parts of everyday communication in which, according to Moores, "The communicative styles of TV and radio are oriented to the everyday realities of viewers and listeners—and in appearing to address their talk and action directly to audiences in local settings of reception, broadcasting's personalities are engaged in the performance of a distinctively modern public drama" (2000:112).

For our purposes, then, the "locale" that this "stretching" of experience is ultimately "pinned down" to, is, in the case of much broadcasting, the home. Here I want to consider how broadcast talk reaches across the mediated space, stretching out face-to-face communication to produce new forms of communicative action.

Broadcasting as Speech Communication

Broadcasting has been described as "an institution in everyday life" (Rath, 1985) that historically had to find a way of communicating with its audiences appropriately in domestic settings (Spigel, 1992). This was not necessarily obvious, as early broadcasting in the UK privileged monologue over dialogue. In 1928, Hilda Matheson, as the first Head of Talks at the BBC, conducted experiments that suggested it was "useless to address the microphone as if it were a public meeting, or even to read essays or leading articles. The person sitting at the other end expected the speaker to address him personally, simply, almost familiarly, as *man to man*" (Matheson, 1933:75–76, my emphasis).[9] The lecture style, as if speaking from a pulpit to a congregation, was inappropriate to a technology embedded within the private space of the home. Broadcasting could not speak to its audience as a single mass but instead had to develop modes of addressing its audience personally and intimately. It is not just the talk show that endeavors to create this kind of relationship with its audience; this is a feature historically associated with the nature of broadcasting as a domestic medium. While broadcasting constitutes part of the mass media that is distributed to "many," it adopts a form and style that seems as though it is communicating directly with "you."

Scannell (1991a) refers to the subsequent development of a broadcasting style as its "communicative intentionality," which has a double articulation: "It is a communicative interaction between those participating in discussion, interview, game show or whatever and, at the same time, is designed to be heard by absent audiences" (1991a:3). It is this articulation to the audience and how that is received that concerns me most here. While broadcasting as "mass media" is mostly thought of as one-way communication (characteristic of "old media") from which its ideological imperative has been deemed most efficient, some authors have begun to think about its communicative ethos in terms of interaction. Thompson (1994, 1995) has discussed the kind of electronic channels presented by modern media as "mediated quasi-interactions" that supplement face-to-face communication interaction. Therefore, across a new time-space continuum, from dispersed physical locales, new forms of interaction might be emerging.

One can find a similar, but much earlier, understanding of mediated forms of interaction within psychologists Horton and Wohl's (1956) essay on "para-social interaction," which has recently been the focus of revived interest and has been deployed by theorists of the talk show to explain the "down-to-earth" style and thus the popularity of the host. Both descriptions of either "para-social interaction" or "mediated quasi-interaction" contain prefixes that refer to the apparent monological character of broadcast communication, that is, its inherent lack of the reciprocity that is characteristic in face-to-face, co-present communication. There is instead a simulation of mutual interaction, what Horton and Wohl call the simulacrum of conversational give and take.

In this way, broadcast communication has been effortlessly incorporated into the humdrum routines (and sounds) of everyday life. Indeed, so ubiquitous is its presence that its *style* of communication has often gone unnoticed. Horton and Wohl's early essay presents us with some of the features that characterize such a relationship. Television in particular relies on the enigmatic role of the "persona" on the screen. The presentation of personalities in this way encourages the formation of "relationships" with their audiences that approach intimacy—what they call "intimacy at a distance." The regularity of the presenters' appearances and the direct mode of address with which actors speak to audiences delivers a bond that allows the audience a feeling of "knowing" them personally. This is how the personality system[10] works in television, where the realm of the "ordinary" reigns, precisely breaking down the distance between the performer and the audience that is seen to distinguish the talk show. The distortion of these traditional boundaries occurs through television's quotidian qualities, creating an everyday feeling of intimacy and thus problematizing its theorization solely in terms of the "spectacle" of the text.

Talk TV: An Intimate Relationship

Daytime talk television offers an ideal case study through which to empirically research this "para-social" phenomenon, precisely because of the way in which it seemingly exaggerates these features that might be seen to outline the very nature of television. In his history of the talk show, Wayne Munson (1993) describes the way in which the 1960s American show, *Art Linkletter's House Party* (which he argues led the way for audience participation programming such as *Donahue*), develops new forms of spectatorship through its involvement of "ordinary" people, anecdotes, and the studio audience in a type of folk culture.[11] This apparent co-presence of the housewife and the studio is explicit in British broadcasting in the mid-morning talk television that concerns us here. Moores's (1997b) description of the para-social phenomenon in broadcasting draws precisely upon the daytime magazine program and the talk show. He points to some of the textual features that help facilitate this feeling of a para-social relationship. For instance, the magazine show's title, *This Morning* (ITV) draws our attention to the immediacy and co-temporality with which we are to experience its daily programming. The original presenters were known by their first names as "Richard and Judy," now replaced by "Phil and Fearn," as were the presenters of *Good Morning* known as "Ann and "Nick. Any viewer who has regularly tuned in to these programs has been privy to intimate knowledge of the presenters as themselves. For instance, we know that the husband and wife team Richard and Judy have twins who have occasionally appeared on the program and have been brought into the discussion by the presenters to validate their authentic experiences as parents. Similarly, Oprah's personal narratives of weight loss, life with Stedman, and a difficult childhood as a black woman from the American South, contribute to her success through creating a sense of intimacy with her audience. The personal, private topics that are covered on the shows produce the revealing of presenters' lives as they validate their performance as "one of us" with ordinary domestic concerns.[12]

The organization of the studio set of *This Morning* and *Good Morning* helps to replay the arena of the domestic. The presenters sit upon sofas with coffee tables, lamps, and flowers, suggestive of the domestic space of the living room. Guests sit on armchairs with cups of coffee and are thanked for "dropping-in" in the same way in which the audience is greeted at the beginning of the show. After the commercial breaks we are welcomed "back" to share the same space and time of the visitors on the show. Their living room is extended into our living room. The domestic experience of the home is shared within the televisual space of the studio as well as the *real* domestic space of the viewer at home. The space of the studio is "lifted out" and re-embedded within the *real* living room of the home in a mediated phenomenon of shared and "doubled" homely space.

Similarly, this valorization of the "ordinary" is extended to other talk show programming, whereby the programs rest on the persona of the presenters, such as *Kilroy* and *Vanessa*. Although *The Time . . . The Place* did not headline its presenter, John Stapleton, in quite the same way, the show's particular emphasis was to move around the UK to different towns for its studio audience. In this way, *The Time . . . The Place* replicates the here and now of this "communicative ethos" of broadcasting. In studio discussion programs, ordinary people talk about their lives, replaying domestic issues through the control of the host. The hosts appear as "down-to-earth" and style themselves as "one of the people," drawing upon common sense on "our" behalf.

Although in some talk shows the television studio is not always set up to reflect the home environment (except for the show *Vanessa,* where guests would often sit on armchairs) the textual conventions still attempt to produce a co-present effect of "being there." For instance, at the opening of *Kilroy,* we see the set and rows of participants as though on a stage, but once Robert Kilroy-Silk addresses us through direct address, the subjective camera angle then moves with him into the studio audience. We walk up the steps with him and are then positioned within the studio audience space where ordinary people debate. In this way the home and the studio are co-spatially organized together in such a way that the viewer at home is encouraged to experience a feeling of co-presence, inhabiting the same space as the studio audience. (The staging arrangements of the programs are explored more extensively in chapter 3.) In these programs, therefore, there is a continued relationship whereby televisual reality unfolds in parallel with the everyday lived experience of the viewers. Television allows itself to emerge as though "live" and co-temporal with daily life. One only has to think of the embedding of temporal rituals like Valentine's Day or Christmas Day in the soap opera world that are similarly reproduced in the magazine and talk shows.

Sociability and Conversation

The co-temporal and co-spatial organization of broadcasting assists in the development of intimate para-social relationships in which an "illusion" of intimacy is sustained through the regular and ordinary omnipresent nature of television broadcasting. The conversational gestures employed by the host/presenter are interpretable as though he or she is talking to friends, not, as in early broadcasts, through a hierarchical position of talking down to the masses. Television's *mode* of speaking mainly assumes a relationship of equals. When referring to TV hosts, Horton and Wohl suggest that, "to say that he [or she] is familiar and intimate is to use pale and feeble language for the pervasiveness and closeness with which multitudes feel his [or her] presence" (1956:357). Meyrowitz even suggests that "the evolution of the media has begun to cloud the differences between stranger and friend and to weaken the distinction between people who are 'here' and people who are 'somewhere else'" (1985:122).

Scannell (1996) refers to the development of such a relationship as related to "sociability" as a strategic feature of broadcasting's communicative ethos. Other authors refer similarly to an increasing "personalisation" occurring in TV discourse (Silverstone, 1994). The medium of sociability is conversation—talk for talk's sake. Here Scannell takes direction from Simmel: "In sociability talking is an end in itself; in purely sociable conversation the content is merely the indispensable carrier of the stimulation, in which the lively exchange of talk as such unfolds" (1950:136). Again, this reflects how the talk show has been interpreted, in terms of its commitment to "ritual," rather than transmission forms of communication (Grindstaff, 2002).

One of the imperatives of broadcasting's communicative intentionality is that it assumes some kind of, if not mutual, then at least conversational relationship with the audience at home. This might be interpreted within wider cultural trends such as "the conversationalisation of public discourse," a concept that suggests a wider ideological drive within consumer culture (Fairclough, 1984). I analyze the conversational (spoken) genre of television in order to generate an alternative assessment of its communicative relationship with its audience. As well as considering the substance and production of media messages, should we not also pay attention to how that "substance" is assembled and generated dynamically in actual media "talk"? How is it that we are addressed by radio and television? Who is it that television speaks to? For Scannell, these questions propose a crucial distinction between a structuralist approach to the media that is concerned with the relationship between text and subject, and a more dynamic interactive perspective whereby "the oneself so addressed by radio and television is a *someone,* not just anyone; that is a person, not a subject as in Althusser's notion of ideological interpellation" (Scannell, 1996:13). Therefore, we should think about the ways in which programs address someone—what he refers to as the "for anyone-as-someone" structure. He argues that this structure "is a necessary precondition of any cultural product that can (a) be found as meaningfully available, without any difficulty, by anyone, and (b) presents itself in such a way that it appears to be 'for me'" (1991a:14). This leads us to a focus on approaches to "discourse," beyond just *what* is said, to emphasize the importance of context, situation, and the identity of speakers in defining the *communicative* function of mediated language at any moment in time.

Discourse

Chapter 1 discussed the way in which Illouz's analysis of *Oprah* concentrated not so much on an underlying dominant symbolic meaning, but rather on how the self-referentiality of *Oprah* attempted to *achieve* a set of relations with its audience that makes sense in terms of contemporary anxieties. Although Illouz's focus is not upon spoken discourse as such, she momentarily alludes to the kind of analysis proposed here. In keeping with the idea that the talk show offers a type of "ritual" communicative function, she suggests that "Oprah's show produces the very event it reports on, a linguistic one. Indeed confessions, reconciliations, and disputes are speech acts that point to themselves and not to an order of truthfulness or reality beyond" (Illouz, 2003:56). It is the discursive *event* that brings the show into being, where guests embody the speech acts that they dramatize. This is a reference to theories of pragmatics and to J. L. Austin (1963), who describes "illocutionary acts" in which speech acts also *perform* actions, for example, "I name this ship." This way of handling discourse sees language as "behavioral units," as practices that are constitutive of social phenomena, an approach reminiscent of Bakhtin. Searle (1969) goes on to develop a larger taxonomy of illocutionary acts in which there are a number of types of *action* that one can perform while speaking. Language therefore is also performative; we learn aspects of linguistic competence and employ the appropriate rules for the right social occasion to gain the appropriate outcomes.[13]

Communication thus rests upon the pragmatic use of shared knowledge, where the intentions between speakers are understood. "Pragmatics" develops a theory of how meaning in interaction functions through a model of cooperation between speakers. For example, Grice's (1975) concept of "implicature" refers to the way in which a speaker's intention is inscribed not only in semantic meaning, but also in the use of conversational principles, adhering to maxims of quality, quantity, and relevance. Similarly, Conversation Analysis (CA) developed out of ethnomethodology and examines the micro-politics of interaction through an analysis of the "turn-taking system" (Sacks, Scheggloff, and Jefferson, 1974). Conversational turn-taking is part of our communicative competence that ensures the smooth running of social interaction. While an exhaustive account of these approaches is not possible here, it is important to recognize how they can help to explain the mutability of language, the importance of context, and the relevance of the relationship between speakers. The following section exemplifies how context, time and space, speaker identities, conversational turns, and genre can also be important to understanding mediated discourse.

Broadcast Talk as Discourse

There is a relatively small, but burgeoning body of work concerned with the analysis of broadcasting in terms of its discursive functions. Analysts focus on the institutional character of the formation of the discursive features of the televised text, whereby, "If some interaction has an institutional character then the relevance of the institutional context in question must be shown to inhabit the details of the participants' conduct" (Heritage and Greatbatch, 1991:94). Studying the talk of television and radio has received increased attention in recent years, despite the dominant tradition of media studies having neglected a rigorous consideration of "talk" as imperative to understanding television and radio's relationship with their audiences.[14] "Talk" is central to television's protean nature and therefore is fundamental to television studies because "talk thus generates the socio-communicative sphere within which television images operate" (Corner, 1999:37).

This returns us to the observations made by Scannell about television's search for a voice that can be reconciled with the nature of broadcasting's domestic consumption. It is here that discourse analysis can engage with the import of context, since it is the duality of broadcast discourse—its production within the public domain and its reception within the private domain of the home—that provides us with its "double articulation." It is its institutional production and domestic consumption that makes broadcast discourse a remarkable phenomenon. Some basic insights into this peculiar nature of broadcast discourse are outlined here, as they inform the subsequent analysis of the programs in the next chapter.

Context: Double Articulation

Broadcast talk is not merely conversation, but it is conversation produced for an overhearing audience. "Normal" conversational maxims are transformed by the mediation of talk. For instance, Montgomery (1999) discusses the way in which elements of "performance" are central to understanding the discursive structure of the comedy show made for BBC, *The Mrs. Merton Show,* as entertainment. Here, talk is produced for comedic effect and audience response, mainly through transgressing usual conversational maxims. For instance, in *Mrs. Merton,* her character uses ritual insults that breach the "approbation maxim," which Leech tells us, "says 'avoid saying unpleasant things about others, and more particularly, about H (the hearer)'" (Leech, 1983:135). Comedy for the listener at home is created through the discursive undermining of the hearer in the studio—the guest on the show. This requires a disregard for the usual maxims of politeness as outlined by Brown and Levinson (1987), which involve maintaining the "positive face" of the hearer, and may call into question Grice's maxim of "manner" in the production of double-entendres, and so on. (Montgomery, 1999). This element of "performance" is what transforms the discourse from ordinary conversation through the necessary "double articulation" of broadcasting's entertainment bias.

Time and Space: Deixis

"Deixis" refers to "features of language that refer directly to the personal, temporal, or locational characteristics of a situation . . . (e.g., you, now, here)" (Crystal, 1995:451). According to Hanks, the optimal condition for the use of deixis is where both participants "are face to face, mutually oriented, and share detailed background knowledge of referents" (1989:112).[15] One of the key features of much broadcast discourse is that the talk itself uses discursive references that are usually considered to require face-to-face arrangements to be meaningful. Thus, in Montgomery's discussion of "DJ Talk," social deixis is created through the use of direct address, "you," to address the listener. This deixis can be narrowed down by the use of accompanying identifiers, whereby the "you" may be identified by name:

> Alison and Liz you are now official listeners for Ward Eighteen
> Ian Schlesser hello happy birthday to you
> You are now (Marjorie) the official Radio One listener for Princess Street
> Yeh Okay then Bob Sproat in er Worcestershire er . . . T-shirt on the way
>   to you.
> (Montgomery, 1986b:425)

Through these deictic references, absent viewers are treated as though they are capable of responding, thus suggesting co-presence. Social deixis can also be extended to include spatial deixis through references to the environment of the speaker, such as:

> 'er got my pumpkin in the studio here
> I(t)'s really good (I) got a real pumpkin honestly
> I mean you probably think that I'm ninety
> but here hang on
> let me just hold this up in front of the microphone
> so you can see my pumpkin
> can you see that
> a real Halloween pumpkin
> (Montgomery, 1986b:429)

The references to the immediate environment of the speaker (this place, pumpkin *here*, can you see *that?*) according to Montgomery, can be understood as a device for erasing a sense of distance between speaker and audience—assuming a common visual field implies a form of co-presence.

Similarly, for my purposes, the co-temporal arrangements of television are interesting since in some sense television is always "live," unlike film, as it is immediate, "transmitted and received in the same moment as it is produced" (Ellis, 1982:132). Therefore, much of TV, despite the dislocated spatial arrangements of the viewer, refers to a shared "now" of co-temporality. Marriott (1996), for example, discusses the way in which this phenomenological "now" is complicated by the shifting of tenses in sports replay talk; she concludes that the replay, "re-embeds the sequence in a different 'here' and 'now'—the 'here' of the viewer and the 'now' of the television event, unfolding in real shared time. The development of replay technology means that the same sequence can be re-embedded again and again, each time in a different phenomenological 'now'" (1996:84). Deictic references to time and "now" are also therefore central to understanding para-social relationships built through broadcasting. The use of such references is one of the mechanisms that allows for the reconfigurations of space and time that are so liberally theoretically espoused in contemporary media theory.

Identity: Footing

The concept of "footing" was developed by sociologist Erving Goffman (1981). It is premised on his earlier work in *The Presentation of Self in Everyday Life* (1969), in which he explains the constructed nature of identity through the various ways in which the self is performed or presented in response to situated environments and present others. In the concept of "footing," Goffman is concerned to dissolve the unitary categories of speaker and hearer as an oversimplified formulation that does not recognize the parts other bystanders or eavesdroppers might play in the interaction. For Goffman, there are various forms and degrees of participation that can be broken down into more specific interactional "footings." These are the "animator"—the person who utters the sequence of words; the "author"—the person with whom the sentiments originated; and the "principal"—the person whose position is being expressed in and through the utterance (1981:144). An individual may therefore switch between these alignments depending upon the presentation of self in particular contexts.

This concept becomes useful in broadcast talk. For instance, Brand and Scannell (1991) describe the way in which a DJ—in this case Tony Blackburn—can switch footings dependent upon his "performance." Blackburn thematizes himself in a number of self-conscious ways that involve the use of different voices: authoritative, empathetic, camp, or send-up. He can play a variety of different roles embedded within short segments of dialogue. Similarly, Clayman (1992) utilizes the concept of footing to demonstrate how news interviewers can preserve their institutionally prescribed neutrality. By shifting footing the interviewer can remove the inference of themselves as "author," either by attributing the viewpoint to a different "principal," e.g., "Doctor Yallow said earlier . . ." (1992:168) or to a generic unknown principle, e.g., "It is said that . . ." (169). Here the speech is conditioned by the particular footing generated by the journalist's identity and accepted speech genre, a circumstance that highlights the context-sensitive nature of discourse and how this phenomenon can be applied to different areas of broadcasting.

Conversation Turn Taking

Some researchers have adopted a Conversation Analysis (CA) approach to the turn-taking structure and applied it to the specificity of the broadcast context, taking into account the nature of the production of talk for the viewer at home. For example, Heritage (1985) shows how the absence of a "third-turn receipt"[16] in question-and-answer sequences in the broadcast news is predicated upon the production of the talk for the overhearing audience. Also, the interviewer adapts the usual conventions of everyday conversation to formulate information for the viewers at home. Following Heritage, much of this pioneering work into CA analysis of the broadcast text has been concerned with the structural organization of the news interview (Heritage, 1985; Heritage and Greatbatch, 1991; Clayman, 1991), especially with specific turn-type pre-allocations that are contextually unique to the broadcast encounter.

Fairclough (1992) is critical of Conversation Analysis for its privileging of the "turn-taking" system as the fundamental matrix organizing interaction. He argues that Conversation Analysis presents a generalized model of interaction that ignores the fact that social, cultural, and power relational factors affect the talk exchanged between speakers. Ian Hutchby (1996) has provided an analysis of power relational factors in radio call-in shows. His CA analysis of the discourse produced between radio host and caller emphasizes the asymmetry between their contributions in the formation of the discourse. The host is ultimately in an institutionally validated position of power that is located in the turn-taking structure of the phone-in and illustrated in the host's manipulation of the discourse and pursuit of conflict and argument.

Some callers are more adept than others at usurping this power through their conversational strategies, such as interruptions, but ultimately the host retains control through the interaction. This type of analysis draws together the importance of context and the social identities of speakers and allows us insights into power relational factors at work in types of talk. Different styles of talk in broadcasting will therefore offer different turn-taking features, which brings us to the relevance of the notion of speech genre to this type of critique.

Genre

Andrew Tolson argues for the consideration of genre in the analysis of broadcasting's discursive products. Drawing upon the work done in discourse analysis, he argues that, "Genre is at once an analytical concept, requiring formal demonstration; but it is also operational, at a level of practical knowledge of which speakers themselves may be more or less aware" (1991:178). The concept of genre is crucial to the understanding of discourse. As Volosinov and Bakhtin discuss "behavioral genres" that are applicable in the specifics of daily repertoires, so too media analysts can be concerned with the specifics of genre to the patterns of media production. What will emerge throughout this book is a fusing of these ways of thinking—of the genres of lived interaction with the genres of the media's production.

Referencing Halliday, Tolson suggests that discursive genres are located at the point where "texts" meet social situations: "There is a generic structure in all discourse, including the most informal, spontaneous conversation" (Halliday, 1978:134).[17] For Tolson, therefore, one might begin to understand the discursive features of broadcast talk in terms of their generic conventions: "I want to suggest that just as television, and broadcasting more generally, has developed its own particular dramatic genres (e.g., situation comedy), so too it has developed certain forms of broadcast talk which have identifiable generic structures" (1991:179).

Arguing for an approach to speech "genres" in broadcast discourse, Tolson discusses the formulation of "chat." One of the features that he suggests enables us to distinguish "chat" in the context of the news interview is that it is "apparent in a clear shift of *register* within the programme format where it occurs, such that the primary business of the format is temporarily delayed or suspended" (1991:179).[18] We can identify these shifts in register in three ways: a topic shift to the personal (as opposed to the institutional) or toward the private (as opposed to the public), the appropriation of wit, humor, double entendres, etc.; and the possibility of "chat" opening up areas of transgression (e.g., in interviews where the interviewee might be asking questions). Clearly this idea has a direct impact on the topic at hand particularly in regard to the informal and conversational style employed in talk television.

Genres of Sociability

Arguments about the genre of televised chat remind us that broadcasting's search for a voice led to the development of less formal, more "sociable" speech styles across multiple genres, bringing the audience closer to the performer. However, Scannell's (1996) discussion above suggests an undifferentiated "sociability" that is generic to the historical development of broadcasting's modes of address. But it seems clear that it is necessary to complicate this reference to "sociability" further. Scannell's examples refer to programs that were broadcast between the 1930s and the 1960s in Britain: *Harry Hopeful* (1935–36), *Billy Welcome* (1941–42), and *Have a Go!* (1946–67). These are examples of sociability within a particular regional, working-class, and masculine framework; indeed, Scannell discusses Wilfred Pickles's performance as working-class northerner as crucial to the communicative intention of *Have A Go!* What this indicates is that modes of address can indeed have a cultural specificity. The "for-anyone-as-someone structure" can suggest a socially constituted subjectivity rather than simply a textually inscribed notion of the subject. In contemporary broadcasting, for instance, we might consider the particular address implied in youth TV or children's TV. The time-span of Scannell's examples is crucial to the context-specific nature of the discourse and thus his analysis. As Corner points out in his account of British television's development of new "sociable" communicative forms in the 1950s, these modes of address were unmistakably masculine, whereas radio had a clearer sense of woman as consumer: "Television's newly familiar mediations were still predominantly male and middle class however, and though certain programme genres (and advertising too) had developed distinctive and new styles of gendered address, daytime transmission schedules did not yet have the space to court, and in particular to construct, a 'housewife' audience in the way that had become central to radio" (1993:13). Sociability can be genre-specific. There is a periodicity relevant to the development of personalized and gendered modes of address in *daytime* television that has transferred from radio since the 1980s.

Historically, in the 1950s, U.S. daytime television emerged as a specific site to engage the housewife, copying the form of radio programming (Spigel, 1992). However, it was not until the 1980s that the British daytime schedule developed a clear sense of what Spigel calls "Mrs. Daytime Home Consumer."

It seems that since the development of morning television in the 1980s, British networks now have a well-defined strategy of a gendered address that constructs a sense of its audience, possibly more clearly here than in any other time-span on the schedule. Therefore, the next chapter suggests how this gendered sociable address is formulated as a generic structure.

Conclusion

This chapter has argued for resurrecting and re-instating research into speech communication to enhance our understanding of the embedding of mass communication in everyday life, arguing that there were early precedents of this type of cultural analysis in the founding work of cultural studies. However, this calls for a theoretical shift from Saussure to Bakhtin as an alternative framework to underpin our understanding of the communicative relationship between broadcasting and its audiences. To do so requires not only investing in semiotic meaning as the way in which texts are negotiated in everyday life, but also to recognize that broadcasting has a physicality of experience that is based upon broader communicative processes. It is the dominant legacy of structuralism that has hindered the development of establishing the relationships of mass-mediated communication with other forms of face-to-face and interpersonal communication, where pragmatic contexts contribute to the actual lived meaning of communicative events. In this way, why not register that meaning is also located in the *activity* of broadcast communication as it achieves a relationship with viewers, suggesting the dynamism of the engagement as an event that is firmly embedded in the routines and rituals of everyday life? To do so suggests an alternative dynamic to the semiotic text-reader model, which in its attempts at fixing meaning cannot capture the quotidian and can only be explained as time-free encounters of socio-cognitive construction and de-construction of meaning. To locate broadcasting as alive in everyday life and taking place *in time* is to potentially begin to describe the media's role in the re-organization of time-space relations and the re-orientation of experience and social identity as it is *performed* in mediated practices.

Some conceptual tools through which we can draw together an analysis of talk TV by taking *communication* as its premise have been outlined here. Drawing from suggestions about the phenomenology of broadcasting in the modern age, and from discourse analyses into the context-specific nature of broadcast discourse, this calls for a new vital outlet for media research that prioritizes how meaning is *pragmatically* organized. That is not to suggest that arguments about power are jettisoned; power is, after all, normatively invested in the social interactions between speakers, as the field of socio-linguistics overwhelmingly documents. This approach might be able to discover new possibilities for intervening in debates about the politics of our socio-communicative relationships with electronic media in the modern world. The next chapter begins this process by offering a close analysis of the communicative practices of morning talk television, in order to establish the textual features of its socio-communicative framework and how it might address and implicate the audience in its sociable appeal.

3. Daytime Talking

Introduction

Synthesizing themes from theories about the media's embedding in everyday life with approaches to meaning generated in the pragmatics of talk provides the framework for imagining the television text as a "communicative event." This chapter applies these principles to the daytime shows in this study and analyzes the way in which the domestic climate of morning television structures its "chat" through para-social arrangements for the daytime audience. There is no doubt that one of the distinctive features of morning television is the spontaneity implied in its reproduction of a televised "everyday." This "everyday" chat provides a mediated interface between public and private domains that, following Meyrowitz (1985), must have repercussions for an understanding of gender in the modern age. While the conventions of daytime television approximate everyday and mundane conversation, both in form and content, one must also think about the way in which the form is institutionally produced and performed as a media construct.

This study takes the nine o'clock-to-noon morning schedule as the object for analysis, since the programs contained in that slot as "morning television" offer talk shows and magazine programs that we will see share similar features in terms of their feminized mode of address. The first part of this chapter provides an analysis of the audience participation programs *Kilroy*[1] (BBC1), *The Time . . . The Place* (ITV1), and *Vanessa* (ITV1), which preceded the magazine shows in the morning schedules, and then we move on in the second part to discuss the British morning magazine programs *This Morning* (ITV1) and *Good Morning* (BBC1). The particular programs used as examples here are taken from some of the exact programs watched with the women in the audience research of the study. This is a deliberate move to enable the crafting of an account of the communicative process, from broadcast to reception. Although there are obvious differences in style and format between the programs, the chapter concludes by drawing together the fundamental common themes or "orientations" that underpin their communicative intention to their audience, which resonate with the feminized speech genre of gossip.

Part 1: Talk Shows as Space for Ordinary Folk to Talk

The morning talk shows that preceded *This Morning* and *Good Morning* on British television through the duration of this research were *The Time . . . The Place* (*TTTP*), eventually replaced by *Vanessa* (for a short time both were on air before *This Morning*), and *Kilroy,* which preceded *Good Morning.* According to Haarman's (1999) criteria, *Kilroy* and *TTTP* belong to the audience-discussion format genre of the talk show (akin to *Donahue*), which is concerned with public issues, whereas *Vanessa* belongs to the "therapy" sub-genre of talk show (more akin to *Oprah*), which presents some stylistic variations. As we have seen, the phenomenon of the television talk show has often been afforded a privileged position within current debates about the nature of a mediated public sphere. These have highlighted the talk show's emphasis upon the "life-world"; foregrounding ordinary lay people's lives. In the magazine program, although this is central to appeals to participation, ordinary people are present intermittently, if consistently, as callers or interviewees; whereas in the talk show they provide most of the talk continuously throughout the show. As "an exercise in electronic democracy" (Carpignano, 1990:48) the talk show is distinctive in its promise of participation and apparent challenging of traditional hierarchies. It involves real people, talking about real life experiences in real time, which gives them a claim to authenticity that assists in the talk show's performance of the championing of the ordinary citizen. As commentators on the talk show have documented, the reliance on "authentic" personal stories, confessions, arguments, and personal testimonies are what have maintained the talk show's distinctive success. Here, we look closely at how these shows are managed to consider how the viewer at home is positioned in the mediation of apparently spontaneous, chaotic talk.

The Host as "One of Us"

The relationship between the talk show and the audience at home is mostly mediated through the persona of the host that is forecast in the title sequences. On *Kilroy* and *Vanessa* these are made up of montages of the presenters' faces that are cut with graphics. They emphasize the centrality of the personality of the presenter and, as the talk show unfolds, frame their central place as "one of us." *TTTP* opens with an image of a sunrise; followed by an image of someone collecting two pints of milk from the doorstep; then the presenter, John Stapleton, appears in a kitchen apparently at home drinking (by inference) a cup of tea; then a shot of John doing up his tie; John hailing a cab; John getting a train; John arriving in the studio, and the title music stops as he enters the studio to applause. *TTTP* was broadcast live from Monday to Friday at 10:15 a.m. from different parts of the country. Thus the title sequence implies a narrative of John as an ordinary man, getting up for work every day and traveling to studios around the UK. The recorded title sequence of John at home flows into the "live" event occurring in the studio. His real life "now" is part of his televised appearance, blurring boundaries of time and space.

Another strategy occurs before the title sequence of *TTTP* and *Vanessa*, where both presenters directly address the camera to introduce the programs' issues of the day. In *TTTP*, John Stapleton stands backstage, sometimes in front of a busy crew and sometimes so that the studio audience is visible. This location helps to blur the front stage/backstage distinction that is also crucial to the para-social imperatives contained within the magazine programs and will be discussed later. A typical pre-show address sounds like this:

1	John S	**[direct address to camera]** He:llo: good morning how would <u>you</u> feel if your
2		partner said you couldn't see your children again? Well I'm joined today by lots of
3		dads who say they're being denied that right and some mothers who say <u>their</u>
4		youngsters don't need a dad.

        [cut to title sequence]
[June 12, 1996]

The audience at home is addressed directly as "you," assuming a para-social relationship with the viewer at home by asking a question of them. Notice that it is also a "you" that is assumed to have children, again echoing the assumed hetero-normative demographics of those at home in the daytime.[2] The viewers are therefore invited to consider their position on the upcoming issue, thus preparing them for involvement, and importantly establishing them as participants (and here parents), in the upcoming debate. *Vanessa* employs the same strategy except that she is pictured backstage resting on a television set that bears the program's logo:

1	Vanessa	**[direct address to camera]** Do you ever go gr<u>ee</u>n with envy or fee:l you're going to
2		exPLO::DE with jealousy—have you ever been driven to the edge or done something
3		totally unforgivable like chucking paint all over your partner's clothes or chopping
4		up his suits in a jealous rage? Today we'll be grappling the green-eyed monster.
5		**[cut to title sequence]**

[Jan. 16, 1996]

In this example, Vanessa elaborates upon the topic of jealousy and gives the viewers more examples upon which they can identify themselves as participants. Notice also that this is a gendered address to a heterosexual female viewer: "chopping up *his* suits in a jealous rage" (line 4). This direct address foregrounds the place of the viewer as not simply privy to the debate about to take place, but also as a member of the ensuing discussion. After all, talk show debates are doubly articulated, televised for an audience at home, who also offer the potential of being future studio participants.

The viewer at home is firmly located within the terms of the debate that continues in the hosts' openings of all the programs here, *after* the title sequence. For instance in *Kilroy,*

1	Kilroy	**[Direct address to camera]** Hello and good morning. Do <u>you</u> trust the police? Do
2		they do enough: to fight crime? (.) Are they over <u>zea</u>lous (.) heavy <u>handed</u> (.) <u>ra</u>cist?
3		We:ll the courts seem to think they are sometimes (.) Last week one man was
4		awarded one hundred and eight thousand pounds after the police used false evidence
5		against him. Another was awarded three hundred and two thousand pounds after he
6		was brutally treated by the police (.) **[moves up the stage to a member of the**
7		**audience and camera moves with him]** And yet often the police don't seem to do
8		what we want them to do do they Michelle, do they do enough to deal with the
		problem that you've got in your area?

[May 14, 1996]

Again, Kilroy establishes a direct relationship with the viewer by asking questions of them. He also situates the topic for discussion within contemporary real-world occurrences. What is interesting is the way in which the appeal to the viewer is linked to the opening of the discussion with the studio audience. He moves up the stage to Michelle and addresses her by her first name as one of the lay members of the audience. It is almost as though Kilroy knows Michelle, and this familiarity accompanies and reinforces the familiarity with which he has just addressed the viewer. There is an implied connection, therefore, with the viewer at home and the lay member of the audience. John Stapleton does the same thing in *TTTP:*

1	John S	**[After title sequence host walks in to applause from studio audience]**
2		**[addresses to studio audience]** Thank-you, thank-you very much indeed.
3		**[direct address to camera]** Hello::: good morning, good morning to you at home.
4		Well we all know that one in three marriages in this country end up in divorce and
5		there can be nothing more heart rending and difficult than deciding who has custody
6		of the children and how tha:t access will work. But what happens when one partner
7		says sorry no wa::y can you have access to the children? That's what a lot of parents
8		in the audience have decided, **[starts to walk up the stage]** Maria's one of them.
9		**[addresses Maria]** How old is he?

[June 12, 1996]

John here, although he uses direct address, does not address the audience as "you," rather he uses the assumed community of "we" (line 4). He then moves on to talk about parents and access but, like Kilroy, begins the debate by the link to the "ordinary" member of the public, Maria. Moving from direct address to the viewer at home to immediately addressing the lay audience member is important. It implies our sense of belonging within the discourse as another member of the audience made present through the broadcast medium.

The use of the camera assists this implication; it moves up the stage with both Kilroy and John Stapleton, and is then fixed within the studio audience. Once here the camera often uses a subjective camera angle as though we, the viewers, are situated within the studio audience. Throughout the discussion, the camera angles include close-ups of speakers, or the presenter, or a wider shot of a small group of speakers, but we never again get a complete view of the stage and the audience until the show's conclusion. Thus, throughout most of the discussion, the viewer has crossed the boundary of the stage and is located within the action. In this way the shooting of the discussion program attempts to draw in the viewer at home, suggesting their co-presence. While this may not be the domestic space of the home as in the magazine show, the process nevertheless suggests a shared mediated space in the studio.

The spatial organization of the *Vanessa* program operates a little differently, more like *Oprah* and the *Ricki Lake Show*. There is a stage where selected "ordinary" people, who are introduced as "guests" in the style of an interview, discuss their personal experience and respond to questions asked by Vanessa. Vanessa situates herself within the studio audience, moving among them, allowing members of the studio audience to ask questions of the participants on stage. This style is different from *Kilroy* and *TTTP,* a difference that is related to their different discursive frameworks. Nevertheless, Vanessa still employs a similar strategy of engaging the viewer in an assumed relationship before introducing the first guest:

1   Vanessa   **[Host walks in to applause then directly addresses to camera]**
2   H̲ello and welcome to the show. Most of us if we're r̲eally honest get jealous from
3   time to time but what happens if jealousy takes over your life? Well my first guest
4   admits that she is obsessively jealous, to find out more let's meet Marissa **[guest walks on stage to applause]**
[Jan. 16, 1996]

The viewer at home is directly addressed and incorporated as having a relationship with jealousy—"Most of *us* if we're really honest" (line 2)—and we
are then connected to the guest in terms of what might happen if that jealousy
"takes over your life." The subjective camera then works differently as neither
Vanessa nor the camera move up onto the stage; rather, we are situated with
the host and studio audience. We are therefore encouraged to identify with
Vanessa and the studio audience and assume our role in interrogating the
guests' experiences. While the concept of "stage" is more complicated here,
we are invited into the studio audience, which is still part of the televised
stage, through the subjective camera.

Drawing the viewer in as a vicarious participant is also reinforced by
emphasizing the viewer at home as a potential studio participant. In all of
these morning talk shows there are invitations to take part in future shows.
These appeals occur in the same way that the magazine programs appeal for
callers for their phone-in debates. For instance on *Vanessa*:

1   Vanessa   Have y̲ou got the b̲est love story Britain's ever heard? Has your love survived
2   separations, illness, or tremendous difficulties? Perhaps you met when you were
3   both young, split up, and got back together again years later? We want to hear your
4   amazing, unbelievable, and romantic love stories for a Vanessa Valentine's Day
5   special, so if you're sitting on th̲e:: story that will make the country sob, g̲ive
6   Vanessa a call now on o eight nine one, eleven, eleven, sixty-four.
[Jan. 16, 1996]

Or on *Kilroy*:

1   Kilroy   Are y̲ou married to your partner's job? Does their work take up all their time? Has it
2   ruined y̲our life? Perhaps you are the wife of a policeman, or the husband of a
3   teacher, or you're married to a vicar? Either way call Kilroy now, on o double nine o
4   two hundred five six, seven if your partner's career (.) comes before y̲ou and your
5   family and has put your relationship in jeopardy
[May 14, 1996]

Notice the gendered assumptions that are present in Kilroy's appeal—"the
wife of a policeman or the husband of a teacher" (lines 2–3)—replaying

traditional assumptions about culturally appropriate gendered professions. In *TTTP* the appeals are very similar:

1	John S	If your family was susceptible to breast cancer, would you choose to have a
2		mastectomy? Do you think it's better to have no breasts at a:ll than breasts with a
3		ninety percent chance of developing cancer? Or is it wrong to have healthy breasts
4		removed? Perhaps you or your family have already made that decision. Do you think
5		that genetic testing will lead to a healthier nation? Or is it better to know what
6		diseases you'll develop in the future? Whatever your story or you view call us now o
7		eight nine one seven hundred one four five.

[June 12, 1996]

The example above is clearly a gendered topic. But so also is its address: "will *you* choose to have a mastectomy," and not "what if your wife or girlfriend faced a mastectomy?" Many of the appeals were marked as gendered by inference. These examples demonstrate how the audience at home is called to consider their own subjective experiences as potential for talk show debate, a factor that surely affects the viewing experience, which becomes an invitation to the take part in the televised talk. On *Vanessa* and *TTTP* these appeals occur directly after the advertising break, halfway through the program. The viewer at home is addressed as one of the wider network of talk show participants, ordinary people with ordinary, often gendered, experiences: "have you?" "are you?" "would you?" "will you?"

Thus far we can see how the morning talk shows suggest co-presence, co-temporality, and gendered address, phenomena that help create a para-social environment. The talk show also involves the production of apparently unscripted talk from a number of lay individuals coming together to debate a particular topic. How can such a debate be understood as "for us" in terms of Scannell's "for-anyone-as-someone-structure"? How can the boundary between stage and audience be collapsed when more recent commentators have argued that talk shows pursue "spectacle" over true debate? The pursuit of the drama—the fight, the emotional breakdown, what Grindstaff (2002) refers to as "the money shot"—might seemingly position the audience at home outside the discursive framework of the show, as we become voyeurs watching the drama of the debate unfold. But television's entertainment drive is not incongruent with its attempt to establish a rapport with its audience. Television holds these forces in tension extremely well, particularly in the case of the public issue oriented type of talk, where the more a clash of conflict is allowed to emerge, the greater the potential for the host to be on "our" side.

"Being on our Side": The Evolution of Talk on "Public Issue" Shows—
Kilroy *and* The Time . . . The Place

Talk show commentators have assumed that the viewer at home is encouraged to feel an affinity with the "ordinary" people who tell their stories in
the talk show, since these people speak through personal testimony and
authentic voices.[3] The opening sequences and the use of camera-work serve
to discursively and spatially position viewers at home within the studio audience as other (para-social) "speakers." Shared common ground of "lay
experience" emerges through the talk, and it is subsequently validated and
defended by the management of the program. According to Livingstone and
Lunt (1994), the commonsense stories of lay participants are often privileged
over those of the institutional discourses of the expert, disrupting normative
power dynamics. In such a forum, therefore, the traditional polarization of
the public and private is often eroded. This, it is claimed, accounts for an
oppositional public sphere that encompasses the lived experiences of the
citizen ("life-world") alongside the critique of state actions (the "system").
However, I argue that the precedence given to lay experience is not so much
related to the inherent triumph of experiential common sense over abstract,
institutionalized discourse, but more to the management of these discourses
in accordance with *televisual* entertainment requirements that allow the host
to emerge in the role as "our" hero(ine).

   Talk shows are, after all, television programs that are carefully researched,
produced, and to some extent pre-scripted. Grindstaff's (2002) ethnography
of talk show production highlights how this is the case in the re-production
planning and staging aspects of the shows. Ultimately, the talk in question
is produced with an overhearing audience at home in mind, and in this section we see that the pursuit of televisual drama, or "the money shot," is the
main goal that affects the management and construction of talk show debate,
thus enhancing the viewers' alignment with the host and the "ordinary folk"
of the studio audience. Accordingly, questions about the host's role in the
production of the talk and how the "commonsense" and expert discourses
are elicited and managed for televised display need to be addressed.

Us Versus Them

The centrality of the host is therefore established from the outset. Key to understanding the construction of the interaction in talk shows is the knowledge
that the host is ultimately responsible for deciding who can take the floor
in the debate. Mostly this is explicit in the power to select participants to

speak, but occasionally speakers gain the floor through self-selection. Either way, ultimately the host is responsible for allowing speakers to retain the floor. The description of the host as romantic hero suggests that hosts situate themselves against established power.[4] This can be seen in Kilroy's and John Stapleton's performances in the public issue–oriented discussion programs. They maintain their "authenticity" and position themselves (although Robert Kilroy-Silk is a former Labour MP) as heroes on the side of "ordinary" people. This can be explained in terms of their management of the production of talk in the studio. Their orientation as "one of the people," rather than the impartial journalistic figure that is encouraged in other kinds of television interview, is apparent from the opening of *Kilroy* we examined earlier.

After Kilroy's establishment of a relationship with the general wider public—"Do *you* trust the police?"—he moves to cite *real* stories that set the scene for the primacy of the *real* event before moving to Michelle, given authenticity by reference to her first name, to invite her to relate *her* story about *her* area. On the other hand, the police in this introduction remain a faceless, homogenous entity. Clearly the distinction here between "us and them"/ experts versus lay speakers, has already been drawn. The emphasis on the authority of the "authentic" over the "professional" is often marked in these shows, produced to meet televisual requirements through the way in which the contributions are managed by the host.

The talk show hosts clearly position themselves as "on our side"—as they engage in a management cycle of the discussion whereby they:

- assist the lay speakers' production of narrative;
- formulate narratives to produce ultimate tension for the experts;
- defend the lay speakers' rights to the floor, and press the expert to respond to a particular lay person's sense of injustice.

Although Livingstone and Lunt do, to some extent, discuss how the host manages the debate, their analysis is mostly theoretical and does not pay close attention to the way in which turns are taken. A close look at the kinds of "pre-allocated turn-taking system" that apply here outlines the rules of talking that structure the talk show. Despite the appearance that talk shows may give of being open and random, the discussion is actually rather neatly executed and artfully managed in favor of lay speakers on behalf of "us."

Knowing the Audience: Helping Stories Unfold

The pre-scripted nature of the show is evident in the hosts' knowledge of the spatial orientation of the speakers and the roles they will play in the discussion. In most instances, the host selects both lay and expert speakers by reference to their first names. At the beginning of the management cycle outlined above, the host selects a narrator by choosing a member of the audience to relate their personal story. If the host addresses them by their first name, prior knowledge of their experience also identifies the narrative context from which they are to speak. If we take the opening question from the example we have already seen from *Kilroy,* the host has prior knowledge that Michelle has a problem in the area where she lives and here he selects Jonathon, a black man, to tell a story about police racism:

```
1   Kilroy      Jonathon are the police racist? Jonathon?
2   Jonathon    I think in some cases the police are very racist . . .
                    . . .
3   Kilroy      Do they treat you in a discriminatory way?
    [May 15, 1996]
```

After Kilroy's prompting question, Jonathon proceeds to tell a story about having been stopped by the police on several occasions. It is clearly not a "lucky guess" that this man has an experience to tell about racist treatment, as Kilroy accurately seeks Jonathon out among the audience at a pertinent moment in the discussion.

It is evident that the hosts have considerable prior knowledge of some of the experiences of their guests, and they work with the lay speakers to produce the narrative that they already know they have to tell. In the next example it is clear that Kilroy is helping Michelle relate her experience:

```
1   Michelle     Well first of all prior to this they've got my second son Dean hah hung him from
2                the balcony on the second floor by his ankles erm (.) he::'s got learning
3                disabilities so he's backward so=
4   Kilroy       =n: this group of youths you say that they have been terrorizing the neighborhood
5        →       as well as your own sons to the extent that you've had to move to what a safe
6                house?=
7   Michelle     = a safe house
    [May 15, 1996]
```

In this example, Kilroy introduces a piece of detail, referring to Michelle's move to a safe house (line 6), information that she has previously not volunteered. How the host then uses this knowledge of the life-world becomes interesting to the strategies used to control the discourse. Having selected a lay speaker, the host and the chosen interlocutor embark on a question/answer sequence. In everyday conversation, Searle (1969) suggests that there are two types of question: the "real," whereby the questioner asks about something s/he does not know, or the "exam," whereby the questioner tests the other speaker about something s/he already knows. Kilroy obviously has prior knowledge of lay participants' stories and therefore the type of questioning might reflect an "exam" style question under Searle's criteria. However, in this institutional context, the questioning is not so much a test but rather a device involved in mediating communication. The question-and-answer sequence here does not, therefore, approximate those found in everyday conversation, but rather takes the form of an interview where the questions are being asked to elicit information (in these cases personal stories) for the overhearing audience, as in the following example:

1	John S		First of all Jean <u>why </u>did you decide to become sterilized?
2	Jean		We:ll I had three boys I felt we had a complete family we—we were happy.
3	John S		And what were you told about the operation?
4	Jean		Very little just that there was a risk of getting pregnant (.) I could have accepted
5			that but I still wanted to have it done=.
6	John S	→	= you wanted it done so:: you went along to the
7			hospital, you had the operation and then what?
8	Jean		Th<u>en : </u>I- I started to feel ill after about a month. I was gettin' stingin' in me side, I
9			was swelling up, but I went to my GP's and they sent me away:: possible infection
10			and I went back and I went back around <u>five</u> times.
11	John S		To the GP and to the hospital—or just=
12	Jean		= to the GP's and I was just sent away for
13			infection and it's <u>normal</u> and things'll be back to normal and you'll have a period.
14	John S		Had your periods stopped at this point?
15	Jean		I'<u>d had </u>periods before me operation but not afterwards, no:: I didn't have one.
16	John S	→	So they said oh:: it's an infection everything'll come O.K.
17	Jean		Yeh,
18	John S	→	But it wasn't
19	Jean		No
20	John S	→	You found out ?=
21	Jean		= In October=
22	John S	→	=that you had?
23	Jean		That I was pregnant with twins.
24	John S	→	And that you'd <u>been </u>pregnant
25	Jean		I was two months pregnant
26	John S	→	When you [had the operation
27	Jean		[when I had the operation.

[May 20, 1996]

It is clear here that John is helping the woman tell her story, even filling in parts of the narrative (e.g., line 6). As the woman tells her story, John prompts her to produce pertinent points of the narrative (lines 16, 18, 20, 22, and 24) until eventually we have the salient and ultimately contentious point—she was two months pregnant when she had the sterilization operation. The host leads the informant to the key point in the story that can then be further used as the controversial issue with which to continue the debate.

Lay participants' stories, therefore, do not emerge spontaneously and develop freely. Thornborrow (1997) suggests that they are mutually produced by participant and host, and often what becomes of key concern is not so much the story itself but its subsequent evaluation. This analysis goes further to suggest that the evaluation is a result of the narrative's subjection to the host's own framing and evaluation that conforms to an agenda agreed upon prior to production. For instance, the prior knowledge of speakers and their stories not only allows the host to elicit certain material at pertinent points in the show, but it also allows him a kind of editorial control. In Michelle's case, when Kilroy presents her problem in this way he has already made a subjective judgment about the police having not done enough in this case:

> *KILROY:* And yet often the police don't seem to do what we want them to do do they Michelle, do they do enough to deal with the problem in your area?

Similarly, in the case of a woman who was falsely tried for murdering her husband, Kilroy has already framed the point of issue within which the woman is allowed to contribute her narrative:

```
1  Kilroy        . . . we don't want them to be overzealous we don't want them to exceed their
2         →      powers (.) is there a feeling also that perhaps sometimes they make an arrest
3                because they need to make an arrest just to get somebody?
4                [Kilroy takes the microphone to woman who he knows will answer positively]
5  woman         Definitely
   [May 15, 1996]
```

These questions therefore accomplish more than revealing information for the overhearing audience (as in the news interview); they also work to reproduce an agenda within which information is to be interpreted, one in which the host is positioned to defend lay speakers as our representative.

Formulations

After eliciting lay speakers' stories through the question-and-answer sequence, the host must then formulate the narrative so that it can be presented for comment to the rest of the audience or the expert. Heritage describes formulating as "summarizing, glossing or developing the gist of an informant's earlier statements" (1985:100) for the benefit of the overhearing audience. It is more common in institutional contexts such as courtrooms and news interviews than in ordinary conversation. Sometimes formulations can operate in a neutral or even a cooperative way to assist the communication of the lay story. Heritage refers to these as either "prompts" or "cooperative recycles." An example of a "cooperative recycle" in the talk show would be:

[P= Photographer arrested at demonstration]

1	Kilroy		What happened to you?
2	P		I was hit in the face by a policeman, [I was dragged off
3	Kilroy		[wh- where where
4	P		Demonstration, I'm a professional photographer I was photographing a
5			demonstration (.) I had a press card I had my cameras around me the policeman
6			ran up and he smacked=
7	Kilroy		=wh- what were you taking pictures of?
8	P		The demonstration (.)[arrests arrests
9	Kilroy	→	[It was a demonstration arrests so it was arrests. There was
10			a bit of a kerffufle (.) a bit of argy-bargy

[May 15, 1996]

At lines 9 and 10 Kilroy formulates the gist of the photographer's narrative to clarify the information for the overhearer. But, however cooperative these recycles appear, they can still perform a function in the talk show debate that can be understood in terms of the pursuit of televisual moments. This occurs in the next extract from a *TTTP* program about absent fathers:

1	woman		. . . After he left, I had the baby, his behavior continued to be bad, I monitored
2			the situation without introducing him to Samuel as his fa:ther (.) er just to see
3			how the ex-partner would progress (1) his behavior remained the same.
4	John S		Unacceptable- we should make clear that this was socially unacceptable.
5	woman		He's quite a dysfunctional adult
6	John S		To you
7	woman		In my view yes .hh a lovely person but unfortunately his problems are such that
8			he is incapable of being unselfish and nurturing which is what I feel my children
9			deserve [. . .] I'm not against fathers being in the picture but I think when it's to
10			the child's detriment you've got to stop and look at the situation very clearly.
11	John S	→	And you think that the aspects of your second partner's behavior would not be in
12			your son's interest to witness and be with him?

[June 12, 1996]

In the extract above, we see John formulating the woman's perspective and producing the evaluation (line 11) that it would not be in her son's interest to be with him. This is an accurate summary of the woman's position, but the woman's right to the floor has been carefully selected and the evaluation of the narrative reinforced in view of the next speaker. After this formulation, John gives the floor to a woman who believes that all fathers have a right to see their children regardless of any circumstances, a point subsequently reinforced by an expert, the chair of Parent Contact Centres. Therefore, formulations of the lay narrative by the host can assist in summarizing their contribution quite accurately, but in doing so can also help to reinforce the point of tension that is about to be passed to an opposing speaker. Such formulations in the talk show help sustain debate and argument.

According to Heritage, there is a type of formulation present in news interviews, which he terms the "inferentially elaborative probe," that is used by the interviewer to "commit the interviewee to a stronger (and more newsworthy) version of his position . . . than he was initially prepared to adopt" (1985:110). In the next example, we can see Kilroy performing such an action with a Labour MP:

[MP = Conservative Member of Parliament for Bridlington, John Townsend]

1	MP	Right, now I'm saying a number of things. I'm saying that it was <u>not</u> their
2		expectation that they would have to dispossess mainly daughters (.) caring relatives
3		many of whom gave up the prospect of marriage or a career or both to look after an
4		elderly mother or father or <u>both</u> and whose reward for that now is to be told that
5		they've lost the home that they expected to inherit, now ( )
6	Kilroy →	So <u>your</u> answer to my
7		question is <u>yes</u> the low-paid- the low-paid in your constituency should pay for <u>my</u>
8		children to inherit my home <u>that's</u> the answer you've just given me.

[May 14, 1996]

Here, Kilroy has clearly reproduced the MP's answer in a much more contentious fashion than intended and in such a way that reinforces his own position as a defender of the common person. This is reminiscent of what one might expect in a news interview in which the more newsworthy topic is produced for the overhearing audience. The talk show, however, provides a further twist to this function, since rarely would the host produce such a formulation in anticipation of the present speaker's reply. Rather, it is produced to be passed to another speaker, in this case, the "ordinary" taxpayer. The production of "newsworthiness" is no doubt one function of this mediated action for the overhearing audience, but in the talk show it also assists the production of dramatic tension for the audience at home, while reinforcing who is on "our" side.

The power to formulate the narrative of a speaker is also extended to the lay narrative. This can even mean *re*-formulating the narrative completely in terms of the framing already set out by the scripting of the program.

[PW= petrol station worker, Bertram = neighborhood watch coordinator]

1	PW	Well really I was robbed at gunpoint three consecutive times .hh and when I asked
2		one of the police er why it took thirty five minutes for them to travel (?) about
3		half a mile from the police station to the petrol station where I was working I was
4		told well this is in Salford sticks if there's a chap that can come here nine times out
5		of ten he's gonna have a gun if we turn up very quickly =
6	Kilroy	= Salford near Manchester=
7	PW	=Yes, that's right erm, they're gonna shoot at us so we're gonna hang
8		back n take the evidence of the video camera and
9	Bertram	heh, heh, heh
10	Kilroy	That's not funny Bertram heh,heh,heh
11	Bertram:	No, I'm horrified to think that that was the case I thought they'd get there very
12		quickly
13	PW	→ Well, you've gotta take their point of view as well I -I=
14	Kilroy	→ = You mean the police don't get there quickly enough
15	PW	That's true
16	Kilroy	→ They don't take it seriously enough or they don't or are afraid
17	PW	→ No, it's not that, think about it a minute you've got a policeman possibly married
18		with children he's in there in the front line so to speak a::ll the time okay now (.)
19		it's gonna be natural to hang on a second I wanna see my kids tomorrow I'm just
20		gonna hang back just that five minutes just to let them get out of the way=
21	Kilroy	=Ali, it seems to be just from the three things we've heard now that the police
22		seem to do what seems to be—here they won't go to deal with the estate with the
23		petrol bombers and th- th- the thugs terrorizing a hh young innocent family they
24		→ won't a- deal with a man with a gun hh but they'll go to the nice safe e- estate
25		which is patrolled by people like Bertram to deal with a scratched car. Do the
26		police do enough to protect us?

[May 15, 1996]

At line 14, Kilroy produces a cooperative formulation of the gist of the petrol station worker's prior narrative. However, the worker has already embarked on a statement suggesting that he has some sympathy with the police (line 13, "well you've gotta take their point of view"), which Kilroy interrupts with his formulation. Unwilling to accept the worker's progression, Kilroy again reformulates the statement entirely into "they don't take it seriously enough or they don't or are afraid" (line 16). This is clearly not how the worker wanted his assertion to be evaluated, as he makes a straightforward denial of Kilroy's presentation of his point of view (line 17). The man eventually frames his narrative in terms of support for the police, but this direction is not allowed to play any further part in the course of the program. When Kilroy subsequently summarizes the last three lay narratives for the expert Ali (Inspector Ali Dezai of Thames Valley Police) this particular contribution is merely represented as "they won't deal with a man with a gun" (line 24) and delivered to the expert as support for Kilroy's initial agenda on our behalf (which began with Michelle) of "do the police do enough to protect us?"

The key point in these strategies is that predetermined agendas are designed to heighten contentious issues *and* register the televised discussion as *for* the people and won *by* the people, uniting the studio audience with the audience at home. The host's management of lay narratives is therefore about prioritizing televisuality—ensuring that "life-world" experiences are reinforced as potential points of conflict. Periods of argument occur, therefore, when the contentious topic is handed over for response from the experts. Livingstone and Lunt (1994) suggest that the tension is inherent within the challenge presented to expert discourses by anecdotal evidence authenticated by "real" experience. While this may be partly true, it does not explain the role of the host in the mediation of expert and lay discourses. However, when Hutchby (1996) discusses the pursuit of conflict in talk radio, his analysis of the interactional strategies at work provides an understanding of the ways in which the host can wield institutional power. In these talk shows, the host employs a management strategy to exacerbate the tension between expert/public and lay/private discourses.

Undermining the Experts

The difference between the host's management of the experts' space to talk and his management of the lay narratives is marked. Lay narratives are generally produced with the host sitting close to the speakers, encouraging them, even showing emotion with them, and clarifying their stories. John Stapleton often sits down on a step next to the lay speaker and visibly comforts them when they are in distress. The host's acknowledgment of their "pain" assists in the authentication of the lay narrative and in the host's sharing of their emotion:

```
1  Man          . . . I had a complete nervous breakdown and I've been in and out of psychiatric
2               hospitals ever since and I've erm tried several times to commit suicide because to
3               me it's like I have buried my daughter, it's the only way I can cope cos I know I will
4               never see her again. I've tried everything, I've tried private detectives, I've tried
5               South African high commission and still nothing.
6  John S    →  I know it's- I can see just by looking at you as well as listening to you, it's causing
7               you immense distress.
   [June 12, 1996]
```

Often Kilroy guards lay participants' rights to tell a story through interjections such as "listen" and "let her speak." The experts, on the other hand, must fend for themselves; the hosts never align themselves with experts by physically sitting next to them. Experts are rarely given long periods of time in which to explain their point of view and are frequently interrupted by the host. Most interruptions of experts are aggressive,[5] and the reason for this is mainly due to the fact that the primacy of the authentic "authored" narrative of the ordinary speaker has already been established. For example in *TTTP's* sterilization debate:

```
1   John S       Let me ask George [gynecologist] before we go any further. I mean these people
2                gasped, I:: gasped when I heard this story right I mean can you envisage any
3                circumstances in which- I mean what's the procedure, surely, surely people in
4                hospital check whether someone's pregnant before they do an operation?
     [May 20, 1996]
```

After John helps the woman tell a story that he demonstrated considerable prior knowledge of, he presents it to the expert in horror. What occurs when the experts are called to respond is interesting. The experts can only respond in keeping with their institutional persona and policy in an "animator" footing (Goffman, 1981). Thus, their explanations seem inadequate to the personal, "authored" accounts of the authentic experiences that have been presented by lay participants.

Following the example above, this is what occurs when George, the gynecologist, is called to address the woman's case:

```
[G= George, gynecologist ]

1   John S       Let me ask George before we go any further. I mean these people gasped, I:: gasped
2                when I heard this story right I mean can you envisage any circumstances in which- I
3                mean what's the procedure, sure, surely people in hospital check whether someone's
4                pregnant before they do an operation?
5   G        →   You see what happens is when you go and see the necessary people in the hospital
6                and you get an appointment for your operation date. That can easily be like six
7                weeks after the original consultation, anything can happen in that six weeks
8                sometimes even two months . . . [continues with narrative of procedures when
9                arriving at hospital] . . . when you arrive one of the questions they will ask you is
10               if you still have regular periods and there is no doubt that you (.) can NOT be
11               pregnant then  we go ahead and [ do the sterilization procedure
12  John S   →                                   [But you see I:::ve done programs with women on
13               this show who had pregnancies they knew nothing about and they've had periods all
14               the way, so that's no check at all is it?
15  G            No, true but on the other hand you'll have to go and do a pregnancy test, now if you
16               do the pregnancy test (.) the pregnancy test will only show up on a woman who
17               missed her period by a week. So, if a lady says George I have missed my period by
18               a week alarm signals go off and let's do a pregnancy test but on all the women who
19               say they are bleeding a pregnancy test will anyway [show negative
20  John S   →                                                    [Hand on your heart aren't you a
21               bit surprised by that [points to woman] case to put it mildly.
     [May 20, 1996]
```

George, addressing the host, answers the question with a lengthy description of hospital procedures (line 5 onwards). This is in keeping with his institutional footing as a gynecologist, rather than addressing what might have gone wrong in this particular case. His use of "you" is generic and does not address the woman who told the story in particular. This is typical of the news interview in which interviewees prefer not to address the co-interviewee in order to avoid direct conflict.[6] John interrupts with a direct challenge to the expert's description of the procedures (line 12). The place the interruption occurs can be interpreted as aggressive, as John continues with his challenge. What is interesting here is that John's interruption is based upon his experience with "real" women on his show. As the expert continues, still within his institutional footing, John aggressively interrupts again (line 20), this time to press the gynecologist on his opinion of the specific case in the studio. The phrase "hand on heart" is an appeal to the doctor to shift from his professional footing to a more authentic, subjective, and personal response to the issue. George eventually addresses the specific case:

```
1  G             Well, I think it's very sad and it is very unfortunate what's happened to you and
2                furthermore your GP kept saying that there's another condition other than you might
3                be pregnant, whether  it could have been picked up at the beginning it's difficult to
4                say it's always easy retrospectively but it's a difficult case.
5  woman         I was two months pregnant, that was over seven weeks.
6  G        →    You see it's very difficult for me to comment on the history you gave to your GP.
   [May 20, 1996]
```

The gynecologist eventually addresses the woman, but is careful about what he might say professionally. When the woman begins to speak to him directly, not through the mediation of the host, the doctor closes down the interaction—"you see it's very difficult for me to comment"—thereby avoiding direct conflict. Interruptions by the host largely occur when there is conflict between the expert's animated footing as an institutional representative and the pressure on the talk show to discuss the authored *real* stories of individuals.

Kilroy here refuses to let the expert respond to the lay narrative on an institutional footing. A woman has just told an emotive story about being arrested with her three-year-old son and locked in a police cell. The woman is very distressed and Kilroy displays a good deal of caring and sensitivity in helping elicit her story; he comforts the woman and holds her hand at points where she is visibly upset, adding to the liveness and immediacy of the event.

[C = Chris Waterton, Chairman of Local Police Authorities]

1	Woman	I was knocking at the door begging them please .hh can I have a glass of wa:ter
2		after fifteen minutes one of the police officers .hh
3	Kilroy	you were put in a police cell w- w- with your three and a half year old son you were
4		locked in=
5	Woman	=cell yes with my hh=
6	Kilroy	=you were locked in the police cell
7	Woman	.hh I was locked in a police cell
8	Kilroy	Just the two of you
9	Woman	Just the two of us
10	Kilroy	Stop the:re (.) What's goin on Chris?
11	C	Well obviously [this is a very anxious situation
12	Kilroy	→ [This isn't right
13		It's a what situation!
14	C	A very anxious situat [ion-
15	Kilroy	→ [It's a scandal!
16	C	Well hh I-lets understand this [.hh the officer, the officer at the time (.) may or
17	Kilroy	→ [It's not anxious it's a scandal you don't put
18	C	may-
19	Kilroy	a mother and a three and a half year old son in a police cell we don't put sixteen
20		year olds in police cells fourteen year olds in police cells
21	C	→ I'm not condoning bad beha:vior but lets underst:[and what's happened-
22	Kilroy	→ [this is bad behavior
23		is this bad behavior?
24	C	→ a- it is bad behavior ye::s=
25	Kilroy	=it is bad behavior

Kilroy attends to the woman and her narrative sympathetically, formulating the points of issue for the expert. However, the expert, Chris, provides an institutional response that is not satisfactory, and Kilroy aggressively interrupts at lines 12, 15, 17, and 22. In line 15, Chris's description of the events as an "anxious situation" is formulated by Kilroy in a much more hostile manner—"it's a scandal." Chris then begins to embark upon a defense of hypothetical officers, but again this is not satisfactory, as Kilroy presses the expert to deal with *this* situation. He is in constant pursuit of a contentious admission of guilt. Kilroy isolates Chris's statement, "I'm not condoning bad behavior" (line 21), which is detached from the actual narrative, and aggressively interrupts the expert again to insist on his tying of this statement to the woman's predicament.

In a later extract from the discussion of the same case, where the problem is presented to Inspector Ali Dezai, Kilroy is even more explicit in his interrupting of the expert to oust him from his institutional footing (lines 8, 11, 13, 15):

[A= Inspector Ali Dezai]

```
1   Woman        . . . hh I: was the victim (.) but I was treated like an offender (.) and as I said  I
2                was absolutely devastated h—h—=
3   Kilroy                                =and you still are, [you still are (.) Ali?
4   Woman                                                  [And I still are and I looked at my
5                chi :ld
6   A            I think the point I would like to make is this e- for every case I've heard here
7                there are a thousand cases where pe ople  have [been treated properly
8   Kilroy    →                                                [we're talking, we're talking about this
9                child
10  A            I- I appreciate that I am- I am- [yes wh- what the implication what the
11  Kilroy    →                                  [No no Ali I'm NOT gonna let you talk
12  A            implication what the implication is you're drawing here Robert is that one
13  Kilroy    → about the other thousand  we're talking about this woman and her child.
14  A            case depicting the whole serv [ice being not complying with procedures and
15  Kilroy    →                               [well of course it does
16  A         → that's absurd it's simply not the case. We don't always get it right, we don't always
17               get it right . . .
```

The expert, Ali, embarks on a defense of the police's position by suggesting that there is a wider picture. Such a "wider" picture is unacceptable, as it does not deal with the injustice experienced by *this* particular woman. Using figures or percentages as evidence is valuable in institutional discourse as abstract reasoning, but it is particularly unpopular on talk shows due to the primacy of authentic testimony. All of Kilroy's interruptions occur at moments that can be interpreted as aggressive, insisting that the expert address this individual case. Ali maintains his institutional footing by not responding to the specific example. However, in having to address the problem of errors, he does eventually produce the admission "we don't always get it right" (lines 16–17).

Dramatic rows can occur at these points in the show's cycle where experts' institutional responses are awkwardly positioned outside "commonsense" terms. Experts are often interrupted by lay speakers because, unlike the host's "hero-like" protection of the lay speaker, he rarely defends the expert's right to the floor. Under constant pressure from interruptions to respond to the lay narrative on its own terms, one possible solution, other than an admission of guilt as above, is for the expert to interact with the lay participant in a direct way. This usually involves the expert relinquishing their institutional footing. Greatbatch suggests in the case of disagreements in news interviews that "the strength of disagreements is determined in large part by the extent to which speakers opt to maintain or step out of their institutionalized footing in producing them" (1992:287).

In this example, a man begins to relate his experience of the police provoking a riot at a demonstration:

[Man=Man at demonstration, MP= Conservative Member of Parliament for Bridlington, John Townsend]

```
 1  Man              . . . and we had a li:ne of riot police come and move us along (.) and we were
 2                   saying to them "look calm down this is gonna provoke a riot" and they just didn't
 3                   look at us in anyway like we were human beings they [looked at us as
 4  MP       →                                                    [the police have a right to
 5  Man              as if we were scu:m
 6  MP       →  to keep the: roads and our streets open for pe [ople who wanna go about their
 7  Man                                                        [Do they have a right to provoke
 8  MP       →  own business and if the- if the- of they- if they if the police-
 9  Man              a riot Mister Townsend do they have a right to provoke a ri [ot-
10  MP       →                                                     [No, really who
11                   provoked the riot who riot [ed
12  Man                                         [they did!
13  MP       →  They didn't riot, YOU riot [ed
14  Man                                      [Yes they did (.) I- I- rioted I: was a steward trying to
15                   keep the dem [o peaceful
16  MP                           [b-but you said they provoked a riot the [police weren't rioting
17  Man                                                                   [they steamed into a crowd
18                   of peaceful [people what do you expect?
19  MP                          [But who was rioting who was rioting
20  Man              The poli::[:ce
21  MP                        [The police were riot [ing?
22  Man                                             [Did you see the police charge into Hyde
23                   Pa [rk in a crowd of women and children?
24  MP                 [THAT'S not a riot (.) THAT'S NOT A RIOT.
```
                    **[an argument ensues that allows multiple interjections from the studio
                    audience and for a short period of time is clearly beyond the host's control]**

Despite originally producing a response that attempts to address a general issue about the police's role in keeping the peace (lines 4, 6, and 8), the MP switches his footing to take on the actual issue at hand. The MP begins to challenge the man's account of who instigated the riot by suggesting, "No, really who rioted?" (line 10). In so doing, the MP is making the most extreme move in terms of relinquishing his institutional footing and abandoning the rules of formal political debate. He even directly contradicts the man's version of events by suggesting, "They didn't riot, YOU rioted!" (line 13). This accusation leads to the "money shot" as other lay members contribute by rebuking the MP. Kilroy's intervention in this dispute is somewhat dilatory, as this presents, arguably, the desired moment of spectacle.

In the talk show scenario, the expert's direct testing of an ordinary speaker is particularly meaningful because of the privilege already afforded to the lay narrative by the host. Therefore, when the MP declares, "you rioted," he is questioning the truth value of the lay speaker's bona fide version of events, but life-world experiences are never questioned in the framework of the talk show. Personal experience is the talk show's generic epistemology (Livingstone and Lunt, 1994), and so to question the truth value of the authentic provokes the greatest conflict and gives us "the money shot." It is not simply that the discourses of ordinary people and their "life-worlds" emerge as naturally oppositional to the discourses of institutional representatives, but that the careful management and construction of the discourse makes such heated debate inevitable. Importantly, this handling of the talk favors "real stories" by ordinary folk, and for the viewer, since the mediation constructs us as another lay participant, we may be encouraged to feel that our stories have been validated as well. In the therapy sub-genre of the talk show, common sense is the privileged mode of evaluation, and thus the experts are completely expunged.

The Evolution of Talk on Vanessa

Vanessa offers a different sub-genre of the talk show that is representative of the therapy genre. There are no experts on *Vanessa* because the studio audience and by implication, we the viewers, are the experts. A characteristic of this sub-genre of the talk show is that the studio audience is called to appraise the dilemmas of the ordinary guests who have been elevated onto the stage. Show topics are formulated around their particular stories as they are introduced one by one. For the most part, the topics of these shows are not "public issues" as such, but are more personal issues related to relationships and family, in a style similar to *Oprah*.

The talk process usually begins with Vanessa, like Kilroy and John Stapleton, helping guests to produce their narrative. However, Vanessa displays an even greater knowledge of her guests than in the public issue format:

1	Vanessa		We haven't established a picture of what you're like towards your boyfriend. You
2			phone him on average, how many times a day?
3	Marissa		Four
4	Vanessa	→	I heard it was eight
5	Marissa		Yeh, well, heh, heh, four to eight
6	Vanessa		You phone his mother to check up where he is. You follow him when he goes out
7			in the evening. Tell me about that birthday evening, it was his birthday wasn't it?-
8			His birthday this year . . .

[Jan. 16, 1996]

It is obvious here, more so than in the other two talk shows, that control of the narrative belongs to the host. Vanessa even directly challenges the accuracy of Marissa's statement (line 4). Here Vanessa is evoking the parts of experience that she wants Marissa to tell, in the interests of stressing the extent of her jealousy. Since there are no experts, this is drawn out for the studio audience, who take the expert's place. Their ability to give advice is based upon their own "common sense," often by using examples of their own experience to address the moral dilemma at hand. Members of the studio audience then put themselves forward, possibly even removing themselves from their seat to a constructed platform, where they give their opinion or advice based upon what they have just heard.

Speakers from the floor rarely adopt the detached "animator" footing of the expert; rather, their right to speak is based upon personal experience, adopting an "authored" footing of shared experience. This was one woman's response to Marissa:

```
1   Woman       yeh, well your situation is exactly the same as mine was two and a half years ago
2               an' believe you me I never showed my jealousy and in the end I exploded. I lost tha
3               man, I lost him and believe you me you are both very insecure people. I::'ve now (.)
4               got friends who have spoken to me and said to me he's not worth having you're
5               worth more than him [. . .] and in the end they're not worth having guys like that
6               and I now realize, I'm worth more than that.
            [audience round of applause]
    [Jan. 16, 1996]
```

Here the woman does not actually address Marissa's problem, although she does speak to her directly, and her own story takes over instead. In another example, one woman utilizes her experience of having been subjected to domestic abuse, which gives her a legitimate and authentic platform from which she can challenge the "guest" speaker:

```
1   woman       Have you had any psychiatric help or even asked for any because you certainly
2               need it. I was married to a man like you for eighteen years and he gave me so many
3               injuries, you need help now not later before you kill somebody.
    [Jan. 16, 1996]
```

These examples illuminate the key difference between these and the more public issue orientated shows. All speakers here, apart from the host, are speaking from the same footing, which can encourage empathy, "my experience is like yours," as well as direct conflict, "my experience is more valid than yours." For instance, in this discussion about female bouncers:

[MB= male bouncer who objects to women in the profession and thinks that women should be traditionally "feminine," Woman 1= first woman from the floor, Woman 2 = second woman from the floor]

1	Woman 1	Don't you think in <u>this</u> day and age you're being a bit old fashioned? I mean you
2		can't tell anybody how to <u>look </u>as long as they can do a job it doesn't matter <u>how</u>
3		they look, what they are, who they are, they're just doin a job=
4	MB	= yeh, but point two,
5		do you have to look like a <u>bloke</u> to do a bloke's job, NO!=
6	Woman 1	=you CAN'T TELL PEOPLE HOW TO LOOK! (2) LOOK this is a lady
7		who commands respect and you shouldn't tell [her how she should look when
8		she's doin'
9	MB	[But do the Spice Girls look like
10	MB	blokes,
11	Woman 1	the job JUST AS WELL AS YOU:::
12	Woman 1	NO , they're millionaires
13		**[audience applause for woman's comment]**
14	Vanessa	Lady there **[holds microphone to another woman in the audience]**
15	Woman 2	I think you're just afraid of a woman being more dominant than yourSELF!.
		[very loud audience applause and cheers for the woman's assertion]

Here the women from the audience directly challenge the male bouncer, without any mediation from the host. Their right to this confrontation is grounded in their right to proclaim "common sense" in the absence of an expert opinion. Conflict clearly emerges as the man is allowed to respond from the stage and the speakers interrupt each other at aggressive moments in the exchange. This kind of talk show creates its dramatic tension through conflict *between* lay speakers, giving each the right to an authoritative voice. Notice the applause after the "commonsense" declarations of the speakers, which are lauded and appreciated as performances.

The positioning of the viewer within the studio audience suggests that we too must have an authentic voice from which we have something to say. Recall Vanessa's direct address to the audience at home, "Most of us if we're really honest get jealous from time to time." Personal topics about relationships, personal dilemmas, and family crises are the fabric of everyday life and, as Illouz (2003) points out in her evaluation of *Oprah,* these are the spaces of ontological insecurity in the contemporary world. In the examples from the talk shows discussed here, it is clear how the production devices and structuring of talk implicates the viewer at home both spatially in the studio and discursively in the debate. As viewers we are encouraged to see our own lives in relation to these lives, these dilemma as also our dilemmas.

Even more explicitly in morning magazine shows, the home becomes the mediated site through which a closer intimacy with the studio is fostered; therefore surely we have something to say as the discussions are played out in our own homes, in the very locale of our own personal dramas.

Part 2: The Sociability of Morning Magazine Programs

Morning magazine programs continue to reproduce the everyday through their concentration on domestic issues within a cozy climate of chat on the sofa. *This Morning* and *Good Morning* ran for two hours every morning on ITV and BBC1[7] during the period of this study, and comprised a patchwork of magazine type "features," each segment different in content, including some recorded segments such as short films on travel or cooking. Therefore, over five days each week, with at least ten segments each day, the content of the program is a constellation of different parts, constantly shifting throughout the day and the week. Live presentation provides important continuity, stitching together live interviews, recorded films, live makeovers, live cookery sections, live phone-ins, and live music at the end. Much of the stability of the program is therefore provided by the prominence of "liveness" and the spontaneity of the presenters' performances.

Addressing "Mrs. Daytime Home Consumer"

The content of the magazine program represents obvious ways in which the texts' appeals have a gendered focus. Its staple daily content reflects typically socially constructed feminine pursuits such as cookery, soap opera stories and celebrities, hair and beauty sections, and consumer product advice, as well as phone-ins on health, relationships, and psychological issues. These domestic pursuits are reinforced by the regular hosts (at the time of the study)—on *This Morning,* the husband and wife team Richard Madeley and Judy Finnegan, and on *Good Morning,* Nick Owen and Ann Diamond—along with other regular presenters—advice experts, doctors, psychologists, hairdressers, make-up artists, and chefs.

That the content of the magazine program offers a relatively traditionally coded set of feminine concerns that frame normative heterosexuality is obvious, but, like the talk show, its appeal is also achieved through its mode of address. In terms of its sociability, how does the magazine program's conversational style imply a gendered audience? In other words, how is its "for anyone-as-someone structure" (Scannell, 1996, 2000) explicitly gendered? As Scannell points out, "The radio [or television] must speak to a listener as someone in particular, with the attributes (the face needs) of a person" (1996:24). The most obvious way in which this is achieved is through the extensive use of direct address. All segments are sandwiched with direct address, presenters looking straight at the camera, confirming the viewer at home as the primary addressee rather than an overhearer.[8] Much of the discursive approach in the magazine program replicates what Montgomery finds in DJ talk, which is "obsessively concerned with its own conditions of production and consumption. It tends to foreground the relationship of the DJ to the talk, and the relationship of the talk to the audience, rather than the relationship of the talk to 'the world at large.' Unlike news programmes, for example (where the role of the newscaster in particular and the broadcasting institution in general is often elided from the discourse so that its preferred mode is third person, past tense, with little direct reference to the audience), DJ talk operates much more frequently along the axis between first and second person, between *I* and *you*" (Montgomery, 1986b:424).[9] In DJ talk, the use of direct address is part of establishing a social-relational dimension of talk that usually exists in co-present face-to-face communication. In many ways, the magazine program is reminiscent of a radio show; however, here the coupled presenters work to include the viewer into the social community of the show; the communicative axis is rather between *us* and *you*. Consider the opening of this edition of *This Morning*:

		[Show opens with men doing DIY to the *This Morning* theme music.]
1	Richard	What's with the <u>nipple</u> [tape?
2	Judy	[ye:s heh, heh, heh
3	Richard	what's with the nipple tape
4	Judy	He's just very sensitive (.) [it certainly will be when he takes it off.
5	Richard	[what about when he takes it off, my gom
6	Judy	**[direct address]** Erm the- that:'s it's actually happening, that was live up on the roof,
7		right now, the men <u>nom</u>inated by you loving wives, girlfriends, and mums as the sexiest
8		handymen in Britain. Which of all that lot will be going through to our finals? You can
9		find out in just a couple of minutes <u>plus</u> Olympic gold medallist Linford Christie on his
10		latest victory in the courtroom. He'll be talking about the allegations made by former
11		convict John McVicar that he took drugs to enhance his performance and despite
12		winning he does face legal bills of up to a quar:ter of a million pounds.
13	Richard	So that's Li:::nford Christie <u>live</u> on the show and she's b↑ack after her first appearance
14		on the show five years ago. Doctor Ruth oh:: yes she'll be taking your calls on the
15		phone-in on sex problems and you kno:w what she's like so you can ask what you like
16		you don't have to use your real name as usual on those phone-ins (.) Another tiny bundle
17		of energ- energy rather in the studio over there is Nancy Lamb cooking up Singaporean
18		food **[shouts across studio]** <u>Hi</u> Nancy **[shot of Nancy waving]** mad as ever and ↑WOO
19		HOO win a holiday for two in Jamaica keep watching this screen for details and there's
20		more it's a:ll changed down in Weatherfield Britain's first ever soap transsexual Hayley
21		joins us live.
22	Judy	Nicky Clarke making dreams come true in today's hair clinic the styles you always
23		wanted ten forty. **[montage shots of Nicky styling various women's hair]**
	[July 7, 1998]	

The most obvious point is that we enter Richard and Judy's conversation as though we are eavesdropping, interrupting them chatting to each other. Then at line 6 there is a shift, as Judy turns to directly address the camera. The rest of the introduction contains many references to "you" that are suggestive of some kind of a reciprocal relationship as they are also usually accompanied by inferences to viewers' perceived actions: "you can find out in just a couple of minutes," "you can ask what you like," "keep watching," and so on. Montgomery (1986b) labels these "response-demanding" utterances that are more usually prevalent in co-present communication.

DJs also use "identifiers" such as star signs, or actions, "people on the way to work," or region, "any Midlanders out there," and so on, to make more specific connections with listeners. In keeping with *This Morning's* continuous appeals to reciprocity, identifying viewers is usually linked to the appeal for participants for the live "phone-ins" and constantly asks viewers to identify themselves in terms of a particular issue. In this case it is related to the "sex clinic":

```
1   Judy      That's our phone-in with Doctor Ruth, if your sex life is er not working out and you can't
2             get no satisfac-[ (.) oh god no I'm sorry about that
    Richard                    [No, no don't do it
4   Judy      Give us a call on the usual number.
    [July 7, 1998]
```

Viewers are asked to identify a problem in their sex lives to take part and "Ruth here will put a smile on your face." In fact, appeals to the viewer to recognize themselves in relation to the daily phone-in topic are constantly reiterated throughout the early parts of the programs:

```
1   Richard   . . . and if you're desperate for a baby and one of you is infertile then do:: ring one of
2             Britain's best experts in the field he could have very good news for you. That's the
3             number [number comes up on the screen] o, three, four, five double five, one thousand
4             and we'll see you in eight minutes . . .
    [Jan. 18, 1996]
```

In *This Morning*, the reiteration of the phone-in topic, to ensure that there are enough callers for the slot, often means that they suggest a number of "identifiers" through which members of the audience may feel themselves personally addressed. For example:

```
    [Link from talking to Raj, the psychiatrist, about differences in relationships]
1   Richard   Okay, well thanks for now Raj and erm (.) [direct address to camera—close-up] if
2             you are at logger heads; over any issue with your partner, whether it's religion,
3             politics, sex or morality, give us a ca:ll .hh on o one five one treble five one thousand
```

4   and Raj will try and sort (.) you and your relationship out- maybe you can't agr<u>ee </u>about
5   how to bring up the kids as he said .hh maybe you're being <u>for</u>ced to submit to your
6   partner's beliefs or (.) per↑haps you've both made a compromise and it's all
7   worked out. Do::: let us know . . .
[June 30, 1997]

There are repeated attempts to encourage the audience to recognize themselves in terms of the show's concerns that, like the radio call-in, offer a route through which broadcasting can provide some kind of reciprocity, reminding the viewer/listener that the show is after all for *you*. In terms of the discourse, these petitions assume spatial deixis and co-presence (as discussed in chapter 2) that is predicated on the invitation into an interpersonal relationship with the presenters and life of the show. We begin to see how a shared sense of space, time, and sociability is accomplished.

However, while Scannell and Montgomery both imply a kind of generic sociable address, in these texts there are obvious ways in which the invitation is also explicitly gendered. The programs assume a feminized community in much the same way that women's magazines have been described as postulating a "synthetic sisterhood" (Talbot, 1995). Consider the way in which Judy, in the opening to *This Morning*, refers to the nominations of sexiest handymen by "you loving wives, girlfriends, and mums" (table 29, line 7), assuming an audience made up of women belonging to traditional heterosexual relationships. Most of the phone-ins, especially on *This Morning*, refer to "personal" issues that usually belong to the feminized private sphere—here infertility and sex advice. These inferences show how the communicative ethos of broadcasting also helps reinforce ideologies of normative social relationships.

These observations may seem rather banal, but there is an unmistakably feminine mode of address at work. This sociable style is sustained by an intimate conversational simulation of mutual friendship. One might say that this type of talk shares features with the speech genre of gossip, which in chapter 1 helped to explain the disapproval that these programs receive from the popular press, as they represent a feminized form of cultural expression.

Getting Closer: The Breakdown of the Text as Spectacle.

This Morning and *Good Morning* establish an intimate relationship with their audience by utilizing a number of strategies that serve to close the distance between text and spectator. These include constant reminders of the live text as "in progress," a text that the audience is privileged to be seeing in its making. It is this "liveness" and a sense of process and progress that characterize the experience of broadcasting as it takes place in the home and that make it a particular type of media event that cannot entirely be thought of as flatly "read." Magazine programs do not appear as polished, complete texts, already artfully produced and then simply screened. Instead, they evolve seemingly *with* us as viewers, as we are included into their world, and made privy to their production processes.

For instance, mistakes made by presenters help constitute some of the program's spontaneous appeal. In the world of the magazine program there is no need to excuse or feel embarrassed about stalling on the show, being unsure of what happens next, or even making a complete error. It is simply part of the appeal of the "liveness" and spontaneity of the "ongoing" *now* of "this morning":

1	Richard	. . . Right, are we gonna move on then?
2	Judy	oh, have we still got more to do? (.) Right **[claps hands]** everybody if you can all come in again
3		**[models return to the studio, continue talking about the DIY models]**
4	Judy	**[to Richard]** Right, it's your turn now
5	Richard	We're massively over time. I think it's your turn now
6	Judy	Is it? Where are we (.) oh, we're there . . .

[July 7, 1998]

Admitting that you have miscalculated the timing of a slot and lost your place in the script are all events that can be comfortably worked out in front of the camera and not hidden from the spectator "backstage," as one might usually expect in traditional forms of theater and broadcasting (Goffman, 1981).

In this phone-in, there is a fairly lengthy period of time where things are apparently going wrong:

1	Judy	. . . w- we'll go to Helen first from Bedfordshire- Oh (.) **[hearing something in her earpiece]**
2		we can't start with Helen Ok↑ay we'll bring **[turning over sheet]** Helen in later- we'll go to Kay firs
3		who's calling from Bedfordshire **[looks at sheet]** no, Bedfor- um
4	Richard	Get on with it woman-
5	Judy	Right um **[clears throat]** we start with Kay who's calling from Lincolnshire, this isn't religious
6		though, hello Kay
7		(2)
8	Judy	Oh dear (1) Oh::[:: dear
9	Richard	[Shall we do some tap dancing? Raj can you sing? Can you do any turns?
10	Raj	mmm some quick therapy heh, heh,heh
11	Judy	Are you there Kay?
12	Caller	Hello:::
13	Judy	Oh, heh, heh, thank god for that. I thought you'd completely disappeared. You are Kay aren't you?
14	Caller	No. I'm Debbie
15	Judy	[Oh, right, heh, heh, heh
16	Richard	[heh, heh, heh
17	Raj	[heh, heh, heh

[Jan. 18, 1996]

This is common on *This Morning*, as the presenters joke about the delay, "shall we do some tap dancing" (line 9), rather than attempt to cover up the problem with the telephone relay by perhaps showing a recorded segment. This is a convention to which sophisticated audiences have become accustomed within live television, a convention that produces dramatic tension from the anxiety over "what might happen next" but is smoothed over by the ease with which the presenters involve the viewer in the apparent interruption. Even aside from these seeming "errors" and "misjudgments," which are part of the performance even if they are not exactly scripted, daytime television allows us further into its behind-the-scenes production.

Alongside making the audience witness to the hosts' mistakes, we are also made to feel as though we are privy to production developments within the show. While more obviously the viewer is encouraged to call in, play a game, win a holiday, etc., we can also be party to the planning of new slots for future programs. For instance, in this next example, while talking to the popular sex therapist, Dr. Ruth Westheimer, about the introduction of the drug Viagra, Richard apparently has a spontaneous idea for a future program:

[Interview with Dr Ruth Westheimer, Richard has asked Dr. Ruth
whether Viagra helps orgasm]

1	Dr. Ruth	. . . Now, I'm not saying that it might not help some people, It might help
2		her not only with the arousal but also psychologically. The idea of having
3		taken that (.) it costs in the States ten dollars it's expensive to have taken that
4		she has to use it so maybe that idea is orgasmic=
5	Richard	=there's a way we can test that
6		which we might do in a proper way on this programe ha
7	Judy	No, we won't!
8	Dr. Ruth	On this program? Not with me sitting here, heh, heh, heh, heh
9	Richard	No, on this program, no listen it's going on prescription September-October
10		of this year in Britain, right. What we do is we could set up a couple of- with
11		Dr. Chris who's our GP we could set up a couple of control groups and we
12		could have one taking it and one not and couples, married couples taking it
13		and I bet you that a proportion of people who have taken the placebo will
14		nevertheless report an enhanced=
15	Dr. Ruth	=because they th [ink they're taking it
17	Richard	[because they think
18		they're taking it.

[July 7, 1998]

In September of that year, as the drug was released for sale in the UK, *This Morning* hit the tabloid headlines for screening a test of the Viagra drug by sending three middle-aged couples to a hotel and asking them to return later to the program to report on the drug's success.[10] This example highlights the program's commitment to "liveness," immediacy, and to its evolution within real time. As the drug was released, *This Morning* tested it, and so the program, like a soap opera, evolves contemporaneously with our own lives.

Similarly, topics used on magazine programs are often referenced through "real"-world events that are happening "now." For example, all of the openings of *Good Morning* begin by chatting about a news story in that day's papers. *This Morning* often bases its topics for phone-ins on topical news stories; for instance, the phone-in on relationships that need to overcome major differences was prompted by the wedding of celebrities Imran Khan (Pakistani cricketer and politician) and Jemima Goldsmith (heiress):

```
1   Judy      . . . on a::ll the front pages is the glamorous Imran Khan  and the stunning twenty-
2             one-year old Jemima Goldsmith [cut to the days newspaper front pages]. They
3             finally went and did it. Last night in Paris in an Islamic wedding ceremony and
4             judging from the kind of doom and gloom articles that have been written about
5             them you'd think the bri:de had just sentenced herself to a life in jail.
6   Richard   Yeh, but it certainly wasn't a last tango in Paris for Jemima- she wasn't even
7             allowed to hug or kiss the groom at their ceremony cos' of the ru:les- they're
8             obviously in love  and good luck to them- but we're fascinated here by this kind of
9             marriage and we'd love to hear from YOU this morning, if you and your partner
10            have had to overcome some massive basic difference (.) religious, political,
11            sexual, whatever. So if you're at loggerheads whether it's working ou:t or it's
12            falling apart, give us and psychiatrist Raj Pursaud a ring
    [June 30, 1997]
```

The emphasis on "real" time and the "real world" within the content is central to the viewers' experience of simultaneity, of the "everyday," quite literally every day.

These programs therefore appear as though they are constantly in motion, and our involvement in them as "in-process," helping to muddy the waters between stage and audience. Indeed, in magazine programs the "backstage" often becomes "front stage," partly through the frequent references to the production staff on the program. This often happens when camera crews are consulted as to where they want the presenter to look, a feature that is often generic to live TV, but more often in *This Morning* and *Good Morning* the camera crews', make-up artists', directors', and editors' *real* lives (as well as the presenters') become part of the content of the show.[11] We are constantly reminded of the personalities and even private lives of the production staff. In this particular example, presenter Judy Finnegan is filling the viewer in on why the program is auditioning for a D.I.Y expert:

Judy: . . . Well, looks like we've got all these guys who've been nominated by mums, girlfriends, wives, sisters, whatever 'cause they're gorgeous and very handy, because just to get the, y'know, background, our editor's wife Zoe is looking for a new handyman, hence our program, so as usual whatever Nick wants we have to do.
[laughter in the studio, noticeably from the studio crew too]
[July 7, 1998]

Here we learn the name of the editor's wife and some relatively innocuous, although personal, detail about her, which apparently informs the content of the show. This type of information begins to stretch our relationship with the show beyond what is screened, not only to those responsible for making the show, but also to their personal relationships and their "real" lives. In the world of the morning magazine program, "personality" ranges beyond the presenter, as the production crew can also be the "ordinary" stars of the show.

On some occasions the breaking through of the backstage into the front stage can also enhance the immediacy of the live broadcast event. Later in the same program, the director's comments are incorporated into the phone-in conversation, despite the viewer not being able to hear her voice:

		[On "Dr. Ruth's sex clinic" Dr. Ruth gives advice to a caller, Emma, which she suggests she should act on tonight]
1	Richard	But isn't it the Brazil game tonight?
2	Emma	I think so yeah
3	Richard	We::ll:: it's all over then isn't it?
4	Emma:	I could cope if it [was just the World Cup
5	Dr. Ruth	[Well you might have to wait until tomorrow
6	Judy	It probably is the World Cup **[shrugs]** you know it probabl-=
7	Richard	=This's been going on
8		for four months, it's only been on for three weeks
9	Judy	We:ll [t.hh .hh. hh
10	Emma	[the World Cup feels like it's been going on for four months
11	Richard	**[holding his earpiece]** That's what our director just said, that's just what our
12		director just said.

[July 7, 1998]

Here the production equipment, the presenter's earpiece, which is a link to the director and intended to be an invisible aid to the smooth running of the show, becomes a visible prop and part of the show's performance. Richard's inclusion of this comment here also works to suggest that the caller and the director are thinking alike: they share in common an irritation with the duration of the current football tournament, which one might regard as feminine common ground. Therefore, the distinctions between "front stage" and "backstage" is clearly blurred in *This Morning* and *Good Morning,* transgressing conventional boundaries of spectatorship. These features help create the impression that the viewer is part of the wider production of the show, having a role beyond that of a "spectator" who has knowledge only of a show as finished product, as a "text," thus drawing the viewer into greater proximity to the experiential "world" of the magazine program.

Chat: Getting to Know You

Paddy Scannell might describe these features as part of "sociability" (1996), a less formal speech style used across a number of genres that has traditionally accompanied the domestication of television since early broadcasting. A characteristic of such a style is "chat," preferred over more imposing and hierarchically ordered forms of discourse. In his discussion of the genre of chat, Tolson (1991) regards its structure as apparent through topic shifts to the personal, through clear shifts of "register." These features are identifiable in the conversations that occur on daytime television. In fact, the shift to the personal is used at the opening of almost every *This Morning* interview or introduction of a guest or presenter. Consider this opening of the segment with Nancy Lamb, *This Morning*'s Singaporean chef:

		[After segment on "hunky" DIY men]
1	Richard	Did you enjoy that Nancy?
2	Nancy	Very much lovely body
3	Richard	Did you enjoy that Judy?
4	Judy	er::m (.) it was alright (.) erm now erm you know **[puts arm around Nancy]**
5		Nancy's daughter's just graduated, she's got a really g[ood degree hasn't she?
6	Richard	[What in?
7	Nancy	[I'm very pleased
8	Richard	What in?
9	Nancy	Economics and computer science all she needs is to=
10	Judy	=two one?
11	Nancy	Two -one [with honours ye:::h.
12	Judy	[two- one oh good for her (.) what's she called?
13	Nancy	Augusta
14		**[conversation continues about Nancy's daughter until there's a topic shift**
15		**to the food segment that Nancy is to present]**
16	Judy:	Now tell us about this food festival . . .

[July 7, 1998]

Although Nancy has been on the program before, she is not one of the regular slot presenters. The way of introducing her therefore communicates to the viewer her ordinariness. It is reminiscent of an introduction in daily interaction since it suggests "this is what she has in common with you." We are told details of something that has just happened in her life that involves her family and her private life. Nancy becomes "one of us," fitting the world of the show, displaying conventional motherly pride in her daughter's achievements, which exist in the real world, in real time. Through the show, Nancy Lamb has acquired some celebrity status, but as we see here it is through the construction of her as "ordinary" that she becomes a personality that accords with Langer's (1981) personality system.

In the world of daytime magazine shows, the emphasis on intimacy also extends to those who might elsewhere be afforded "expert" status. For instance, Dr. Ruth Westheimer is introduced as though we have met her before (and indeed she has been on the show previously); she is an old friend returning:

1	Richard	**[to camera]**Well she's an old friend of This Morning, **[to Dr. Ruth]** hello **[back**
2		**to camera]** Dr. Ruth is here **[back to Ruth]** lovely to see you again.
3	Dr. Ruth	Hello there, glad you've moved to London, [easier for us yes
4	Richard	[well it makes it easier for you doesn't
5		it that was one of the reasons behind it to be honest erm, well how <u>are</u> you? It's
6		been a few years since we saw you.
7	Dr. Ruth	I'm very good
8	Richard	Yeh? you still doing the radio stuff in New York?
9	Dr. Ruth	I do a lot of radio a lot of television. No:t my own show which is wonderful
10		because this way I have my Sunday evenings free but I still talk about sex. I'm a
11		grandmother of three no:w and I still talk as explicitly and as clearly about these
12		issues. **[to Richard]** I see you are smiling
13	Richard	no, no I'm [pleased
14	Dr. Ruth	[I have to say the word sex. Guess what happened to me last night. I
15		went . . .
16		**[Ruth tells a story about her visit to the theater and getting kissed backstage**
17		**by the male lead]**

[July 7, 1998]

Sociability is clearly marked here. The introduction of Dr. Ruth is presented as though she is visiting old friends, not delivering a performance for television. The interaction begins with greetings that are more usually associated with daily conversation—"lovely to see you again"—and notice how Ruth remarks on how glad she is of the move to London. *This Morning* moved from Manchester to London to be able to attract more famous guests, but it is discussed in this extract not so much as though the show, the studio, has moved, but more as part of the presenters' lives, "*you* have moved to London." Indeed, the fusion of the life of the show with the life of the *real* world was suggested at the time of the show's move by press articles about Judy's worries about leaving her home town and the children switching schools. Thus the "world" of the show is blurred with the "life-world" of the presenters as we "drop in" to this mediated domestic space.

The extract continues as though we are catching up on the life of an old friend—Dr. Ruth is not initially introduced in terms of the function she will provide on the show, which is later revealed as hosting a sex therapy phone-in, but rather in terms of a personal emphasis related to her relationship with Richard and Judy, and her private life while she has been away. She even relates a narrative of "guess what happened to me last night?" that reasserts both co-temporality and the importance of her daily, routine life as "one of us." What is remarkable about extracts such as these is not that there is a *shift* to the personal "such that the primary business of the format is temporarily delayed or suspended" (Tolson, 1991:179), but rather that the personal emphasis on chat provides the structuring frame through which guests are allowed to inhabit the domestic world of the show.

As viewers of daytime television, we are privileged to a "para-social" *knowing* of personalities (Horton and Wohl, 1956). Langer suggests that it is the element of disclosure, as we have seen in the extracts above, that suggests we are seeing celebrities "as they really are" and not in terms of their public selves (1981:361). Tolson argues that in the chat show celebrities perform "synthetic personality" in the interests of good television and through such instances, through interviews over time, the viewing audience may build a "para-social" relationship with them. However, in the morning magazine show the main presenters sustain this kind of relationship through the daily iteration of real-life experience, which is fundamental to the creation of the show's familiar world. Many of the links are inflected with personal experience. For instance, in this next example from *Good Morning*, Nick is introducing a topic for viewers to call in and give an opinion:

1   Nick   . . . and also something I've seen in the paper today er a <u>very</u> sma:ll story and I think
2   it's worth more in <u>The Mirror</u> "new man is dead." It says the eighties wimp who
3   changes nappies, cooks, and shares chores is officially dead- ye::es **[laughter from**
4   **crew]** cor what a relief- I can go back to being normal again **[laughter from crew]**
5   the worst moment was when I was pushin' the double-buggy aroun:nd on a Saturday
6   afternoon- <u>Saturday</u> afternoon, round the shops when I should have been on the
7   terraces at Luton shoutin' things like **[sings]** you're goin' 'ome in a Luton ambulance
8   **[laughter from crew]** anyway:: anyway the number to call o, one two one, four, one
9   five, five thousand. <u>Is</u> it good that new man is officially dead, according to the new
                    survey?
[Jan. 26, 1996]

The topic is introduced not only as contemporary news, but also something that relates to Nick's personal experience. The style of talk is rather "tongue-in-cheek," drawing upon conventional, and arguably within these shows, compulsory, heterosexuality. Nick's para-social address involves a flirtation with an assumed "community" of female viewers; much of this can also be detected by the non-verbal visual cues given by Nick that are difficult to capture in transcription. The socio-communicative sphere generated here is clearly one of intimacy: the presenters share their life with you, as you might want to share your life with them (call in, write in, go on the show, or simply "drop-in"/turn on).

Revealing private lives is consistent in the magazine show format, but it is not revelation in the sense of uncovering shocking secrets of the type that constitute the main fodder of the tabloid media (although that can occasionally be the case). It is more the case that we learn the mundane and routine details of the lives of the presenters, which reflect the content of daily conversations with friends, repeated in the humdrum of daily life over time. Consider this extract from the *This Morning* hairdressing section with hairdresser, Nicky Clarke:

1	Nicky	. . . and of course on Fleur she's got <u>dead</u> straight hair and she would just wash and
2		leave her hair. She's just had it all cut off hasn't she?
3	Richard	Yeh it used to be long didn't it?
4	Nicky	I'm <u>really</u> gonna have to work with it today but I thought we could actually show how
5		to do some really nice curls which are very much the look for [the summer
6	Richard	[ye- ye know what? (.)
7		Fleur has just actually told us for the fi- cos you've actually been with us for a long
8		time **[turns to Judy]** were you aware of this? Really weird this but when we stayed
9		on holiday for the first time in Clearwater in Florida with our kids <u>you</u> actually stayed
10		in the same hotel
11	Fleur	Yeh, with my mum and da[d
12	Richard	[yeh
13	Judy	**[to Richard]** And do you know how old she was?
14	Fleur	About ten
15	Richard	Ten
16	Judy	thank↑you
17		**[laughter from those on set and crew]**

[July 7, 1998]

Here, Fleur is introduced as a model who has "been *with* us for some time"; she clearly belongs to the shared community, to the "us" of *This Morning*, which Richard reinforces by recognizing her change of hairstyle (an observation usually associated with "women's talk"). A loyal audience inhabiting this world would recognize this also, since building an intimate knowledge of people who appear over time is part of the routine. We are also privileged to information about Fleur before the lifetime of the show and her coincidental meeting with Richard and Judy at an early age. Again, this is not treated as a random coincidence between performers to be discussed "backstage," but rather this kind of information is what builds the very fabric of the show's world around the other topics. The "chat" assembles a picture of the presenters' relationships to each other, at the same time as it assumes and substantiates the viewer's relationship with the show. Chat therefore performs a discursive function: it builds an intimate social setting where the purpose of the talk is not so much the transmission of information, but rather to confirm sets of social relationships, knitting together hosts, crew, guests, and us the viewers.

Part of the appeal of *This Morning* was the relationship between then presenters Richard and Judy as husband and wife; Ann and Nick were not married, although they attempted to imitate heterosexual coupling. The British press made much of this in the alleged "sofa wars" between the two magazine programs. Indeed, it was suggested that this was the reason why *This Morning* beat *Good Morning* in the ratings war: "Why then when like played like, was one liked more than the other? The answer is almost certainly sex or, anyway, marriage. . . . The whole point of ampersand celebrities is their physical relationship. Viewers like watching Richard and Judy for subtle clues as to what goes on in the bedroom or, for more decorous members of the audience, at breakfast. Otherwise routine appearances by the doctor, the agony aunt, the cook and the financial adviser are enlivened by the search for hints of frostiness between the couple on domestic issues. . . . This was the key to their gender appeal. As the Archbishop of Canterbury said last week in a different context, alternatives to marriage are not, in this slot, quite the same" (Lawson, 1995). Indeed, the private relationship between presenters in their home life is incorporated into the "textual chemistry" of their on-screen relationship.[12] For example:

[Introducing the day's contents]

1	Judy	. . . er hot foot on the footsteps of The Corrs, Boyzone and Bewitched, Ireland's latest
2		pop export Kerry Ann, she's with us live at ten past twelve
3	Richard	Actually, I've met Kerry Ann outside my dressing room she was in the corridor,
4		standing waiting to be ( ) she's <u>really</u> nice=
5	Judy	=as long as it wasn't <u>inside</u> your
6		dressing room
7	Richard	↑I'm old enough to be her grandad heh, heh, heh. Anyway there's <u>nobody</u>, nobody
8		ever comes into my dressing room, my hallowed portal

9	Judy	Apart from me
10	Richard	Only if you knock
11	Judy	Come on
12	Richard	Come on let's get on.

[July 7, 1998]

In this exchange, Richard and Judy are splicing the presenting of the show with banter that is expected of them *as they really are* as husband and wife, displaying jealousy and teasing each other. The chat here is meaningful in its heterosexual display, reinforcing a dominant and ideological traditionalism in which being "like us" is a particular, conventional "us" that it is assumed can be comfortably occupied by "Mrs. Daytime Home Consumer." These particular cues to a para-social relationship are not only built through disclosures that are *asides* to the more dominant course of the program, but rather they provide a broad knowledge, accomplished daily over time through chat. Here the viewers at home are encouraged to engage intimately with the experiential world of the television program as though it is part of a set of "real" relationships akin to those formed through face-to-face interaction.

Authenticity

The "sincerity" of these relationships must surely be considered in relation to the mediated process of television. When Andrew Tolson talks of the chat show he points to the *knowingness* of television performers' construction of personality: "There is a sustained and highly self-reflexive metadiscourse about television as a cultural institution. Here participants not only invoke the cultural knowledge of the viewer, they also draw attention to the construction of their own performances" (1991:183). Self-reflexive "knowingness" belongs to the genre of comedy (Cardiff, 1988), but is ambiguously marked in the magazine show.

There is often no obvious sense of "performing" the sincere, since comedy is not the main genre of the talk. Allusions to the real world do not stand out in the text as extraordinary as they have no sense of irony, even if they are self-reflexive in terms of the knowing unraveling of the show. For instance, this next example appears seamlessly within Nancy Lamb's cookery section:

[Nancy Lamb is cooking banana fritters]

1	Nancy	. . . let it sit for an hour and then let it fry (.) Do <u>not</u> let your oil [get] too <u>hot</u> because
2		this is raw er banana so when you cook it slowly and you get cri<u>spi</u>er and crispier
3		each time.
4	Judy	mmm, mmm

5	Richard	We had erm we had Sunday lunch with Vanessa on Sunday (.) because it was
6		Sunday lunch -
7	Nancy	Yes
8	Richard	- .hh and she did baked bananas, didn't she=
9	Judy	=baked in the oven=
10	Richard	=just put them in the
11		oven, yeh that was all and they were deli::cious

[July 7, 1998]

Richard's personal anecdote is not recognized as a dramatic shift in register; it appears as perfectly unremarkable within the program's discursive style. In this case, the easy inclusion of personal anecdotes like this one are more accurately described as shifts of "footing" (see chapter 2): "A change in footing implies a change in the alignment we take up to ourselves and the others present as expressed in the way we manage the production or reception of an utterance. A change in our footing is another way of talking about a change in our frame for events . . . participants over the course of their speaking constantly change their footing, these changes being a persistent feature of natural talk" (Goffman, 1981:128).

Implying a shift in "register" suggests that the speaker leaves behind one style of speech address and takes up another, but the concept of "footing" suggests a much more fluid usage of speech styles wherein one can "sustain more than one state of talk simultaneously" (1981:155). Therefore, by thinking about moves to the personal in this way, we do not have to consider that there is one dominant state of talk, relegating other states to asides. As seen in the introduction of Nancy Lamb and Dr. Ruth on *This Morning*, it is usual for the personal to be the framing theme of some conversations, where the footings of "animator" (expert discourses on psychology or cookery) and "author" (discourses of personal experience) can easily merge.

To return to the extract above, then, the shift of footing is significant in terms of the viewers' proximity to, and occupation of, the habitat of the show. The reference to "Sunday lunch at Vanessa's" is unremarkable in terms of the show's norms, but interesting in terms of its "communicative intentionality." This aside about Sunday lunch at Vanessa's, without any other elaboration by Richard, is meaningful to the show's audience. The assumed community of "Mrs. Daytime Home Consumers" is expected to share the knowledge that the "Vanessa" referred to here, is actually Vanessa Feltz, another personality of morning television who previously had a slot on *This Morning* and, at the time this particular program was aired, had her own talk show directly preceding *This Morning* on ITV's schedule (discussed earlier). Thus the private relationship and the public one are fused, at the same time as the exchange contributes to the seamless structuring of the morning schedule, implying an even wider world of "morning" television in the UK.

"Inferentiality" is common on the program; consider the way in which a soap star was introduced in the opening introductory segment by Richard: "It's all changed down in Weatherfield, Britain's first ever soap transsexual joins us live." There is no reference to the actual name of the soap opera, just Weatherfield, which it is assumed that "Mrs. Daytime Home Consumer" will know and understand to be the setting for the long running ITV UK soap opera *Coronation Street*. Knowledge of soap opera is part of the assumed feminine cultural competence that belongs to the world of morning television. This background knowledge is part of the communicative intentionality of the program, where any distinction between the real world and the life of the show is blurred. Intentionality produced through references to intimacy and chat reproduces a feminized mode of address that is traditional and hetero-normative.

The prominent "meaning," therefore, invested in morning magazine programs is about the production of a series of para-social relationships. The televised real selves here are also mundane and conventional, white, heterosexual, coupled if not always couples, who address their audience with an assumption that they are "just like us." To think of this as a television "text" does not entirely capture the way in which the audience is encouraged to feel intimately involved in the sociability of the show and its production both spatially and discursively. An audience sharing these pragmatic communicative cues might occupy the discursive space of the program. Thus, the socio-communicative sphere of the program, and what it performs, is also what it *means*. This book seeks to home in on how the audience is implicated in this framework, not just in the semiotics of content, but in the discursive and spatial registers in a manner that assumes a type of relationship, offering a space where the viewer is immediately articulated within the format of the show. It is here that we can begin to understand the "power" of these formats in terms of their relationship with their audience.

Conclusion: Morning Talk as a Mediated Gossip Genre

The programs discussed here have different formats and their topics and contents shift and change through their daily repetition. However, the para-social appeals to lived reality endure throughout all of these formats. Therefore, with reference to a more flexible concept of genre, morning talk programs share a similar focus, or "orientation" (Neale, 1980). Following the suggestion in chapter 2 that Bakhtin's call for more accounts of speech genres can also be applied to broadcasting (and other media), this section looks to establish a generic framework. These texts are commonly orientated through their emphases upon the relational and experiential that accords with styles of speech associated with "feminine" modes of gossip (see chapter 1). We can compare these strategies of morning television to characteristics that have been attributed to gossip as a feminine speech genre using Jones's (1980) essay, "Gossip: Notes on Women's Oral Culture." The elements of gossip are detailed following a socio-linguistic approach presented by Ervin-Tripp as a "verbal framework" that is studied "in terms of the relations between the setting, the participants, the topic, the functions of an interaction, the form and the values held by the participants about each of these" (Ervin-Tripp, 1964, cited in Jones, 1980:195).[13] Each element is considered in turn to explore the relationship between gossip and morning television.

Setting

Setting refers to both time and place and the more general sense of cultural situation. According to Jones, "The private, the personal domain—this is the cultural setting. In concrete terms, the setting is the house, the hairdressers', the supermarket: locales associated with the female role both at home and outside it" (1980:195). There are, of course, the obvious ways in which the studio space created in the morning magazine program simulates a domestic setting through familiar surroundings of the home, but also some segments exactly reproduce both the hairdressers' and the supermarket, with spaces for the resident hairdresser and the various consumer experts. While the talk show does not conform to these physical locales in such a straightforward way, it does help reproduce the more general cultural setting of the private and the personal and can invite the viewer to experience the parallels with their own domestic circumstances. Both kinds of shows foreground personal experience and private discussion, which is constructed through various strategies, as we have seen, and can be summarized more accurately in relation to the other elements of gossip.

Participants

Under this category, Jones suggests, "Gossip is essentially talk between women in our common role *as* women. Gossip is a language of intimacy . . . an intimacy arising from the solidarity and identity of women as members of a social group with a pool of common experience" (1980:195). The programs present interesting strategies here. First, both kinds of programming assume an audience demographic (female) that shares common experiences. For instance, consider the "implicatures" that refer to assumed shared "feminine" knowledges (such as recourse to the soap opera), but also the talk shows' specific assumptions of shared experiences: "would you let your child?" . . . "would you have a mastectomy?" These are assumptions about women's subjectivities in their traditional roles *as* women: mothers, wives, daughters. Recall Judy Finnegan's opening to the show in one of the examples from *This Morning,* "you loving wives, girlfriends, and mums."

These strategies help to constitute an ideal shared experience of "Mrs. Daytime Home Consumer" that continually reasserts women's position within the private sphere. However, there is also another sharing of experience within the specific mediation of the discourse. This refers to the co-temporal and co-spatial orientations that are embedded with the texts. All of the texts present simultaneity as though they are happening "here and now." This allows the viewer access to a text in production, privy to errors and misjudgments that not only break the spell of spectacle, but also assist in the creation of a shared and mutual intimacy with the broader community of the show. Across the constructed space of broadcasting, through deictic references and camera angles, the suggestion is one of a mutually unfolding and communal experience between the studio and the home. Therefore, both talk shows and magazine shows offer a mediated discursive space for an assumed community of women *as* women.

Topic

According to Jones, topics for gossip are always about the roles involved in the occupation of "being a woman," and whatever the specific topic, she suggests that its relevance is always related to the personal. In both the morning magazine show and the talk show, the "authored" voice (Goffman, 1981) is important to speaking directly, unaffectedly, and from personal experience. In the morning magazine show, the structure of its "chat" means that both presenters' and guests' discourses are framed in this way. In the talk show the points of the dramatic spectacle appear through the pursuit of the "authored" voice: through the hosts' defense and support of the lay narrative, the hosts' pursuit of conflict through the "experts'" relinquishment of an institutional footing, or simply through the validation of the right to speak from personal experience—"this happened to me." While it might be obvious how the topics related in these shows gender the discourse, it is the primacy of personal experience in the business of being a woman, no matter the actual topic, that prevails.

Functions

Jones describes four functions at work in gossip: "house-talk," "scandal," "bitching," and "chatting." "House-talk" obviously refers to the domestic is-sues that connect women's lives and is replayed in the topics on the morning magazine program as well as, to a lesser extent, on the talk shows. "Scandal" refers to the moral judgment of the behavior of others and is possibly most visible on the talk show, especially on *Vanessa,* which creates dramatic ten-sion through onstage "lay" judgments upon the participants' private lives. But scandal is also related to the way in which talk show conflict is often pursued through the hero-like defense of the ordinary public who have been wronged. This also relates to Jones's suggestion of the cathartic category of "bitching," which is where we can berate those who have done us wrong or locate our experience in relation to another's experience to feel superior, operations that might, in Illouz's (2003) terms, help us cathartically to feel more ontologically secure.

The other interesting function here is "chatting," which Jones describes as "the most intimate form of gossip, a mutual self-disclosure" (1980:197). These programs assume a "sociable" conversational style that is both personable and intimate and that involves the mutual self-disclosure of both present-ers and lay participators in the studio. However, this reciprocity, which is characteristic of gossip, is also here a particularly mediated phenomenon. The para-social appeals to participate also implicate the self-disclosure of the viewer at home. In the magazine program we are encouraged to phone in and in the talk show we are encouraged to understand ourselves as participants during the viewing experience as well as for future shows. This is mediated "chat," wherein mutuality is created across broadcasting, drawing in a wider community of potential "chatterers."

Finally, Jones suggests that all these forms are criteria founded upon women's everyday lives. We have seen how the quotidian is reinforced in these programs through daily inferences to what is happening "now." This mediated "dailiness" potentially embeds these personal discourses within the daily experience of the home. The creation of an intimate shared community is not simply one played out upon the screen, but one that utilizes these strategies to suggest the erosion of a distinction between text and spectator, implying a reciprocity that includes viewers at home as also *participants* in the broadcast space.

This situation presents an intriguing phenomenon at the interface of pub-lic/private spheres. The apparent staging of the closure of the spectator/spec-tacle distance, the appeals to participate, and the defense of the lay narrative are all part of the talk's emphasis upon relational, contextual experience that is the backbone of what, more popularly, we might call "gossip." In this instance, private and intimate self-disclosure is mediated by television as entertainment and is at once transformed into public dramatic spectacle while also being "re-embedded" within the local context of the home. It remains then to assess how these televised strategies are encountered in the daily experience of women's lives. The next chapter sets out the implications of these ideas for drawing up a methodological framework for audience research.

4. Method

Texts-in-Action

Introduction

Morning talk programs have a particular "communicative intentionality": strategies of embedding themselves into a communicative framework of the everyday, the routine, and the personal. Talk shows and daytime magazine programs draw upon "para-social" imperatives that suggest reciprocity with their audience, and much of this address is specifically and ideologically gendered around hetero-normative social and cultural frames. However, despite research into the features of broadcast talk utilizing the concept of the "para-social" to explain the address to the viewer, at the time of this research there are no similar studies that attempt to explore the impact upon the "real" viewer at home. This chapter sets out a methodological framework for researching the particular matrix of the gendered construction of intimate broadcast talk and its communicative impact upon a female audience.

Existing methods of audience research are briefly summarized to make way for an alternative methodology for researching the ritual communication of broadcasting with its audiences. The methodological approach is eclectic, bringing together methods from media audience research with linguistic approaches to language and discourse, thereby going some way towards overcoming demarcations in the field between mass and interpersonal communication. The chapter begins by establishing some of the limits of the well-established traditions of audience research in the field, for the type of phenomenon that is explored in this book, outlining the space for considering a more dynamic model for capturing audience responses to television. There are also implications for doing feminist research with women when developing a methodology based upon pragmatics. A post-structuralist account of gender as performative contributes to the broader analytical frame of analyzing language in situ. And finally, the chapter describes the practical stages of carrying out the audience research in this study, giving a sense of the group of women whose voices help to paint a more vibrant picture of the socio-communicative sphere of daytime television.

From Uses and Gratifications to Cultural Studies' Approaches to Audiences

Audience-studies paradigms generated from cultural studies were born from wanting to grasp the complex negotiations of the media's role in the circulation of meaning. Such studies provided a challenge to both the overdeterministic and linear "media effects" (transmission) model from mass communications research, and the overly functionalist "uses and gratifications" model. Uses and gratifications research suggests that media use depends on the perceived satisfactions, needs, wishes, or motives of the prospective audience (Katz et al., 1974) and there have been attempts from within this paradigm to research para-social interaction with the media as fulfilling basic psychological and social needs for interaction (Rosengren and Windahl, 1972). Much of this type of research is not premised upon either understanding the significance of particular media genres, or upon any social theory that might account for the implications of social or cultural distinctions, but rather it focuses upon a mentalistic account of "need" within which the para-social replaces some kind of "lack" in personal human development.[1] Such a model works with deficit measurements of communication that can be quantified, dangerous apparatus given the contentious history in which women's pleasures have been too easily associated with failing personal traits.

The most significant criticism of uses and gratifications research is that it fails to engage with questions of power (Moores, 1993:7). In contrast, the breakthroughs made at the Birmingham Centre for Contemporary Cultural Studies (CCCS) in the 1980s took into account the relative power of text and reader in cultural struggles over "meaning." This development was initiated by Stuart Hall's (1980a) influential "encoding and decoding" model, in which the semiotic construction of meaning from a Marxist perspective is explored in terms of the encoding of messages in production and the decoding of those messages in reception. For Hall, both processes involve structures of meaning. This approach shifts the emphasis away from the older communication models of "sender-message-receiver" and into a process whereby, "We must recognize that the discursive form of the message has a privileged position in the communicative exchange . . . and that the moments of 'encoding' and 'decoding' though only 'relatively autonomous' in relation to the communicative process on the whole are *determinate* moments" (1980:129). In terms of ideological impact, the process of decoding the discursive structure of the message is as central to making meaning as the process of encoding the structure of the message. Hall points out that these processes may not be symmetrical, and here he draws upon the work of Volosinov, who, as we have previously discussed, stresses the multi-accentuated nature of the sign. Thus, the text becomes open to alternative readings depending upon cultural power and social relations, and Hall posits hypothetical situations of decoding that mark out the territory for audience research.

Hall's essay opened the way for a more complex understanding of text-reader relations in media research. It is important to stress here that the *social* subjects implied in Hall's work make use of the symbolic resources around them to decode messages.[2] David Morley (1980) empirically tested Hall's hypothetical decoding positions within audience research. He attempted to assess the ways in which audience members were incorporated into the dominant paradigm or resisted the dominant ideology according to their socio-economic position. His investigation of different socially oriented audience responses to *Nationwide* (an early evening magazine news program) supported Hall's hypothesis.

Morley's study has generally been heralded as a landmark in cultural studies research that proved relationships between ideological readings and social positions within the broader attempt at the Centre to orient the media's role to the relationship between ideology and subjectivity as influenced by Althusser, and to the maintenance of the status quo as influenced by Gramscian critiques of hegemony. Other studies have followed this tradition, utilizing the encoding-decoding paradigm. Seiter (1999) considers three such studies: Corner, Richardson, and Fenton's (1990) *Nuclear Reactions*, which focuses on readings of programming on nuclear power; Jhally and Lewis's (1992) *Enlightened Racism*, on reception of *The Cosby Show*; and Schlesinger et al.'s (1992) *Women Viewing Violence*. All of these studies reveal group readings of material shown in an institutional context—usually the university department. They are all concerned with how different groups deconstruct the messages as transmitted by the media, a research principle that can only be carried out if one is reasonably certain of the meaning of those messages in the first place. Consideration of each of these studies leads Seiter to suggest that "the 'encoding-decoding model' seems to work better for news and non-fiction programming than it does for entertainment programming, where it is much more difficult to identify a single message, or even a set of propositions with which audience members could agree or disagree" (1999:20–21). Similarly, we have seen in chapter 1, it is difficult to find overarching ideological meaning in talk-based programming where the discursive framework turns any stable sense of the politics of representation into a constantly moving target.

Morley's early work is generally acknowledged as leading the way for audience research that takes into account the social dynamics of the viewer, but he does make clear some of the problems that were inherent in his early method. The issue of "contexts" of viewing most dominates his immediate concerns with method, since decoding does not "naturally" occur in the institutional context; television viewing usually takes place in the domestic environment influenced by family members or cohabitants. This insight led to a change in direction, and audience studies began to focus upon the domestic conditions of media consumption and as a result drew its methodological apparatus from "ethnographic" approaches. This approach involved spending time with informants in their local environments and homes, carrying out "participant observations" and usually semi- or unstructured interviews. Key examples of early ethnographic media research included Hobson's (1980) research into young mothers' use of the media in the home and her research with soap opera viewers (1982), Lull's (1980, 1990) expansive study involving the observation of over two hundred family households,[3] and also Morley's (1986) follow-up study, *Family Television*. Of course, research on media in the home has been considerably influenced by a feminist agenda framed around the politics of the domestic sphere and family power dynamics (e.g., Gray, 1992). Following this trend, studies that turn to the site of consumption apply a sociologically grounded consideration of technological appropriation in the domestic environment (e.g., Silverstone, Hirsch, and Morley, 1992; Livingstone, 2002).

Dominant directions in cultural studies' audience research therefore largely involve a triumvirate of concerns around texts, readers, and the contexts of consumption. These represent shifts from considering encoding and decoding as a theoretical principle, to it becoming a methodological principle, and then turning to contexts where sometimes the analysis of the text is lost altogether. A methodology appropriate for this study cannot be concerned with any *one* of these dimensions alone, and the very terms of that trinity are inappropriate for capturing the *experience* of broadcasting. Audience research in cultural studies has shifted from positioning audience members initially as "readers" of texts to then locating them as "users" of technology. My emphasis on the process of communication resists both of these labels to consider audiences as communicators in the broadest sense.

Morning-television texts have been described in terms of their ritual communication, with a particular interest in understanding the programs' communicative relationship with their audience to reach a broader contextual understanding of the operational power of daytime talk. This leads me to want to dissolve the distinction between texts and readers as entirely separate entities, one that is predicated on the systematic dualism of encoding and decoding. As Moores suggested almost two decades ago, "The time has come to consolidate our theoretical and methodological advances by refusing to see texts, readers, and contexts as separable elements and by bringing together ethnographic studies with textual analyses" (1990:24). To some extent, this call has been heard by researchers who are increasingly bringing together an analysis of the text with analysis of reception, which mostly involves conducting research in parts: an analysis of the text, followed by interviews or focus groups with audiences.[4] While this does make steps towards mobilizing audience responses back into an understanding of the text, it tells us little of the phenomenological experience of texts in ethnographic contexts. I offer a separate textual (discourse) analysis, but this chapter is dedicated to finding a method of research that can bring text and reader together in situated contexts.

Of course, the significance of talk about television viewing to the broader production and circulation of meaning within the cultural sphere has received considerable attention in the ethnographic audience research (Hobson, 1991; Fiske, 1992; Brown, 1994; Gillespie, 1995). It is well documented that television promotes gossip and kinship among social groupings. In earlier chapters we have seen how Mary Ellen Brown (1994) discusses the way in which soap opera in form and content echoes forms of orality that mesh with women's oral culture and helps foster cohesion among women. Similarly, Gillespie (1995) provides an interesting account of young British Asians living in Southall in London talking about the Australian soap *Neighbours* within their peer groups. The soap provides a platform for discussion whereby they can compare and contrast their family lives and kinship networks with those in the fictional world of "Erinsborough." It also generates discussion about cultural difference significant to their diasporic experience. The traditional method of investigating people's talk about television with their peer groups gives insights into the way in which social formations and lived realities are assembled into the reading of the television text.

Audience research of this kind often relies on "naturally occurring" social networks as viewers, rather than the construction of a panel of viewers placed together for the purpose of the focus group. However, what this produces is information about how television texts take on subsequent significance within social networks and also serve to enhance social cohesion. This is *one* important way in which television enters in the discursive field of the cultural sphere, but can only take place *after* the program has literally and physically entered into the life of the home (or bar, café, airport, etc.). In my study, the actual moments of viewing are essential to capturing the communicative event of the text *in action* with its audience. Therefore, while my interviewees do talk *about* the text, this research also gets a stage closer to the act of viewing. What happens as the women watch the television program? Is it possible to observe and pay close attention to the text/speaker and the reader/hearer union? Thus, as with the textual analysis, the audience research does not conform to the encoding/decoding process where symbolic meaning is constructed and deconstructed as a dual process that is separately conceived. Registering Hall's emphasis upon the "determinate *moments*" of the communication process, the present study will make progress towards making sense of the *mechanics* of television in time and space.

Moments of Television

Finding a method for removing the binary distinction between texts and/or readers may enable an investigation of "para-social" viewing strategies. In Fiske's 1992 essay, "Moments of Television: Neither the Text nor the Audience," he also suggests a dissolution of the categories "text" and "audience." First, he argues that the concept of "audience" is difficult to understand as an empirically accessible "object" since it is difficult to find its boundaries. For instance, he asks us to think about what is not the television audience, since we are constituted at different moments in time as different members of different audiences. But the most provocative point is that he asks us to rethink how we conceive of a "text." Increasingly, "postmodern" textual analyses suggest that (particularly television) texts are open, polysemic, refuting solid definition, and indeed we have seen the talk show defined in this way. Many television texts (particularly, say, in opposition to film) cannot be understood as complete and unitary objects. Ellis's (1982) use of the term "segmentation" describes the way in which the television text is different from its cinematic relative in that it is broken up into segments that constitute television's particular aesthetic form. We have seen how this "incompleteness" works in relation to the talk programs that concern us here, and this has considerable consequences for reception. Incompleteness requires something of the viewer: it opens up syntagmatic gaps and begs the viewer to "write" in their own missing parts. Fiske therefore adapts Barthes' theory of the "writerly text" to invoke a concept of the "producerly text": "A producerly text does not prescribe either a set of meanings or a set of reader relations for the viewer: instead it delegates the production of meaning to the viewer-producer. It differs however, from the writerly text in that it is not avant-garde and does not shock the reader-writer into learning new discursive competencies in order to read-write it: rather it offers provocative spaces within which the viewer can use her or his already developed competencies" (Fiske, 1992:63).

The analysis of morning talk television in the previous chapter argued that it appears as though it is in progress and not "finished." The programs evolve "now," contemporaneously with daily life, suggestive of a "producerly" text foregrounding "liveness" that works to diminish the authority of the author.

It is important to offer a short caveat here, should my argument become aligned with the various appropriations of Fiske's ideas with the label "active audience theory," which suggests that audiences necessarily resist the ideological power of a text through this very openness. All communication is active, but it does not follow that action should necessarily be equated with resistance. Here, Fiske's point is useful because it allows us to move beyond the binary distinction of text and audience, offering a sense of the relationship between text and viewer as mutually produced. Fiske suggests research should take into account, not so much the text, but the *textuality* of the viewing experience whereby "the correspondence between subjectivity and textuality is so close that the two leak into each other at every point of contact" (1992:57). However, Fiske's appropriation of the "writerly" text still proposes an unsatisfactory literary framework. I suggest that it is possible to stretch the concept of textuality to also embrace physicality. These "points of contact" or "moments" could be analyzed for how they sustain a particular socio-communicative sphere in which *textuality* can be used as a means to open out the *lived experience* of texts in particular "moments of television."

A "moment" refers to a small portion of time, an instant or an exact period of time; in which case thinking of moments of *television* can be suggestive of television taking place, dynamically, *in time,* now, in the everyday. Secondly, in a physical sense, a "moment" can refer to a mechanical process—a product of force from a line of action to a particular point—in which case television's moments might imply enactments at work with dynamic and physical force, rather than simply as two-dimensional texts. This study, therefore, crafts a methodology for capturing significant "moments" of talk television as having a *third* dimension outside of the text-reader (or even product-user) binary set of relations that is related to the experiential and phenomenological *act* of watching television. It is logical then, given the appeals to para-social interaction that are embedded within these texts, that realizing the viewing relationship as a communicative event would illuminate "moments" of mediated talk that can unlock, in some real sense, the *physicality* of reception.

Text to Text

To detail particular interactive moments of television requires a methodology that enables both the program and its reception to become simultaneously visible. The resultant method, "text-in-action," is new, but the idea of reproducing the text and the context together has of course been mobilized in a few other studies. My approach owes a great deal to Walkerdine's (1986) account of family video viewing.[5] Having viewed the film *Rocky II* with the Cole family, she provides a description of the narrative of the film alongside the occurrences in the home. For example:

Rocky II, the video

	000
Fight scene, possibly the 15th round.	R: (untranscribed) F: Watch, watch. Cor he ain't half whacking him, ain't he, Do? Watch, here.
	010
	F tells J to go and ask M to make some tea. J goes to the kitchen. M's friend is with her—Scottish accent—with her young child. [. . .]
	125
	F pauses video or winds back to the closing round, because M is handing out the tea and cakes.
Rocky fighting championship round, pitched against huge black opponent. Things aren't looking good. Rocky is taking a beating. The crowd is going wild, cheering, shouting.	R: Mum, hurry up. F: You ready? M: What? F: We've yet to see the end of this. R: This is the 5th round. F: Fifteenth, watch it.

From this example we can visualize the points in the film marked out as central for the family's engagement. This type of transcript enables Walkerdine to see the parallels Mr. Cole draws in his identification with the protagonist Rocky. She begins to understand the association with the film within the framework of class struggle: as Rocky must "fight" for a better social position for his family, so must Mr. Cole physically labor for his. Would Walkerdine have got to such a close evaluation of Mr. Cole's identification with Rocky had she not charted the viewing experience in such a way? Had she simply asked Mr. Cole what he thought about the film after the event, is he likely to have articulated such a relationship with the fight scenes that could have been understood in any other way than pleasure in the spectacle of the event?

It is important to remember that when we ask audiences questions about relationships with media forms, they are not necessarily used to critically reflecting upon their viewing experiences in such a way—or interrogating their pleasures and practices in terms of subjective involvements and senses of self. Hermes (1995), in her study of magazine readers, remarks on the way in which magazine reading is actually very nonattentive, casual, and not always "meaningful."[6] Hermes makes comparisons between daily magazine reading and daily television use that are useful here since she draws attention to the half-attentive ways in which texts are consumed. Such analysis reveals a crucial methodological point, because when Hermes interviewed her subjects they often had little to say about their experiences of reading women's magazines. Practices that are embedded in everyday experience are not reflected upon, and therefore gaining data by asking people to account for their everyday experience can be frustrating and unproductive. Just because everyday media is not necessarily registered as meaningful by its consumers, we should not conclude that it is not meaningful at all. It is precisely because of the way in which media forms have become so ubiquitously implicated in our sense of the everyday that we hardly notice them. This is a social phenomenon that requires more significant attention, requiring research to look for the "determinate moments" embedded in the ritual *experiences* of media consumption.

Walkerdine's study presents one of the very few examples that display the action in the home alongside the media text, although there are significant differences with the present study. Walkerdine analyzes a video text that creates a different viewing environment from that created by the normal flow of television. In addition, Walkerdine, as a participant, is generally interpreting the physical actions of the family during the viewing experience as part of her ethnographical study. She pays relatively little attention to the detail of the text. Here, we are concerned with broadcast texts that flow into the space of the home, constantly employing direct address that cannot be understood as having a contained and unitary textual focus like film.

There are clues in other television audience research studies to the type of research methodology introduced here, although they take place in the focus group setting outside of the home. These seem to be accidental moments when research that involves watching television with audiences produces unexpected unsolicited talk during the program in question. For example, in Liebes and Katz's book *The Export of Meaning,* they transcribe one of the Moroccan group's discussions while viewing. Their notes on the methodology report that, "Taping was discontinued here on the assumption that there would be little or no conversation during the viewing. Fortunately, the observers took notes verbatim until the recording resumed" (1990:41). The accidental nature of this incident is obvious, since there was an assumption that viewers would not speak while watching the program. Anecdotal experiences of watching television, especially with others, suggest that this would not necessarily be the case. Perhaps the dominance of text/reader models in media theory predisposes media scholars to align television viewing with the silent act of reading. But after all, television is a noisy medium too that demands our attention directly in our living rooms.[7]

While Liebes and Katz do make note of the talk produced while their audience watches television, the talk is not documented in terms of its exact relationship with what is occurring on the screen, but rather the content of the data is used in the same way as other focus group data, as part of the process of decoding, rather than as a response to the immediate ritual responses to the communication taking place. Liebes and Katz are working with the narrative text of the soap opera *Dallas,* which presents a different genre with which this methodology has not yet been tested, but David Morley's focus groups with the more openly conversational BBC news magazine program *Nationwide* also invoked unexpected commentary. Interestingly, Morley does document a few extracts of the television text in parallel to the audience commentary, and looking at them we can begin to see how the text is negotiated while it is *alive.*

The mapping that Morley provides here is useful, although neither he nor Liebes and Katz grant much significance to how these utterances have been induced. Morley attributes the commentary to the group finding the program unacceptable, but does not pay any attention to this as an active discursive encounter outside of his exploration of the content of what they

Table 1.

Program	Commentary
Link after Vox Pop *interview:* "Well there we are most people seem to have agreed that the tax system is too severe . . . "	"That's a bloody sweeping statement, isn't it? . . . from four bloody edited interviews!"
Interview with Mr. Worthington	"Is this chap a tax expert? Seems like a berk . . . " "Poor old middle management!"
" . . . ambitious people . . . "	"Aaaagh" "Avaricious people, did he say?"

(Morley, [1980] in Morley and Brunsdon, 1999:230)

say as discursively produced. Can it be seen as part of a ritual communicative encounter provoked by the discursive register of the text in which the viewers felt a compulsion to *participate* in the discourse, as they decode it? Clues exist in these canonical studies as to the dynamism of television texts in process, yet there has not since been a longer study into the significance of these moments of television. Therefore, this research into *texts-in-action* is concerned with the precise details of what the women *say* as they watch programs that reach out to them "conversationally."

Gender and Performativity

This research has focused upon a feminized mediated speech genre and seeks to outline its relationship with women viewers. Traditionally, feminist research has been concerned with making visible the marginalized voices of women in an attempt to evaluate practices and pleasures that have been previously excluded from serious critical concern within the male-dominated academy. Take for instance Oakley's (1974a,b) study on housework or Radway's (1984) study of romance reading wherein the "feminist consciousness, feminism itself, is deeply and irrevocably connected to a reevaluation of 'the personal' and a consequent refusal to see it as inferior to, or even very different from, 'science'" (Stanley and Wise, 1983:6). I endeavor, therefore, to make sense of the gendered evocation of the personal as a mediated experience, one that is routinely played out in everyday experiences.

However, post-structuralist concepts of the self have disrupted the ease with which feminist researchers can comfortably add territory to the map of women's experience. In media studies the challenge has been most clearly articulated by Ang and Hermes' argument that research into gendered practices of media consumption has led to the essentializing of gender as an a priori category, advocating "against a continued research emphasis on women's experience, women's culture, women's media consumption as if these were self-contained entities, no matter how internally differentiated" (1996:333). This argument poses some problems to the accepted paradigms of feminist research and has also opened up questions about *which* women are referred to in the acknowledgement of difference. Seiter suggests that there is a conflict between the theoretical frameworks through which the post-structuralist accounts of gender are arrived at and the modes of doing empirical research: "Ang and Hermes construct media subjectivity through postmodern *theories* of ethnography, through theoretical discussions informed by Michel Foucault, Jacques Lacan, Judith Butler, and others—based at times in textual analysis, but rarely in empirical field research" (Seiter, 1999:29).

Empirical research has struggled with how to conceive of subjects in this theoretical terrain, but it is time that the advances made in post-structuralist thought are made to speak to our methodological approaches in feminist media studies. It is not incompatible to test subjectivity as an unfinished process in which gender is constantly in flux as an unstable category, and yet still carry out empirical research, because these observations, to make sense at all, must be discernible in lived and real subjectivities. It is possible to suggest that Judith Butler's theoretical insights are in tune with the propositions made here in relation to media and the *pragmatic* accomplishment of meaning.

Butler (1990) asks us to consider gender as a process of enactment, of "doing" gender rather than "being" gendered, such that it becomes a mutable practice. Gender, therefore, becomes an "act," constituted in its performance rather than in its essence. This concept rests upon an undoing of fixity that she later attributes to Austin's theory of pragmatics (discussed in chapter 2 of this book). In this context, she asks what it means for a word not only to name (semantics), but also to perform what it names (pragmatics). In the space between the two lies the pragmatic negotiation of meaning, which for Butler becomes the performativity of gender. *Doing* gender therefore *becomes* gender, a perspective that is conducive to the arguments building throughout this book that calls for an account of how meaning is pragmatically constituted through the *act* of television viewing. Similarly, in the work on talk shows, Illouz (2003) also argued that the meaning of *Oprah* lies in the events that are performed: testimony, therapy, reassurance, and so on. This surely registers that audience research needs to get up to speed in accounting for the active pragmatic relations of meaning making.

Central to my position is Butler's emphasis upon the dynamism of the process of gender enactment: "Gender ought not to be construed as a stable entity or locus of agency from which various acts follow; rather, gender is an identity tenuously constituted in time, instituted in an exterior space through a *stylized repetition of acts*. . . . This formulation moves the conception of gender off the ground of a substantial model of identity to one that requires a conception of gender as a constituted *social temporality*" (1990:140–41).

In later work Butler (1993) is at pains to clarify how this repetition constitutes performances as not simply choices but as material acts that are central to embodiment.[8] I have placed considerable emphasis upon the idea that the reception of broadcasting, and how it comes to be meaningful, is also constituted through its physical, experiential dimension *in time*. So we might ask, what role does the media's temporality play in the "tenuous" temporality of gender as an identity? Feminist media studies must surely ask questions about how gender performativity is mediated. Therefore, this methodology suggests investigating "moments" where specific discourses of the private meet across a mediated experience. In the same way in which the text here is not conceived of as whole and unitary, neither are the women in this study. It might be possible to situate the responses of the women in the study as "performances" of gender, where we can make insights into the role of television in the active repetition of gendered and ritualized acts of identity.

Speech Analysis

In some senses, working with speech acts allows an obvious route through which we might accomplish the task of marrying post-structuralist thought to methodological practice. For example, empirical research on gender and language-use has followed a similar theoretical trajectory whereby linguistic performances of gender are not considered fixed as stable entities in sexed bodies, but rather understood as strategies and competences deployed to suit changing social contexts (Cameron, 1995b, 1998a,b). I place greater emphasis on the speech acts informants produce during the broadcasting of the program, rather than relying entirely on their construction of the viewing experience after the event, which also addresses another issue in relation to the analysis of informants' speech.

There is an interesting debate within social science research about the nature of analyzing the responses of informants as we "let them speak for themselves." Part of this debate has focused upon the power of the researcher to interpret the meanings produced by the subjects of the research. Geertz comments that, "What we call our data are really our own constructions of other people's constructions of what they and their compatriots are up to" (1973:9), and Buckingham (1991) expresses doubt about the merits of simply taking the words of informants as they are given, without reflecting upon the conditions in which they are produced. McRobbie (1982/1991) too is concerned, with feminists in particular, about oversimplifying the nature of the spoken word and attaching to it a "spurious authenticity." These researchers are therefore asking us to be aware of not only the semantics of what is said, but also *how* expressions are arrived at, since they are influenced so heavily by the context from which they are derived. Thus when making use of what research subjects say, researchers should consider the discursive (and pragmatic) production of those words in the first place.

In audience research, Morley's (1980) *Nationwide* study suggests the importance of thinking about the language informants use in investigating decodings, working with actual speech, rather than only the content of those responses, to get some sense of the order of expression. Corner, Richardson, and Fenton (1990) also stress an "ethno-discursive" approach to their findings, wherein they were interested in the interviewees' framing styles of their accounts to gain insights into the subtleties of "interpretative processing." These studies, though, must take into account the discourse produced as part of the constructed focus group encounter, but this study also wants to capture the communicative event of television viewing itself. The speech recorded here will be concerned with the conversational style with which viewers respond to the text: whether they use direct address, whether they respond to questions produced by the presenters, whether they contribute their own compatible life narratives with the genre's form. In short, whether the audience takes up the para-social invitations that chapter 3 argued are fundamental to the programs' ritual contribution to the socio-communicative sphere of daytime television. This might suggest a search for a "purer," less *re*constructed picture of the audience experience. Indeed, immediacy is important since it is one of the primary features of television as a distinct medium, but the speech itself is also treated in terms of the details of its contextualized construction, in line with a more socio-linguistic, or ethno-discursive methodology paying greater attention, not only to the content of that speech but also to how that speech is pragmatically produced in the context of television viewing.

There are approaches to the study of language in action that stem from an ethnographic approach to culture. In his series of papers in the 1960s and 1970s, Dell Hymes (1974) shifts away from understanding socio-cultural forms and content as a "product" towards their study as "process," whereby language use is part of our broader set of relativistic cultural competences. Therefore, "Our knowledge of what words and meanings are appropriate for a given time, place, and purpose, etc., is cultural knowledge. The use of contextualization cues to convey the contextual presuppositions of an utterance displays our communicative competence as a member of a certain culture and situates us in a particular web of beliefs and actions specific to that culture" (Schiffrin, 1994:144).

In the "ethnography of communication," linguistic accomplishments are researched in terms of their cultural specificities, recognizing diversity and searching for variation across cultural distinctions. This practice assumes that speakers are aware of the rules governing the appropriate use of language in different social situations, suggesting wider knowledge than simply linguistic competence. They need "communicative competence," which takes into account wider socio-cultural and lived influences. It seems clear that one of the newer and potentially more diverse ways in which speech cultures have developed, as the "drive belts" of social change to employ Bakhtin's term, is through the impact "mass" communications may have had upon interpersonal communications. In this case, the possibilities of local and cultural competences produced in the communicative process of watching television (or engaging with other media) require much more rigorous investigation than is currently available.

Transcriptions

While I want to take the ethnographic imperative from this approach and think about the *accomplishments* of language through specific *competences* in context, scholars in the field of "ethnography of communication" have largely concentrated on particular speech events (courtroom, classroom, doctor's office) other than everyday conversation. However, in Conversation Analysis (CA), one tapes naturally occurring speech rather than using other kinds of sociological methods such as surveys or in-depth interviews. As Sacks notes, "Social activities are observable; you can see them all around you, and you can write them down. . . . If you think you can see it, that means we can build an observational study" (1992:28). My study, therefore, does not only rely upon interviews involving the women's responses *about* what they do, but also relies upon observing and recording the women's interaction with the broadcast form, recalling that "the objects we record, examine, consider and write about occur *in the course of social interaction*" (Moerman, 1988:7, my emphasis). Obviously any claim made for this as a "naturalistic" method is problematic; my presence as an observer means the research setting is distorted. This does present some complications to the findings and will be discussed later in the book. Some elements of Conversational Analysis's usefulness for the analysis of broadcasting were discussed in chapter 2, but here it is necessary to provide a short note on my methods of transcription.

The data from women watching the program is transcribed and subjected to analysis using tools from CA and discourse analysis. In this vein, women's utterances are explored in terms of how they *accomplish actions* during the viewing process, focusing on the dynamic mechanics of television. Therefore, much of the method in this study relies upon the transcription of the simultaneous data produced from the program and the viewers. It is important to note that in CA the transcriptions themselves are not thought of as the complete data (Hutchby and Wooffitt, 1998). The data are the tape recordings of naturally occurring interactions and the process of transcribing is thought of as the first stage in its interpretation. Elinor Ochs (1979/1999) discusses transcription as theory and draws attention to the particular decisions made during the transcription process, such as the fact that selection and layout of data are critical in understanding and assessing the generalizations reached in a particular study. Transcription, therefore, is a process that reflects the goals of the research, since it embodies a hypothesis; it is not possible to think that there could be a neutral transcription system.

The central features that a CA transcript attempts to capture are the dynamics of turn-taking—the beginnings and ends of turns and the precise details of overlaps, gaps, and pauses—as well as the characteristics of the speech delivery, such as features of stress, enunciation, intonation, and pitch. The data from the television programs was collected from my VCR, pre-programmed at home. I then watched television live with the women individually at each of their homes. A boundary microphone made the television text audible on the tape recording of the women's utterances. The transcriptions, therefore, involved setting out the data in two halves, with the broadcast talk on the left and the home talk on the right, mirroring Walkerdine (1986) and Morley (1980). In CA, transcription turns are marked down the page in chronological order and overlaps marked in square brackets. In my transcriptions, overlap occurs between the studio utterances and those at home, and therefore the exact moments when the women spoke were carefully marked against the televised talk, side by side, as it took place in time, on the page. This gives us a unique way of envisioning the audience's speech in terms of "interaction" with a text.

Practicalities, Methods, and Problems

In planning the recruitment of subjects for this research, it was important to keep in mind the theoretical criteria developing. The extent to which this research is experimental suggested recruiting a relatively small and homogenous group of women in order to test out the methodology. At the time I decided to access a group that could be described as a "speech network" (Milroy, 1980), requiring that there would be some connection between the women who could be constituted as "community" of speakers, sharing their own set of communicative competences. This would provide some consistency between speech patterns in the analysis of their discursive practices with the texts. The group of women therefore already had a sense of group cohesion. I did not create a community, but since I am also one of the speakers involved in the research, I recruited a group of women with whom I am familiar, and with whom I shared a regional accent from the Midlands of England. Hence the women in this research are all white and working class, although of different ages, and all from around the town of "Chinnock"[9] in the Midlands of England, which is heavily influenced by the legacy of the coal mining industry.

Most of the women regularly met on a Monday evening in a village near "Chinnock" for a Ladies Guild Meeting of the local Catholic Church. The gatekeeper was my mother, referred to as "Polly" in this study, and the group of women consists mostly of her friends from the local town. Using a "snow-balling" technique, some of the women recommended their friends to the study too. I attended some of their weekly meetings around the time when they were organizing the Christmas fete. Talking to them about their viewing habits and watching television in the daytime solicited the usual suspicion about judgments around TV viewing practices, possibly compounded by the negativity associated with daytime talk TV in the press at the time. Informal discussions took place in and around these meetings, which I did not record at the time, but their conversations together also prompted me to add in a focus group to the research method, which had the added benefit of enabling me to see how they would talk together as a "speech community." I watched these daytime talk programs with each of the women alone in their own homes, recording the "text in action," and then interviewed them about the programs afterwards. I carried out thirteen individual interviews (ten of which are used in the study) between 1996 and 1998 and one focus group at the end of the research period. Some of the women were only involved in one part of the research, depending upon their responsibilities and what contribution they felt comfortable with, which is indicated in their biography outlines in the appendix.

The individual "text-in-action" process generated the most interesting re-sults, although it also raised issues, some of which I am unable to resolve. When entering the women's homes I turned on the tape recorder to record us watching the program. At no point were the women prompted with gestures towards the significance of what they said during the program; the process was framed very much as an interview in which we would watch television and then record our conversation about the program. My hunch that women would talk through these programs is substantiated by other audience research into talk shows. For example, in Engel Manga's (2003) study, one of the women reports that she likes to watch talk shows in company because she feels the invitation to comment: "Karen: Because like, when I'm watching by myself, who am I going to comment to? It's like, 'Oh I had a really good joke there for someone'" (Engel Manga, 2003:84). But Engel Manga frames this comment as a para-social substitute for the longing for community, rather than asking questions about how that dynamic, the compulsion to respond, works in relation to *mediated* communication in the contexts of television viewing.

As far as possible I wanted the women to feel uninhibited in terms of their immediate verbal responses to the televised text. However, of course, my presence will have undoubtedly affected the viewing environment. Although I had asked the women to continue about their daily business as they would usually do, that was difficult, as I was also in a sense an invited guest as well as a researcher. Some of the women had clearly rearranged their schedules and what they would have normally done while watching television in order to accommodate me being in their homes. This presents a methodological query because in the interviews many of the women reported that they did not usually "sit down" for long to view, but rather, listened to the text while doing other household chores. If "sitting down" is a criterion for more attentive viewing then this may have altered the findings of the research. It is impossible to tell how significant this is. It may be possible in future research to ask the women to switch on the tape recorder without a researcher present, but this would mean losing some considerable insights into the viewing context that, as will become evident later, can be quite crucial to the interpretation of the data. My presence also *adds* something to the findings, as the women also begin to reveal personal experiences in relation to the text that might have gone unrecorded had I not been present, and I explore this dimension in the following chapters.

Conclusion

The theoretical threads from previous chapters have been drawn together to outline their methodological impact upon the research design. This has plotted a route towards a method designed to capture the *text in action,* in order to portray how the communication process is mutually constructed in *moments* of broadcasting. To think of "moments" of reception is a key methodological imperative to enable us to encounter the *mechanics* of reception, how it evolves, and how television viewing may be incorporated into the vital business of everyday life. Therefore, the method requires thinking about the text and audience simultaneously as an active encounter where meaning is established through the pragmatics of communication. This focus also enables the research to be located within a post-structuralist understanding of gender as performative, with the potential to provide new data on how the act of watching television might help to mediate acts of gendered identity. And finally, this chapter has begun to introduce the group of women who took part in the study, to give some background to the voices in the next chapters that complete the more colorful picture of the socio-communicative sphere produced through their encounters with daytime talk.

5. Talking about Daytime Talk

Introduction

The methodology outlined in the previous chapter pointed to a research focus on the experience of watching talk as it takes place in the home. Hence this book appreciates that television texts take place phenomenologically *in time* within social contexts. Before we get to those findings of this research, this chapter will contextualize television viewing as (para-social) interaction. It provides insights into the impressions that the women in the study gave about the pleasures and reasoning behind their viewing of daytime talk shows. In this sense, the chapter reflects conventional modes of audience analysis, drawing from interview and focus group data that provides background to the contexts in which the mediated exchanges discussed in the next chapter take place.

The data in this chapter is transcribed in accordance with some basic Conversational Analysis conventions in order to represent the women's actions as *speakers* as well as informants. While offering up the women's own accounts of the pleasures of watching daytime television, this chapter also provides a second function: to present the women's responses as dialogue produced through the discursive context of the interview or focus group's discussion. Since the women of the study from "Chinnock" in the Midlands of England are all socially connected to one another, they can be seen to constitute a "speech network" (Milroy, 1980). Therefore they share similar features of talk in terms of their vernacular, but also in terms of their intimate relationships and shared understandings as a social group. In some of the focus group data, therefore, we are able to see how the women accomplish certain readings (through features such as simultaneous and overlapping speech) facilitated by their collective discursive competences.

The transcription style draws attention to the women's competences as speakers as well as to their views as informants, thus serving my interest in locating the dynamism of television discourse in everyday life. What is interesting is the turn-taking procedure that the women adopt in producing their readings of the texts as a group. Transcribing this data was complicated due to the amount of simultaneous speech that the women produced. However, this was not to be interpreted as aggressive argument, since the women were not aggressively interrupting each other. Rather, they were joining in each other's turns and producing overlapping speech, two elements of what Coates (1994, 1996) understands as cooperative speech among women friends, where they utilize a "shared floor." For example, here the women jointly produce a comparison of the talk programs with magazine problem pages as a gendered form:

1		Cathy	Men don't like discussing any of that though do they?
2		Angela	Not mine though, he'll read mine, 'e likes reading my magazines, heh, heh, 'e wouldn't
3			go buy one
4		Patricia	Well, that's it y'see [Jo's] in the sixth form and she ses boys always 'ave the magazines
5	→		n' read out all the er problem=
6	→	Jenny	=problem pages
7	→	Cathy	= problems, yeh

Jenny and Cathy both latch on to Patricia's turn without a gap and simultaneously produce the key issue that men apparently find both intriguing and embarrassing, "problems." And in the next example notice how the overlapping of the women's turns helps produce the reading of the talk show as talking therapy:

1		Jana	Sometimes some people are [just so angry they want to share it with other
2		Cathy	[It's therapy, isn't
3		Jana	people, 'look this [is-
4	→	Angela	[This is the only way they can get it out by telling everybody—some
5			people go into themselves and not say anything where others wanna tell everybody—n'
6			that's their way [of doin' it
7	→	Jana	[Tell everyone
8		Cathy	Part of the healing process, in 'it?

At line 4 it is as though Angela is finishing Jana's turn and at line 7 Jana responds by overlapping and reinforcing Angela's point, "tell everyone." This concept of a *shared* floor, rather than a speaker/hearer dynamic assuming only one speaker at a time that is the usual framework in CA's "turn-taking" systematics (Sacks et al., 1974), becomes particularly crucial to the next chapter of the book in the analysis of para-social interaction.

The topics and issues raised in these discussions loosely followed three areas. These are related to: previous findings about women's viewing pleasures and habits in the home, the contemporary debates about talk-based programming and, finally, the intimate and direct address that characterizes these programs as a socio-communicative sphere.

Morning Television in the Home

In terms of the daily routine of television viewing and its place within ritualized practices, the women described how morning programs fit into their daily routines. Those who are married and run their own homes all describe their practices in terms that echo media research into women's consumption of the mass media a decade or more ago. For instance, this is one woman's description of her typical morning:

> SANDRA: Well I'd be u:p and busying meself (.) I'd've probably go:ne- I'd have had me *dry*er on- I've got a basket of washing there to dry and I'd've been ironing what's in the ba:sket and I'd've gone up the sho:p and got me bit of me:at and I'd have been preparing the dinner and might have washed me ha:ir and gone and *too*tled round the bathroom you know I'd have been busyin (.) I'd come and I'd have had me a coffee and I'd've sat and watched it a bit but I mean I might have sat and watched it for half an hour—I'd have sat and watched it for half an hour having me breakfast.

The *This Morning* program that Sandra watches begins at 10:15 a.m. Sandra works as a cleaner at the local school first thing in the morning, from around 7:30 a.m. until 9:00 a.m. Note the amount of chores that she is able to do around watching the program—drying clothes, ironing clothes, washing her hair, tidying the bathroom, shopping for the "bit of meat," and beginning to prepare dinner. The program is two hours long and amongst all that Sandra will also allow herself to have breakfast. Many of the married women tell similar narratives of how they organize their household jobs around watching morning programs:

> HELEN: How would you fit it [*This Morning*] into your typical day?
> ANGELA: erm, I'd put it on in 'e:re [the kitchen] probably either washing up or doing the ironing or all so::rts just in there, I'll put it on and then if there's something *really* interesting on then I'll sit down and watch it. But it's background I'll *lis*ten to it more than anything.

The most common response was that they tend to do the ironing or other tasks and "listen" rather than sit and attentively "view," a response that replicates the way in which other researchers have discussed how television viewing for women is bound up with the expectations of domestic arrangements, which encourages "distracted" rather than concentrated viewing (e.g., Morley, 1986; Hobson, 1980).

The women's responses also reflect the complicated boundary between "leisure" and "work" that emerges in research into women's domestic labor. They express feelings of "guilt" if they sit and watch television without at least occupying themselves with some other task. Alice says:

> ALICE: I've always li:ked it [*Kilroy*] but the problem is (.) I've got itchy feet to get away. I feel guilty to sit down and in the daytime and watch the telly. I think that's cos I do:: find them interesting.

The issue of "sitting down" reappears in some of the women's responses. Sitting down becomes associated with not doing anything else and with attentive viewing. As Sandra stresses:

> SANDRA: I'm not one for just sitting. I'm not a sitter, so if I really need a break and I have a cup of coffee and sit down it's like as if I've got company in the room.

Therefore, "sitting down" to watch television becomes something that is only acceptable if it is for a valid break. Watching morning talk programs is embedded within the structuring of daily tasks for the married women and associated with "guilty pleasures" and half-attentive viewing practices that have been described by earlier researchers (Hobson, 1980; Morley, 1986; Gray, 1992).

One of the other common responses is that the television provides "company" for the women who are mostly at home alone in the daytime. This replicates Hobson's (1982) early findings about the mass media providing women at home in the daytime with companionship. These issues are brought together in the focus group discussion along with some interesting nuances:

1		Helen	What are the app<u>eal</u>s of watching TV in the daytime and how does it fit in with your
2			daily lives?
3		Chris	Some't to watch while I'm doing the ironing—n' the <u>clean</u>ing.
4		Patricia	A lot of it's background isn't it.
5		Others	yeh
6	→	Jana	Something to watch so I DON::N'T have to do the ironing.
7		Others	Heh, heh, heh.
8	→	Cathy	<u>I::</u> was thinking that =
9		Sandra	=I like IT! (.) we:ll I tend to just watch it if I'm having a
10			coffee break or whatever er n' put it on then y'know. If I'm workin' I 'aven't gor it on,
11			but if I sit down to 'ave a drink, than I pur'it on, whatever's on, usually I'll watch it.

12	Patricia	I think I must be strange because I 'ave it on more in the winter than now in the
13		summery mornings, I seem to 'ave the radio on, I don't bother s'much with the telly. I
14		suppose doors and windows are open more n' you're doing different sorts of jobs,
15		<u>don</u>'t you? Whereas in the winter telly goes on an' you set the ironing up an' the
16		fire's on
17	Cathy	that's right
18	Patricia	and you, yeh, yeh=
19	Cathy	=gas fire's on (.) I suppose it's company really, is[n't it?
20	Patricia	[that's right n' ya
		just watch then 'cos it's on y'know—n' you carry on doing your ironing ( )

In this discussion the women touch upon many of the issues that have been raised in previous research that suggest that women's viewing practices are structured around relations in the home and the companionship provided by broadcasting for those alone during the day. Jana produces a response that might be interpreted as a "resistive strategy" as she says that she uses the programs as "something to watch so I DON'T have to do the ironin" (line 6), an observation that Cathy supports. Noticeably, Jana and Cathy are both single parents and possibly their response might be related to the fact that their domestic environments are not entirely organized around dominant patriarchal relations.

In the interviews with the two youngest women, who both live with their parents, one would watch morning programs in bed and the other while she was getting ready for her lunch-time shift working at the pub. Thus, while the older women's viewing habits reinforce the older studies, even after more than a decade of "change," there are some differences among the younger women, who perhaps are head of their household or work part time, which alters the relationship between work and leisure at home. What is important for the crux of this study is the way in which morning programs are deeply embedded in the daily routines of a feminized domestic world. We can begin to see how the dailiness of the programs' address might easily harmonize with the habituated performance of household responsibilities, what Modleski (1983) referred to in the case of soap opera as the "rhythms of reception."

Gender and Genre

The centrality of the gendered address in the discourse of daytime talk television begs consideration in terms of television and the gendering of taste. Most previous audience studies support a distinction between women preferring fiction, while men prefer factual programming (e.g., Morley, 1986), a finding that is sometimes nuanced by variables of class and education (Press, 1991;

Gray, 1992). Some more recent research has put such a clear distinction into question (Gauntlett and Hill, 1999). However, most of the women in the study replicated gendered viewing patterns of taste. They reported watching a lot of soap opera—in fact soap opera was the one time where they insisted that their taste takes preference over the rest of the family or their partner.[1] Many of the women reported that they like films, while they often suggested that their male partners preferred documentaries.

However, this question of taste provided some complicated answers that were not reducible to a gendered fact/fiction distinction. Angela's immediate response was that she and her husband shared similar television tastes:

> ANGELA: Yes, I'd probably watch m*ore* soaps if he let me but he doesn't like watching them. If I wanna watch one I'll watch it on my ow:n or something. Like *Coronation Street* or *Emmerdale* [British soap operas] he doesn't let me have it on. We::ll (.) he'd just go out of the room I think (1) but I'm not that bothered about it. Yeh, we both like documentaries and real life things really. We've got the same taste (.) we only watch the same programs. He's a bit more space-ified than me. He likes space things.

This is curious, since it is clear that their preferences are not the same at all, and she reports that her husband censors her viewing when he does not approve. Angela still suggests that they have the same tastes because they watch documentaries together—it is not clear whether this is due more to her partner's authority or to her own taste. Perhaps it is in the interest of spending time together, since "he'd just go out of the room" during a soap opera, that they "watch the same programs," as Angela points to a difference in choice of documentary content—his preference for programs about space.

Interpreting Angela's answer probably suggests that their practices replicate the conventional distinction more than she directly admits, but what this draws attention to is that the distinction is certainly blurred by relations in the home. One of the women, Eve, suggests that her and her husband's preferences are opposite to prevailing ideas about taste. Her husband prefers cooking programs, whereas she prefers documentaries. While there may be a general trend that accords with expectations, taste in general was by no means consistent.

However, more critical to this study are the straight women's responses when asked about their male partner's impressions of morning talk shows. All of them reported that their partners would not watch any of the morning talk-based programs that we discussed. The gendered nature of morning talk programming was articulated very clearly and consistently:

ANGELA: He wouldn't watch TV in the day. He'd put the radio on or listen to music. I don't think he'd like it if he was here. He'd be like *"ooh I* can't be bothered with tha::t" typical male attitude.

HELEN: Why's that?

ANGELA: He'd find it all too *wo::men's* [**stress implies derogatory reference**] stuff. He'd find it all too artificial. They don't have cars or space do they? I think it's more geared to women. [Stan] wouldn't be interested in fashion or cookery. They're geared up for women. They don't put sports on. They might do the occasional decorating thing.

Angela's suggestion that her husband would not like it is, as one might expect, based upon the content of the programs—the fashion and cookery sections of the magazine program. But her remark about how he would find it "artificial" is significant in relation to what he might consider more "real"—possibly documentaries about the world out there—cars and space. Considering talk programs as a "genre" presents interesting complications to the generic fact/fiction—masculine/feminine—distinction. One of the women's responses complicates the traditional findings:

HELEN: Why do you think these programs are on in the morning and not at night?

SANDRA: Because the me::n, when the men come home from work they don't want to be sitting watching, they'd think it was a load of *twa*ddle wouldn't they?

HELEN: Why?

SANDRA: I don't think [Terry] would be very interested to sit and watch all *that* I think they put it on for women. I don't think [Terry] would be very interested to sit and watch women have their faces plucked and babies jumping up and down in the water, I, I don't think any of that would interest [Terry]. He'd come in and switch over to channel 2 and find a fiction, something more (.) like a Western.

This response draws attention to a significant nuance in the fact/fiction, masculine/feminine distinction. Here the preference for Terry is for fiction over the live show, *This Morning*. Talk programming clearly is not fiction in any sense, yet neither is it popularly deemed "serious" enough to be categorized as "factual" programming, in the same sense as the documentary, despite the emphasis on "real" people. An interesting discussion emerged in the focus group when we talked about the same issue:

1	Jenny	Well, it's a majority of the women that are watching the programs isn't it?—at 'ome
2	Patricia	That's right, so it, they are geared to [women
3	Jana	[Men don't par-, would men participate as much
4		though?

5	→	Angela	Well they don't talk as much do they (.) they don't discuss things like women.
6		Patricia	Occasionally you get a man ring in=
7		Jana	= Why isn't he at work at this time of the day?
8		Sandra	Well if my 'usband pops in for a coffee n' I've got something on like then e'll
9			generally turn it over n' find an old film on BBC2 or somethin'
10		Patricia	'E doesn't want you to know about the sexy bits see 'e's [protecting you.
11		Angela	[and men don't really read
12			many magazines do they really?
13		Patricia	No, they don't=.
14	→	Polly	= Men don't like the real world do they?
15		Patricia	No, they don't=
16	→	Sandra	= they like to see old cowboys n' [things.
17		Jana	[Most men read the problem pages
18			n' they think it's funny.
19		Angela	Mind you [Stan's] bought a men's health magazine, though, only 'cos it got some sit-
20			up n' things in
21		Cathy	Men don't like discussing any of that though do they?
22		Angela	Not mine though, he'll read mine, 'e likes reading my magazines, heh, heh ,'e
23			wouldn't go buy one
24		Patricia	Well, that's it y'see. [Jo's] in the sixth form and she ses boys always 'ave the
25			magazines n' read out all the—er problems=
26		Jenny	=problem pages
27		Cathy	=problems, yeh
28		Helen:	The women's problem pages?
29		Jenny:	Yeh, they do, yeh.
30		Patricia:	Yeh, yeh, the boys always say that, [Jo] ses, they say, 'oh lets 'ave a look in your
31			magazine
32		Helen:	Yeh, apparently loads of men read their partners' *Cosmo*.
33		Patricia	Is that because they've not been talked to as little boys, so they need to know all the
34			little intimate bits.
35		Angela	Well, I must admit, I read that <u>Men's Health</u>, as it gives you the men's point of view
36			on certain things
37		Jana	They 'aven't quite worked out women [yet 'ave they, so they 'ave to read the problem
38		Jenny	[*Cosmo* sorts em out.
39		Jana	pages to see
40			**[indecipherable, simultaneous talk]**
			[. . .]
41		Helen	Don't the men you know get involved in these discussions?
42		Patricia	Oh, no, they've always gotta watch their image more than the women.
43		Angela	They probably watch more, like the <u>Question Time</u> at night, but not=
44		Sandra	= not the day ones.
45		Helen	Why do you think that is?=
46		Angela	=My 'usband 'd '[ave the radio on.
47		Sandra	[They shut off, like [Polly] ses, they dow
48		Patricia	wanna be involved, they do wanna know, do they?
49	→		They think all that's silly women's talk.
50		Others	mmm, mmm, mmm

The women are clear here that the men they know would not be interested in the programs we were discussing. It is interesting that women's magazines, presumably with their gossip columns, problem pages, consumer advice, and so on, are compared to this kind of programming, which discusses women's private world, and that they also claim that men find such magazines secretly intriguing. Polly says that it's because "men don't like the real world" (line 14), which Patricia supports, and Sandra reproduces the example she had discussed in her interview, where her husband would prefer the fictional world of a "cowboy" film (line 16). Seemingly, their partners appreciate the factual world of the documentary but not the "real" world of personal experience that is the mainstay of morning talk. This draws our attention to differences in what the "real world" means in gendered terms. For these women, "reality" refers to personal immediate experience, whereas for their partners apparently the "real world" is the world "out there" detached from personal experience. This echoes the discussion about the gendering of talk and gossip in earlier chapters and has interesting implications for this book in terms of the ontological relevance of personal experience for women.

Gendered Debate

Sonia Livingstone's (1994) study, taken from the more representative research findings of *Talk on Television,* focuses on gendered differences in audience responses to television participatory programming. She sums up the main differences in men's and women's readings: "Compared with men, women are more likely to consider that the genre offers a sphere in which they can participate, feel involved, and that the issues are relevant to their own lives. They are more likely than men to believe that the genre offers a fair and valuable debate within this sphere, and hence to disagree that debates are too chaotic and biased. Men are more likely to consider experts more worth hearing than the laity while women especially emphasize the importance of giving a say to ordinary people. Also women, in particular consider that the debates are of *social* value, while men were more likely to consider them pointless in that they reached no clear conclusion and were considered to have little influence" (Livingstone, 1994:435). There is little point in a lengthy reiteration of the women's responses in accordance with Livingstone's more representative findings, but I want to tease out the relevance of some of these points about the gendered appreciation of the shows, to reassess their implication in terms of para-social interaction.

One key feature that permeates the women's discussion of gender difference in approaches to the television form is the references to "talk." Angela

says in the focus group extract above, "well they don't talk as much do they
... they don't discuss things like women" (line 5) and then at the end of
the extract Patricia suggests that "they think its all silly women's talk" (line
49). The reference to orality is critical here, as it is ensconced in the way in
which the women reproduce common cultural assumptions about the topics
of male and female speech. The women are clearly aware of the notion that
talking about things that are "real" to them is downgraded—recall Sandra's
mention of her husband thinking that it was all "twaddle." These programs
may not be fiction but they "talk" about the same world as the soap opera—
the private and the personal—rather then the public world that is the focus
of the evening show, *Question Time,* a BBC political discussion show that
has a panel of public figures. This returns us to the kind of debates that have
provided some of the backdrop to this research. Women's talk has traditionally been derided as inconsequential under the term "gossip" in alignment
with a political gendering of the spheres of the public and the private. Sandra
recognizes this in her interview:

SANDRA: My 'usband would say its a wa:ste of time to sit and watch. "What a
wa:ste of time is there nothing better to watch" he'd say. So I think that's why
they put it on because that's what *wom*en like to sit and watch.

HELEN: Why a wa:ste of time?

SANDRA: I don't know maybe it's because I'm small minded and sma:ll things
interest me and I can't watch things that are deep. I mean the things [Terry]
puts on I'm *tot*ally bored with.

HELEN: And yet one of the discussions that was on *[This Morning]* just was
about a woman that made a big decision about having a termination, it
wasn't something small.

SANDRA: No, that was really serious but er well it isn't *less* important but it
would be to a man **[assumes a different voice]** "that's her business what's er
comin"- y'know they just wouldn't consider *that* anythin they wanna listen
to. [Terry] e'd rather sit and watch who's conquered Everest and God knows
when you know who climbed some North Pole or whatever, he wouldn't be
interested in who had a termination (.) he'd think that was just gossip and
yet I *love* it.

What is important here is the way the women perceive their practices in
terms of their material experience with their male partners. To Sandra, her
interests are "small" things while her husband's are "deep." He is interested
in the "serious" public world of mountaineering for instance, whereas her
private concerns, such as in this case pregnancy termination, are deemed
inconsequential. Despite the fact that abortion constitutes a major public
and political issue, particularly in contemporary America, the *mode* of the

discourse in which the discussion is elicited locates it as less serious subject matter. Sandra has internalized the dominant discourses that register the gendering of debate as unequal. Again, this public/private distinction is registered in terms of its orality as "*just* gossip."

Livingstone interprets her findings in terms of a feminist reevaluation of the public sphere, where feminine forms such as gossip are compared to masculine forms of rational debate. She draws upon Gilligan's (1989) argument about women's moral judgment as contextual and not "woolly," as the more traditional (masculine) form of moral reasoning would imply. This contextual emphasis means that in television viewing women become immersed in the details of relationships and narratives, as evident in the findings on soap opera viewing pleasures (Ang, 1985; Liebes and Katz, 1990; Hobson, 1991). Therefore, Sandra is interpreting her interests in direct relation to her husband's form of reasoning and finds them "small" and inconsequential rather than recognizing any value in her situated engagements with the personal realm. Gilligan argues that men "intellectualise to an inappropriate extent, denying the complex claims of interpersonal situational details" (Livingstone, 1994:437). It is the dominance of this position, also partially adopted by the women in this study, that preserves a masculinist, formal, and philosophical approach to the moral domain, maintaining the invisibility or a "privatization" of women's experience (Benhabib, 1992).

Expert versus Lay Discourse: Class

The relevance of "talk" and contextual "experience" emerges from the women's discussion about how they feel about the programs in question. As in Livingstone's study, the women were more critical of experts' abstract intellectual responses and sympathetic to the lay person's expression of experiential context. In Eve's interview she describes the experts as too "goody goody" and Cathy uses the phrase "do-gooders." There is clearly some animosity here about official and abstract discourses, and the women in the group articulate their objections to "experts," as in this extract from the focus group:

1	Angela	They do have the professionals on though, don't they, to give their point of view.
2	Patricia	They usually slau::ghter them don't they?
3	Others	Heh, heh, heh,
4	Cathy	A lot of 'em are goody goodies though [aren't they really?
5	Sandra	[ye:h, they get on your nerves sometimes
6	Jana	heh,heh,heh
7	Cathy	Do gooders, I mean there's been a really bad kid n' 'e really needs a good beltin'
8		doen'e?

9	Others	heh,heh,heh
10	Patricia	Inste:ad you've gotta analyze this one an' send 'im bars of choc [olate everyday
11	Sandra	[yeh , yeh.
12	Cathy	Send 'im on a holiday somewhere like to Barbados for a couple of weeks n' 'e'll come
13		back=
14	Patricia	= a real beautiful boy=
15	Cathy	=yeah

The women jointly account for the way in which expert opinion can some-times confound their commonsense experiential knowledge. Here, they are talking about the treatment of young offenders and the way in which they sometimes get rewards in accordance with social and psychological (and liberal) explanations of behavior, rather than with the commonsense solution of punishment for individual deviancy.[2]

As the women talk they begin to reason about why there appears to be such an incongruity between expert opinion and their own:

1		Helen	Are the experts necessary then?
2		Patricia	I think sometimes they can make it more frustrating though can't they, y' know if
3			you're watching something and you can see, like [Cathy] 'as just said 'oh:: send 'em
4			off for a holiday—y'know, we've sort of analyzed this and what 'ave ya and the answer
5			to this is that 'e needs to be sent on a holiday n' your thinking well no 'e doesn't that's
6			not right so you're on-
7		Others	( )
8		Cathy	or tend to make excuses for 'em like they've
9			come from a deprived background. Well not a::ll kids who are deprived go off and <u>do</u>
10			things, so really, you can't put it down to that, but the experts always do.
11		Jana	Well that's 'cos the experts don't <u>come</u> from deprived backgrounds=
12		Cathy	=EXACTLY (.)
13		Jana	imagi [ne how( )
14		Cathy	[the experts 'ave gorra keep 'em , sending ['em else thay 'aven't gorra job.
15		Jana	[They probably come -
16	→	Patricia	It's the pigeon-hole answer isn't it when everybody 'as got to go: into the li:ttle box
17			y'know.
18		Helen	It sounds like the experts come off quite badly then?
19		Sandra	Oh yes
20		Patricia	They do
21		Others	( )
22	→	Cathy	I think the experts tend to stereotype everybody. Like [Patricia] just said they go into
23			all the different types of boxes.
24		Angela	The experts are only gonna do what they, they're gonna look at just their field n' that.
25			It's y'know what they've been taught. That way that's how it's gonna come out
26		Patricia	Yeh
27		Angela	Textbook (.) they're not gonna see [it as a whole so much, they're just-

28		Patricia	[that's right
29		Sandra	[yeh
30		Angela	-gonna' give what they've [been taught to say.
31		Others	[yeh, yeh, yeh
32	→	Patricia	But the part of the training really is that you do your textbook and then you take your
33			textbook and put it to one side and then you go out into the re:::al world, you use
34			your textbook to widen your image, in't it really? But a[lot of those they still use, as
35			you said, use th[eir textbook—n' them
36		Angela	[probably on TV they've gotta show the facts
37		Patricia	that's right, yeh, they never allow for Mr. So-and-so or Mrs. So-and-so or=
38		Angela	=they
39			probably do when they're not on tv (2) but they'[ve gotta use the facts 'aven't
40			[but they're not allowed to
41		Angela	they=
42		Patricia	=otherwise they'd be pulled over the coals wouldn't they so maybe they get a raw
43			deal because of that
44	→	Cathy	I dunno, some of them really ar::e TWITS though aren't they?
45		Others	heh,heh,heh,heh,heh.

It may be that some of the critique of expert discourse is compounded by the dual impact of classed and gendered forms of discursive identity. The women here are working class. One of the immediate objections to the expert's knowledge of deprivation is their inability to access authentic experience. In relation to that deficiency, their professional discourse is encountered as alien because it is not grounded in lived experience. This is articulated by the women in classed and gendered ways. The evaluation of the form the "expert" discourse takes begins with Patricia's comment (line 16) on the "pigeon-hole" answer, which is further categorized by Cathy as stereotyping (line 22). The women are clearly describing the experts' academic language, which interprets and orders behavior into theoretical types. As the experts suggest reasons, they are also imposing rules, something that the women find unrealistic. They connect this kind of categorizing as standardized, related to the intellectualized "textbook" learning that experts receive, whereby their role is to produce "facts" (lines 32–35). The disdain here is also aimed at forms of education that have traditionally been argued to conform to middle-class discursive aesthetics that help to lock into place the underperformance of the working classes. The women begin to make allowances for what might be expected of the experts on television, but this is closed down by Cathy's comment, which everybody appreciates, "some of them really are twits though aren't they?" (line 44). Expert discourses therefore appear too far removed from experience, both in terms of the feminized appreciation of immediate context and in terms of the masculinized and classed discourses of the theorizing of debate.

Cathy probably feels most negatively about the "experts." She continues this theme with me in her interview:

HELEN: What do you think of the experts then?
CATHY: It's li::ke (2) if you take your child to the hospital or whatever and they explai:n things but they don't explain it on *your* level, they tend to think we're all on their plai:n and though *I'm* not thick by any means I don't understand a lot of their technical jargon. It needs to be broken down into basic English and I feel like I'm thick and I think I don't understand a lot of their techni- cal jargon. It needs to be broken down into basic English and I think this program erm particularly it is and if anybody uses the jargon that's way over them Kilroy brings them back down to earth and says that you know *we* don't understand that we're *or:*dinary sort of people.

What this response highlights is not simply that expert answers seem ob- jectionable to commonsense thinking. I would still agree with McLaughlin (1993) that common sense should be observed with caution as often ideo- logical and problematic. But I would also suggest that sometimes there is a distrust that stems from power relations that are operationalized through dis- course and that may be based upon personal and classed experience. Cathy's son is epileptic and she has been to the hospital many times, where she had been confronted by the explanations of a number of professional medical practitioners. While the privileging of common sense might not necessarily be something we want to applaud per se, it is important to recognize that the pleasures some people find in its televised display come from unequal power distributions between speakers in certain institutional conditions.[3] Cathy's evaluation is based precisely upon incidents located in personal experience and not in abstract argument. Whereas in previous contexts she has been made to feel "thick," discursively located in interaction as lacking education and subjectively positioned as working class, here, in a reversal of dominant hierarchical discourse relations, being "down-to-earth" is the most power- ful discursive style, championed and reinforced by the role of the host, as outlined in chapter 3.

In contrast, lay speakers are applauded for their "honesty," authenticity, and their ability to "speak from experience." The women's impression of the value of this form of talk for those speakers in the studio, the "ordinary people," was that it offers a kind of therapy:

1	Helen	How do the "ordinary" people come off then?
2	Polly	Some of 'em get <u>really</u> get, go through the mill don't they, don't they, really feel sorry for
3		some of 'em, I do.
4	Patricia	yeh, some of 'em you wonder why they've come on because they get themselves so upset
5		and they really [dig deep into their own personal life to tell you things -
6	Polly	[yeh
7 →	Patricia	you think oh how brave'
8	Cathy	yeh
9	Patricia	I'd never go on and say things like [that (1) tell everything, all
10	Polly	[No, no, some of 'em, really feel sorry for
11	Patricia	the world my problems
12	Polly	some of 'em 'cos they really 'ave a go at 'em don't they?
13	Sandra	It isn't as though- I mean, your <u>fa</u>ce is on the screen isn't it, it isn't as though you're sort of
14		er anonymous or anything—just a voice—when your face is there for
15		everyone to see in 'it?
16	Helen	Why do you think people do that then?
17	Jana	Sometimes, some people are just so angry they want to share it with other
18	Cathy	[It's therapy, isn't
19		people, 'look this [is
20 →	Angela	[This is the only way they can get it out by telling everybody—some
21		people go into themselves and not say anything where others wanna tell everybody—n'
22	Jana	that's their way [of doin' it
23		[tell everyone
24 →	Cathy	Part of the healing process, in 'it?

Lay experience is marked by the revelation of private issues that the women regard as a very "brave" thing to do (line 7). They talk in the conventional terms of popular therapy about "getting it out" (line 20), which resonates with the notion of the "talking cure," until Cathy even says "it's part of the healing process" (line 24). The women in the interviews replicate such a view. They assume that being a lay member of these programs is probably "good for you," especially for people who need to talk. When talking about the phone-ins on the morning magazine programs:

HELEN: What do you think of the phone-ins?

EMMA: Well, they do everything don't they? They cover it from like they've got every sort of person that can deal with all the different issues like what's her name-

HELEN: Denise? [*This Morning's* agony aunt]

EMMA: Denise and like they have those phone-ins where you can ring up and speak to any of them—that's a good idea and sometimes I think people who watch it really depend upon them and like think oh yeh I'm gonna ring Denise.

And:

> EVE: I think people just want to tell their problems to somebody don't they obviously. Sometimes if they're lonely and haven't got anybody to talk to they relate to them and they think they're quite nice to talk to.

In general, the women felt that ordinary speakers on the programs probably needed someone to talk to and empathized with their position. Again, these responses echo Livingstone's findings, as she suggests that "there were a number of often quite lengthy attempts by women, but rarely if at all by men, to understand and empathize with the position being expressed" (1994:440). This can be understood in terms of the women's search for context and the generic distinctions related to gender and class that are similar to those found by soap opera researchers—that soap opera fans (mostly women) make paradigmatic readings of the genre focusing on the possibilities of narratives based around characters and events, whereas non-fans and critics (mostly men) make syntagmatic readings stressing the repetition of events and the lack of narrative conclusion (e.g., Allen, 1985). For Liebes and Katz, the fans' reading would be described as a "referential" rather than a critical reading of the genre, whereby "viewers relate to characters as real people and in turn relate these real people to their own real worlds" (1990:100).

Personal Experience

Much can be made about the point of gendered comparison, but in the terms of this study, how is it that private and personal discourses of viewers are induced in relation to the television shows themselves? In this study, personal experience is fundamental to the ways in which the women felt involved in the program (recall Cathy's discussion of her experience with doctors). For instance, they often suggested that they use the programs to make themselves feel better:

> CATHY: Some of it's very helpful things that you didn't realize and some of it's really sad and I think some days if you're having a bit of a depressive day, manic depressive, and you see something on there, I think it puts things in the right perspective.

Jenny reiterates a similar theme in her interview:

> HELEN: Do you think people like listening to other people's problems?
> JENNY: erm yeh because they can relate to them ca::n't they really and think oh yeh I'm in that situation or I know someone in that situation a:nd if you

have got a problem of your own and you're sitting there listening to it and you think o:h perhaps I'm not *so* bad after all you know cos these people ring in they've *got*ta be at the end of their tether ba:sically. Yeh I do like listening to other people's problems because it makes me think, oh well all *I* wanna do is lose a bit of weight you know what I mean, like I'm not financially in a mess you know and these people that are hard up and have their kids taken off em and all this business and you think it makes you feel better.

Notice in Jenny's description that she moves between the first person "I" and the third person "you." It seems to be clear that these programs can be used in terms of schadenfreude, taking a kind of pleasure in another's misfortune. Everyday concerns can be measured against the "sadness" that appears on the screen and be used to "put things in the right perspective" or "make yourself feel better." The display of personal tragedies calls upon the viewers' senses of self to "relate"—which was a common term in the women's descriptions of their viewing pleasures.

Engel Manga's (2003) study of women viewers of talk shows mirrors some of the main themes here. She describes how her respondents understand talk shows as legitimate discourse, particularly in relation to accounts of authenticity. Crucial here though is how they feel involved and inculcated into the discursive regime: "The women encounter the shows as *enacting* discourse about relevant issues by people with whom they identify. As evidence of this many of the women indicate that the shows they watch make a positive difference in their everyday lives. These women become participants in the discourse of the talk shows. Thus, for these women, the shows are useful: they provide a public discourse forum that is otherwise lacking in their lives" (2003:198). In my study the women often used personal narratives in order to explain their relationship to the shows, showing their involvement in parallel with the program's participants. Alice discusses how one of the issues on the programs had significant bearing upon a tragic situation in her own life:

ALICE: Because you learn a lot, because there's a lot about (.) oh gays and AIDS, diseases and I think one I saw was about suicide and an aw:ful lot of people commit suicide and its young me:n as well. Well it's a:bsolutely horrifying cause [Michelle, her daughter] used to go out with a lad a couple of years ago and after they finished, and he finished with her, *thank god* but h::e committed suicide she was devastated cos I met him and he was a caring young man a vegetarian, a friend of the earth, save the whales, save the rainforest, a to:tally like sensitive person and I think how terrible and then when I saw this *Kilroy* on a:ll these people who've committed suicide, oh dear you don't realize what a big problem it is.

These shows can therefore be used to put personal experience into a wider perspective, against the persuasive textual reading of the talk show that suggests that they merely reduce social problems to individual psychological trauma (e.g., Peck, 1995). Many of the women even suggest that they feel they "learn" from these programs. But Cathy discusses how the contextual sources in the programs provide the most valuable type of information, which is not available in other media or public forums:

> CATHY: . . . when something like that talk show, [*Kilroy*] comes on you tend to find a lot more that you can identify with because a newspaper article I think it maybe just covers the ba:sics but if you're listening to people who've *actu*ally got it and *actu*ally experienced erm things (.) like he's [her son] got learning difficulties and he's at a special school and you listen to other children that have got the same but it doesn't say that in a newspaper so you get much more information from those sort of things really.

For all the popular debate about the influx of talk in a postmodern tabloid era, Cathy feels that these programs offer one of the few places where experience is given such a platform. This might indeed be cheap television, but ordinary experience clearly has a personal value. Bette and I watched a broadcast of *The Time . . . The Place* about fathers' rights to see their children after separation. Talking about it afterwards was upsetting for Bette as she thought about her street and her own life:

> BETTE: I just switch on the ones [programs] I know that are going to interest me. Probably because of all the sadness and all this we've watched this morning, you know young wives -their *bloody* 'usbands 'ave *bugg*ered off and left them and you know -typical in my own stree::t (.) it's so sad and I think *wh:::y* wh::y didn't you wait and erm in my own family (.) erm I don't think I would like this on tape [**tape recorder is switched off as Bette talks about her childhood**]

While the tape recorder was switched off Bette used the show as a context in which to discuss her childhood, her parents, and the very personal process of understanding that she is gay, which possibly reverberates so strongly due to the hetero-normative address of daytime talk. The women therefore cite their own personal experience as part of the experience of watching others doing the same. As argued in earlier chapters, the strategies of these shows' discursive address call upon viewers to make relationally significant correlations with their own lives. Some of the viewers claim that it might make you "feel better," but schadenfreude is not a complete explanation, as the resonance with one's personal life can also be painful. For instance, Angela talks about how she feels when people on the program get upset and she recalls an instance when it touched upon her own personal emotion:

> HELEN: How do you feel when people get upset?
> ANGELA: That one the other day upset me. That woman who aborted the baby ten years ago (3) and there was one not long back on cry babies and *she's* a cry baby [**gestures to her youngest daughter in the room**] and they'd got this baby on that was really, re:::ally crying and that upset me 'cos I got reminded me what she: was like and I nearly rang in then 'cos that- to say to that woman if she need someone to talk to (.) but I didn't.

This is what Polly meant earlier about the "real" world. It is the world of direct experience. When asked whether they thought these shows were "trivial," in accordance with popular debate, all of the women replied "no." Jenny takes this further,

> HELEN: What stops them from being trivial?
> JENNY: We::ll it's too *real* isn't it to be trivial, they're using real people n' re::al issues.

This is the real domestic everyday world of women that is experienced in their material daily lives. Women's contextualization of their own lived reality is central to the reasons for watching, hence their repetition of the phrase, "I can *relate* to that." Angela's relationship with this part of the program is completely ensconced in, and produced through, her own experience of motherhood. Subjectivity and textuality are therefore undoubtedly entwined in the experience of viewing. These types of responses represent the limit of the depth that interview research like this (and Engel Manga's) can reach in terms of intervening in the relationship between text and experience. Clearly, the language of traditional media research somehow seems inadequate in this context. Viewers here are not only "decoding" signs or reading messages, but they are *relationally* involved in the mediation of experience. These programs reverberate closely with the women's own reflections of their lives, a point that is vital to understanding the intimate relationship that this style of talk television has with its viewers. To interrogate the *form* of this relationship and how it is formed during the viewing process as a peculiarly mediated experience, I draw attention here to some of the clues as to how the women might begin to take up the para-social invitations of the televised address.

Para-social Involvement

Evoking personal experience is vital to the women's contextual relationship with these programs, a situation potentially fostered by the text's para-social organization as discussed in earlier chapters. Attempting to talk with the women about their immediate relationship with the text is obviously not straightforward, hence the need for my alternative methodology. There are, however, some moments in their discussions that *did* point to some insights into this aspect of the study. The previous themes recounted here—dailiness, the gendering of the genre, and the relationship to context-bound forms of talk and orality—might be held in place by the discursive para-social relationship established by these programs. There are some indications in the women's talk that suggests this might be the case.

An Intimate Forum

All of these television shows are based around personalities, for example, *This Morning* and *Good Morning* became unofficially termed "Richard and Judy" and "Ann and Nick." Much of the women's discussion about why they like the programs is about how they like the personalities:

> ANGELA: John Stapleton he seems just a ki:nd, honest man, I don't know he just seems very compassionate towards- he gets very emotional I supp*o*se and he's got no airs and graces about him. He handles people well. I think he's re:ally good.

Angela's evaluation of the presenter is based upon his possession of personal, not professional, qualities. When Sandra is asked about how she likes the structure of the program, she instantly turns to consider the presenters, not the content:

> SANDRA: I think it's quite good I mean there's things I don't agree with because of my personal views on things but I think they handle it lovely, I personally think they're good they're *very* good. I think they're natural and ordinary and put people at ease . . . I think they're nice they're not stuffy- I mean you used to get the David Frosts [news, political affairs and royal correspondent] and the- but the::se are just nice ordinary people.

She describes her appreciation of the program as related to the style, to how "they handle it." Sandra's mention of "ordinariness" relates to John Langer's (1981) argument about the television personality as opposed to the film star. But there's another distinction here—Richard and Judy are not like David Frost (another older British TV personality more associated with serious news and commentary)—they are members of a breed of TV personality that is even more "ordinary." This distinction is difficult for Sandra to explain when pressed on what she sees as the difference:

> HELEN: What's the difference then between them and someone like David Frost?
>
> SANDRA: Well their to:o I dunno how to explain it but he's too black and white in my opinion whereas they are more (.) I can't explain really they're sort of people I could approach and speak to whereas I put barriers up with someone like him, like on *Question Time* I can't watch it.

Here again the pleasures derived from watching *This Morning* are related to the relational orality of the program and the feminist arguments about the gendering of public debate—not "black and white" (masculine) but the "sort of people I could approach" (feminine). This feeling of intimacy is registered as a discursive relationship, suggesting a presenter as someone she can "speak to," and is encouraged by the textual features of para-social relations that mark morning talk as different from other formal debate shows. Sandra's lack of engagement in formal discussion is related to her lack of relationship to the presenter—with whom she would "put barriers up"—feeling locked out of the socio-communicative sphere of the formal debate show. Interestingly, the program *Question Time*, a late-night political discussion program, is often referred to in the focus group as the antithesis of daytime talk. Here the women begin to compare David Dimbleby and Robin Day (presenters of *Question Time)* with Kilroy:

1		Sandra	Ooh they're just n<u>ot</u> the same are they?
2	→	Cathy	Kilroy's got more charisma, I mean I thi=
3		Patricia	= I'd like to see Kilroy on that, on that
4			program.
5		Others	heh,heh
6		Jana	Dimbleby's just th<u>ere</u> 'e's got no personality as 'e [really?
7	→	Cathy	[you couldn't warm to 'im at all could
8			ya?
9	→	Sandra	Well, he [doesn't move around like Kilroy does.
10		Patricia	[No, well he (.) 'cos like he's—not got an opinion as [Polly] ses, Kilroy as
11			got an opinion, didn't ya? David Dimbleby's just [re::ally there to
12		Others	[mmm, mmm
13		Patricia	say that [Mrs. So-and-so it's their question and "you can answer it first,"
14		Sandra	[that's right
15		Others	[yeh, yeh
16		Patricia	"alright you've said enough," "lets have y<u>ou</u>." He's really there just to keep
17			control [n't 'e?

18	Jana	[But Robin Day was like that but he's got more=
19	Patricia	= yeh, but he could be <u>very</u>
20		cutting couldn't 'e?
21	Jana	yeh
22 →	Sandra	But Kilroy's different, 'e's moving around the people.

For these women, there is a fundamental difference between the presenters of daytime and nighttime talk. Dimbleby is described as being more formal and methodical, while Robin Day is "cutting" and harsh; they display the discursive competences of "rational" argument. On the other hand, Kilroy's spatially moving around the studio members is important (lines 9 and 22) and he is deemed to have more "charisma" (line 2). The women's discussion suggests a relationship that is much more intimate than Livingstone and Lunt's description of the host acting as "hero" figure. One of the most interesting observations on Dimbleby is that "you couldn't warm to him at all could ya?" (line 7). These professional personalities are being compared upon their social potential in terms of whether the women feel they can form a relationship with them. Cathy reiterates this in her interview with me:

CATHY: I think he's [Kilroy] sensitive erm when he saw tha:t lady was upset he was holding her hand and squeezing her erm (.) I think he tries very hard to give people a fair say and he doesn't erm let somebody hog the limelight erm I do think he's good. I think he tends to pick up on everything. I think he's quite gentlemanly . . . I think it depends upon him because I think he's quite warming and I think he's the sort of man that you could- I think he's got a sort of funny happy face so you could talk to him.

Again, Cathy's appreciation of Kilroy is evaluated in terms of his compassion and her *own* perceived ability to be able to talk to him. The potential invitation to "talk," and possibly talk back, becomes central to the enjoyment of these programs and registers that these relational attachments are part of a broader association with the programs as an intimate forum.

The viewers thus often draw upon characteristics associated with forms of intimacy in order to evaluate the television presenters. For instance, the descriptor "compassionate" often surfaces here. In dealing with "real" people, the hosts of these shows are seen to display empathy and appear caring towards their guests. Judy Finnegan, the presenter of the magazine show *This Morning* was seen to be particularly adept in these skills:

PATRICIA: I think she [Judy] can be very compassionate, y'know when you get situations like mothers with children that they've had difficulties or problems and I think *he* [Richard] genuinely does fe:el. I think as a mother herself of little ones she can associate and I think he does feel- feel for them.

Empathy, or being able to "associate," is described by Patricia in terms of the sharing of authentic experience since Judy's role as a real mother is signifi-cant to her ability to care. The "ordinariness" of the hosts is reinforced by the women's references to their own personal and familial relationships, as Angela says about Richard and Judy:

> ANGELA: I think they're very down to earth. I think you can relate to them. They seem ordinary people. . . . They talk about their families don't they? It makes them humans. Its not just people who sit there- and let's face it we're all nosy and like to know what's going on aren't we? People share their lives with them, why shouldn't they share their lives with you? Cos they do: tell you about their problems.

The presenters "ordinariness" in terms of the domestic world resonates with the women's own experience. Angela is pointing to the way in which the magazine programs utilize a subjective approach to broadcasting, which is part of their gendered appeal. Importantly though, she discusses it as a fair exchange, recognizing a sense of, if not quite equality then mutuality, in the power relations between the presenters and the participants as speakers.

This appreciation of the "backstage" world of the presenters registers the appeal of the breakdown of the spectator/performer distinction as discussed in chapter 3. The women comment upon the husband-and-wife team of Richard and Judy and how their private lives are part of the intimate world that frames the televised discourse:

1		Helen	What about the presenters? Richard n' Judy n Ann n' Nick?
2		Patricia	I think Judy's very [good—Richard's a bit wet=.
3	→	Angela	[Yeh, Judy =smarmy
4		Sandra	I like Judy
5		Polly	I like Judy.
6		Angela	n' 'e gives me the creeps 'e does.
7		Patricia	e's alright but e's, e's, oh relies on her. When she's not there I think e's 'opeless, yet I
8			think when she's there on her own she's great. I think 'e leans to her, that's my opinion
9			anyway
10		Others	mmm, mmm, mmm
11		Angela	I don't like 'im. 'E thinks 'e knows everythin' about everythin'.
12		Patricia	Yeh
13		Jana	I don't like 'im=
14		Patricia	= He goes "it's alright dear," "don't worry about that dear"=
15		Angela	=oh yeh 'e
16			thinks e's like=
17	→	Jana	= he' s condescending isn't 'e Richard—'n 'e is t[o the guests isn't 'e?
18		Angela	[Yeh 'e is yeh

9	Patricia	(	)

9   Patricia   (   )

20   Helen   What do you make of them being husband n' wife?

21   Patricia   It doesn't bother me when he'll say things like "oh, we've got a son that age" or

22   "we've got a" it's a sort of bringing in the family a bit, but like if our [Jo's] [her

23   daughter] watching, like she'll say "tut, why do they 'ave to bring the family in? We

24   don't wanna know."

25   Angela   They talk as though they're=

26   = Yeh, it's—they talk about how they go 'ome 'n 'e gets the

27   dinner on n' y'know,

28   Others   heh, heh, heh

29   [. . .]

30   Sandra   Well I quite like it n' I quite like Richard. I quite like 'em both, yes. I think they're a

31   lovely team and they work well together n' I think it's wonderful to be able to work

32   with your 'usband if you can. I'd like to work with mine if possible. (.) I used to work

33   with my 'usband, that's where I met 'im. We fall out now but when we were young

34   and in love we didn't [s'much n'then they get on yer nerves a bit don't they?

35   Others   [heh, heh, heh

Obviously watching and appreciating morning talk shows does not necessarily mean that the women do not have critical perspectives on the programs—contemporary audience research reiterates this point against older and traditional notions of audience passivity, particularly in relation to the female audience. Many of the women voiced objections to the presenter Richard Madeley as patronizing or smarmy, but they all liked his wife, Judy Finnegan. However, *not* finding someone attractive does not necessarily detract from the para-social experience.[4] When the women are critical of the male presenter, it is not on professional terms as a presenter, but on personal terms, in terms of his character traits. They evaluate the personalities in the same way that one might talk about other acquaintances. Therefore, it is their sociality that is in question in terms of the women's critical evaluation of the program content, which is a different performative role to that, say, of an actor on television. For example, pleasure is also derived from watching the husband-and-wife relationship played out on the screen, as "he leans to her" as the couple mention their family and their domestic life. In the following extract the women are talking about when there are sexual issues on the programs and Richard Madeley sometimes reveals intimate details of his relationship with Judy:

ANGELA: She's a bit more shy of it than 'im.

PATRICIA: She gets cross with 'im when he becomes a [bit like that.

ANGELA: [He gets a bit

personal.

PATRICIA: She'll like .hh **[gestures pushing away]**

JENNY: Its so:: funny when that happens

The women enjoy the banter between Richard and Judy that is revealing of their "ordinary" and intimate relationship as husband and wife. This topic returned later in the focus group discussion:

1	Helen	Do you think the viewers 'ave to feel like they know them well?
2	Angela	Well, I like it when she gives 'im the dirty looks when 'e ses some't too personal. I
3		think God 'e's in trouble after
4	Patricia	yes, yes,—she'll say "oh shush," don't she? "Oh shush, Richard."
5	Sandra	Well, that's normal, in't it?
6	Patricia	Well, that's right, it's what we mean, yeh
7	Sandra	It's normal 'usband and wife behaviour, in't it, she would sort of=
8	Patricia	= She'd sort of egg
9		him 'on.
10	Sandra	Whereas if it was your 'usband, you'd say "shurrup!" wouldn't [ya? That's human
11	Patricia	[yes, yes,
12	Sandra	nature in't it with your 'us [band.
13	Patricia	["Everybody doesn't want to know about us!"—she'll say,
14		sometimes to 'im, won't she?=
15	Jana	= She'll always say when she's at fault.
16	Sandra	That's natural in't it, yeh, I think so, I think they're [lovely.
17	Angela	[I think the look she gives 'im is
18		definitely natural. I think "ooh poor"-
19	Sandra	Well, you do that's how ya react to your 'usband, don't ya? [I mean
20	Others	[heh,heh,heh
21	Patricia	He'll say sometimes that Judy's looking at me, won't he, he'll say that yeh.
22	Sandra	If my 'usband ses something personal I'd say "shurrup," wouldn't you?

What is significant is the way in which intimate relationships are played out on the screen. The women show their appreciation that the presenters "talk" like us, as Richard and Judy's banter and interaction is like a "normal" husband and wife. Thus, details of being "like us" are part of the involvement that the women feel in a para-social relationship with the presenters, which probably also motivates the evaluations based upon whether or not you could "talk" to them, since it seems they share some communicative competences from the same discursive register. In relation to broader theoretical arguments about the contemporary functions of broadcasting, we can see how the experience of shared intimacy is a key feature of the mediation of social relations in this context.

One of the discussions in the focus group sums up a common popular position on women's involvement in daytime television, a position that makes addressing the question of talking with/to television sensitive. This discussion occurred when I asked the women if they felt that the programs were useful if they could help with problems:

1	Helen	Do you think they're useful then?
2	Sandra	Yeh
3	Cathy	I think if you've got a friend or summat, you'd go an' ask <u>them</u> for reassurance
4	Angela	Some people haven't got that any though ['ave they?
5	Others	[Yeh, yeh,
6 →	Polly	[There's desperate people with nobody.
7 →	Angela	Who've got nobo [dy, yeh
8 →	Polly	[There [is people with nobody.
9	Others	[Yeh, yeh.
10 →	Cathy	You can ring the Samaritans=
11	Angela	= but people don't always=
12	Cathy	= yeh, but while they're ringin'
13 →		th<u>em</u> you might as well ring the Samaritans=
14	Patricia	= but I suppose that's <u>their</u>=
15 →	Polly	= That's their friend in the home, in't it?
16	Patricia	That's right <u>there</u>, tha:t minute.
17	Angela	They associate with Richard and Judy as being in their house n'=
18	Polly	= it's their friend in't
19		it?=
20	Patricia	= That's what I'm saying, I think it's a shame but mine would say, our [Jo] [her
21 →		daughter] 'd say they're saddos but they're not really saddos, they're just, they're
22		pe::ople that need help sometimes, not all of them, but some of them aren't they,
23		sometimes, not all of them are but some of them are, aren't they? Has
24	Helen	anyone ever thought of phoning in?
25 →	Jana	[No
26	Polly	[No
27	Sandra	[No
28	Others	heh,heh,heh

This extract is interesting and, no doubt, influenced by the dynamics of the group. The women suggest that these programs are useful if you are "desperate" or "have nobody" (line 6) and even equate it with ringing the Samaritans (lines 10 and 13). The people who use these programs are "other" people who have "got nobody" (lines 7 and 8) (and yet all the women report regularly watching these shows since it was a pre-requisite for them being involved in the study). Polly says, "that's *their* friend in the home" (lines 15–16)—the parasocial relationship belongs to someone else. Ultimately, Patricia recalls her daughter's description of people who ring in—"they're saddos" (line 21).

Although the women suggest empathy with people in need, they were also careful to suggest that that need was not their own, as a chorus of voices say "no" to my question about whether they would participate. Notice that Angela, who had previously in her interview with me alone described the details of an incident where she had thought of phoning in, is silent. This says something about the nature of the focus group and what it might hide if it were the only method of audience research, but the extract also points to the women's awareness of popular conceptions of participation in these genres—"saddos"—people who have no friends. It is also interesting that these remarks have a striking resemblance to the assumptions upon which the Para Social Interaction scale from uses and gratifications research is based, and reveals that such a scale simply reflects popular prejudice rather than the "scientific" rationale that it claims.

However, there were moments when the women did recount their viewing experiences as explicitly para-social encounters. For instance, Sandra even suggested that Richard and Judy break across the barrier of the screen:

HELEN: What do you think of the way they speak to the audience, to you at home?
SANDRA: Very ordinary, very, as if they are talking to you in your lounge and not in front of a television camera that's what I think is so nice with them.

Sandra feels that it is as though the camera is not there, which suggests that for her the spectator/performer distinction is eroded. The element of "performance" seems absent for the viewer, so much so that the technical mediation of the experience seems to diminish, making the relationship real and live in the context of the home. Eve points to the gendered nature of this experience:

HELEN: On this program they have some really personal things on don't they?
EVE: I think to a woman it's like having a really good natter to a friend in't it and listening really in a way and- don't you think so?

The grounds of intimacy, as established here, require some approximation to co-presence: the feeling of the presenters appearing in the living room and chatting as though with a friend. Again, here spatial closeness and the ritual discourse are inextricably bound, creating a specifically *mediated* phenomenon potentially emblematic of conditions of modernity.

Contemporary sociology suggests that modernity is characterized by "time-space distanciation," accompanied by the rise of abstract systems, which means that intimacy is being transformed and friendship is becoming a process of re-embedding (Giddens, 1991b). Here, frameworks of trust are established across distanced relationships—recall the example of the air stewardess making face-work commitments to reassure passengers in Arlie Hochschild's (1983) discussion of the commercialization of emotional labor. Therefore, "personal relationships whose main objective is sociability, informed by loyalty and authenticity, become as much part of the social situations of modernity as the encompassing institutions of time-space distanciation" (Giddens, 1991a:120). It is possible to begin to locate these findings about television viewing within such a model of contemporary life. For example, Giddens goes on to suggest that the twentieth century preoccupation with relationships means that trust becomes a personal project to be worked upon, "and where the work involved *means a mutual process of self-disclosure*" (1991a:121, original italics). This insight helps to interpret the reciprocal types of commitment, intimacy, and self-revelation that the women recall about television shows and their presenters. Indeed, Giddens does briefly suggest that electronic media accentuate these forms of displacement, and he refers to the increasing "mediation of experience." Moores reinforces just how prescient Giddens's observations are for a fuller understanding of the media's influence upon social life: "Where we are no longer determines who we are—or who we are 'with'—to the same degree as it used to because electronically mediated communication has the potential to transform situation, interaction, and identification" (2000:109).

Conclusion

This chapter has provided some background on how the women perceive their practice of watching morning talk television. It situates their responses with earlier research and assumptions into women's domestic consumption of the media in the home, as well as more specifically with research into the gendered perceptions of participatory programming. Significantly, these discussions show that the gendered nature of this genre is related not simply to the fact/fiction distinction, which is the common assumption from the tradition of media audience research, but more to the rational/relational distinction about moral "debate" that occurs in feminist arguments about the public sphere. And even more importantly, that distinction here is seen to be coded in terms of gendered, and to some extent classed, forms of orality and spoken discourse.

However, these discussions have also begun to reveal how the women's endorsement of context and personal experience is connected to the parasocial organization of the text. Therefore, it is clear that "talk" and "experience" are interwoven as the women refer to the presenters as "someone you could talk to," observations that code their experiences as participants in an intimate mediated forum. Television viewing of talk-based programs is part of a more far-reaching set of conditions that disembed and re-embed social life and communication. If this is so, *how* is this established and enacted in the viewing process? This is a question that begs consideration, particularly if we take seriously the potential of electronic media to transform the nature of social interaction and thereby the very nature of our own identities. I take this further in the next chapter by considering mediated interaction as part of social interaction, utilizing the data from the *text-in-action* research to unusually bring mass communication (television) into the contexts of speech communication.

6. Talking Back

The Mediated Conversational Floor

Introduction

So far, we have seen how morning talk programs construct a format in which ordinary, real-world, and real-time experience is embedded within the "show." This relies on implied "feminine" knowledge through the build up of "sociable," para-social relationships that assume an imagined community of women. In the last chapter the women's own accounts gave us some clues as to how the viewing of daytime television is experienced as an intimate forum, sharing features of social interaction that parallel normative forms of feminine sociability, potentially creating new forms of electronic sociality. This chapter explores how that experience is achieved in the viewing process.

While audience studies, in particular those associated with cultural studies, have recognized relations of power at each end of the communication process, privileging the framework of "text-reader" relations, the data in this chapter overcomes the text/context distinction and places the communicative "act" itself at the center. Here it is possible to envisage the specifically *communicative* relationship between broadcasting and viewers. The "text-in-action" methodology, as outlined in chapter 4, illuminates our understanding of viewing experiences as pragmatically *negotiated* discursive encounters. Audience members respond to the conversational imperatives and sociability invited by these programs. They engage with the text dynamically as it takes place in real time, and these recordings constitute a "mediated conversational floor," one that is lifted out from face-to-face contexts and stretched across time and space, a phenomenon that reproduces the dislocated conditions of modernity (Giddens, 1991a).

The Mediated Conversational Floor

This book has been interrogating how the relationship between broadcasters and their audiences is accomplished as a socio-communicative sphere. Therefore, the empirical research is concerned with recording the utterances broadcast from the studio alongside utterances that occur in the home, which are then transcribed using a system that makes visible both aspects of the communication process simultaneously. Rather than focusing on the sentence, which Bakhtin points out is a whole unit of grammar, I concentrate on the utterance, which is produced through the interplay between participants in any communicative sphere (see chapter 2). This registers the nature of broadcasting's relationship with viewers as a communicative event by locating the *interaction* between speaker and hearer, rather than accepting the framework of text and reader. Here the broadcast speech and the speech of the viewer at home constitute a mediated communicative framework—one that has barely been documented in the social sciences and that can further our understanding of forms of mediated communication.

This kind of "para-social interaction" is, of course, peculiar to the phenomenon of broadcasting and does not offer complete reciprocity of the order that is assumed in face-to-face conversation. However, the norms assumed about co-present communication are more complicated than the "ideal" model of complete reciprocity suggests. Entirely equal platforms of participation are not available to all speakers across all types of conversation, as researchers in socio-linguistics have continuously shown across different social groups and within institutional structures (for example: Lakoff, 1975; Zimmerman and West, 1975; Fishman, 1980; Thorne, Kramarae, and Henley, 1983; Goodwin, 1990; Boden and Zimmerman, 1991; Mills, 1995). Commonsense assumptions, and those usually followed by the tradition of Conversation Analysis (CA), have tended to assume a unitary speaker/hearer dynamic that is predicated on the model of turn taking. However, Goffman's (1981) model of the "participation framework" is a better guide to the structural features of the conversational floor as identified here, and opens up the narrow polarity of the speaker/hearer dynamic. For instance, he suggests that we may not even be actively listening to a conversation and yet have a place in the talk, or conversely we may have no interactive place in the talk at all, and yet be listening. Much talk takes place surrounded by bystanders who may or may not have a part in the interaction. For Goffman, therefore, "The relations(s) among speaker, addressed recipient, and unaddressed recipients are complicated, significant and not much explored" (1981:133). He acknowledges a broader field of conversational interaction, whereby, "An utterance does not carve up the world beyond the speaker into precisely two parts, recipients and non-recipients, but rather opens up an array of structurally differentiated possibilities, establishing the participation framework in which the speaker will be guiding his [or her] delivery" (1981:137).

A related problem is the concept of "floor" as it is usually applied in CA, wherein a speaker can "take" or "resign" the floor in conversational exchange. Ownership of the floor therefore belongs only to one current speaker and "turn-taking" assumes a general normative framework (Edelsky, 1981). There have been criticisms of this basic turn-taking model established in CA because it ignores the fact that social, cultural, and power-relational factors affect the language between speakers (Fairclough, 1992). These include feminist linguists interested in the conversational discourse of women's groups (Coates and Cameron, 1989; Coates, 1993, 1994, 1996). Jennifer Coates (1994) suggests that the CA model is in need of reconceptualization to account for lived social encounters, stressing that turn taking can be expressive of social relationships.[1] Therefore, in Coates's analysis she suggests that turns can be jointly produced by a number of participants, suggesting that in all-female conversation there is the possibility of a concept of a "shared floor," although there is extensive discussion over the pitfalls of gender essentializing in this debate (Cameron, 1992a, 1992b, 1995b).[2] For Coates, the key difference between the normative turn-taking model and women's talk is in the space where the "no gaps" should occur. In the CA "no gap" rule there is no lapse at the end of a turn constructional unit—at the end of a speaker's turn—and the speaker and the turn are coextensive.[3]

This research suggests that we might apply the concept of the shared floor across the doubled social space of broadcasting. That is to say, it establishes a *mediated* floor where the interaction is para-social. We must therefore critically consider patterns of turn taking in relation to the specificities of the social context. In particular, we must also pay close attention to the genre of this type of broadcasting, the gendered specificity of these forms of television's address to female viewers, as well as to their consumption within the culturally inscribed domestic context. Therefore, this chapter considers television viewing as offering a particular type of participation frame that is mediated across broadcasting's apparatus. Audience reception is part of a discursive framework in which texts are not just made up of flatly appropriated semiotic cues, but are "in-action" and can be analyzed as dynamic *events* of dialogic social action, transcending distinctions of text and context.

Levels of Interaction

The representation of the data must take into account both parts of the mediated conversation, and therefore the events occurring in the studio are carefully transcribed alongside the women's responses in the home as they view, in an attempt to identify any verbal communicative process at work. Initially the transcripts do suggest that there are indeed actual moments of interaction with the program that cannot directly be explained by my presence as an observer. In the first instance, the transcriptions reveal audience responses that suggest the program as the primary recipient, as if the women were engaging in direct face-to-face communication. Further responses are produced in relation to the text or with the text as a pretext, where my presence is taken into account. The utterances produced by the women can then be categorized in terms of three stages that the women pass through at different moments during their viewing experience: primary, secondary, and tertiary levels of interaction with the text.

The *primary* responses are indicative of direct interactive exchanges with the programs that fit neatly with norms of turn taking in non-mediated interaction. The *secondary* level of interaction is indicative of the women beginning to interrogate and reformulate the text for themselves. Finally, the *tertiary* level of engagement appears when the women use the text occurring in the studio as a springboard for making evaluations about their own lives, and they often insert their own narratives in relation to the televised discourse. This is where my presence as a researcher plays a larger role in the participation framework. It is important to note that these categories are produced to organize the analysis and not to suggest that the viewer is any more or less involved (or active) in any of these stages.

Primary Responses

Instances of this primary level of interaction can be recognized in at least three ways in the data by the viewers'

1. use of second-person pronouns, directed at a participant (or voice of a participant in the case of phone-ins) in the studio;
2. use of "minimal responses," "news receipts," or "response tokens" (yeh, mhm, etc.); and
3. completion of a turn taken by speaker in the studio.

Second-Person Pronouns

A viewer at home using the second-person pronoun identifies a studio participant as the "primary addressee" for their responses, which indicates a para-social exchange.[4] For example:

Extract 1. Angela watching *This Morning*, Jan. 18, 1996, "fertility" phone-in

		Studio		Home
1	Richard	Ok well listen (1) let's start with		
2		some real calls here. Let's start out		
3		with Victoria who's 25 years old if		
4		you don't mind me saying Vicky		
5		calling from <u>Buck</u>inghamshire		
6	Victoria	Hello		
7	Richard	Hello, now <u>how</u> long have you been		
8		trying to get pregnant?		
9	Victoria	Erm about eighteen months now.	Angela	You've told us now

Extract 2. Sandra watching *This Morning*, Jan. 16, 1996, "dilemmas" phone-in

		Studio		Home
1	Judy	He's to:ld you that unless you agree		
2		to a termination the relationship's over?		
3	Richard	And you're out of the flat or house		
4		that you live in?	Sandra	You've got a dilemma over THAT!

Extract 3. Emma watching *This Morning*, July 7, 1998, "sexual problems" phone-in with Dr. Ruth Westheimer

		Studio		Home
1	Dr. Ruth	. . . Amanda what you have to do is		
2		to first <u>learn</u> like to today to gi:ve		
3		yourself an orgasm touch the clitoris		
4		think of some ve:ry sexy thoughts		
5		maybe put a sexy movie on	Emma	You ca::n't come out with <u>that.</u>

These examples of viewers' use of second-person pronouns all identify their primary addressee, but also appear as commentaries on whatever it is the "you" has just said. The next example appears as a directive:

Extract 4. Eve watching *Vanessa*, Jan. 16, 1996, chat show about "jealousy"

		Studio		Home
1	Woman	I just wanna say <u>one</u> thing it takes		
2		two to play tonsil tennis it's not <u>just</u>		
3		the woman's fault		
4		<u>he</u>'s doin it as well	Eve	Oh shut up <u>you::</u>!
5		I mean it takes two of em		

Obviously, the viewer here does not expect a response to her demand, but the point is that she has contributed such a remark *as though* the exchange is reciprocal.

Extract 5. Sandra watching *This Morning*, Jan. 16, 1996, "dilemmas" phone-in. Caller Jane has called in because her partner has given her an ultimatum to have termination or end their relationship.

		Studio		Home
1	Jane	I can't- I just don't know what to do		
2	Judy	And are you planning to marry		
3		anyway. If this hadn't happened		
4		would you be planning to get		
5		married?		
6	Jane	Well we are engaged –it's been		
7		nearly a year we've been engaged		
8		now		
9	Denise	Is he saying you must terminate <u>this</u>	Sandra	Send him packing!
10		pregnancy, or that he never intends		
11		you to have any children?		

These first examples, then, establish the way in which the viewers at home are actually taking part in conversation that is directed at speakers in the studio, as though they are co-present, and they foreground the concept of the "para-social" as reciprocated by the audience. In the next extracts we begin to see how these contributions from the viewers at home can be understood in terms of ordinary conversational practices.

Minimal Responses to Studio Talk

The viewers in this study all, at various points throughout watching the program, produce minimal responses to the talk occurring in the studio. "Minimal responses" (sometimes called "response tokens") are usually utterances like "mhm," "yeah," "right," and so on (Montgomery, 1986b). They perform the function of signalling the speaker's presence and involvement in the conversation taking place. In these terms, all the women at home express involvement in the interaction taking place in the studio. Here are a couple of examples:

Extract 6. Bette watching *The Time, The Place*, June 12, 1996, discussion program on "fathers' rights"

		Studio		Home
1	Woman	No matter <u>how</u> old they are if the		
2		father lets them down, if the fa:ther		
3		has a problem- children make up		
4		their own		
5		minds	Bette	Mhm

Extract 7. Alice watching *Kilroy,* May 14, 1996, discussion program on "Should the elderly pay for their own care?"

		Studio	Home	
1	Man	It's not a question of <u>luck</u> it's a		
2		question of responsibility		
3	Woman	Some people don't even earn that		
4		much money in a wee:k		
5	Man	It's a question of <u>mo</u>dern da:y	Alice	right!
6		responsibility		

The examples above suggest straightforward acknowledgement of information, but the following examples can be seen as more affective reactions to the discussion taking place in the studio:

Extract 8. Jenny watching *Good Morning,* Jan. 25, 1996, "D.I.Y" phone-in

		Studio	Home	
1	Caller	erm right I've got a problem with		
2		my polystyrene coving		
3		erm I've	Jenny	Ooo::h **[sarcastically]**
4		bought it and I haven't got a clue		
5		<u>how</u> I'm going to cut it to size		

Extract 9. Cathy watching *Kilroy,* May 15, 1996, discussion program on "police misconduct"

		Studio	Home	
1	Kilroy	. . . you were put in a police cell		
2	Woman	a cell yes **[begins to get upset]** with		
3		my=		
4	Kilroy	=wi- with your three and a half year		
5		old son (.)		
6		you were locked in a police	Cathy	Oh Go:d!
7		cell.		

Extract 10. Myra watching *The Time . . . The Place,* May 20, 1996, discussion program on "female sterilization"

		Studio	Home
1	Woman	. . . I had periods before me	
2		operation but after me operation no	
3		I didn't have one=	
4	John	= so they said	
5		"oh it's an infection everything'll	
6		come full circle" but it wasn't you	
		found out=	
7	Woman	=in October=	
8	John	=that you had=	

```
 9   Woman                    = that I was pregnant with
10                    twins
11   John      And that you'd been pregnant with
12                    twins
13   Woman     I was two months pregnant=
14   John                              =when
15                    you had the [operation
16   Woman                         [when I had the operation
17
18   Audience  .hh.hh..hhh                       Myra      Good God!
```

This kind of response, while watching television, is fairly unremarkable and what one expects from commonsense knowledge about watching discussion programs. However, thinking about such "minimal responses" in terms of speech style illuminates their significance. Jennifer Coates's research on all-female speech groups suggests that the establishment of a shared *collaborative* floor means that minimal responses say, "I am here, this is my floor too, and I am participating in the shared construction of talk" (Coates, 1996:143). Such cues indicate "active listenership": "Through signalling the active participation of all participants in the conversation, minimal responses play a significant role in the collaborative construction of text and of the maintenance of a collaborative floor" (Coates, 1996:145). Concepts such as "active listenership" and "the collaborative construction of text" are significant in terms of interviewees' responses to the broadcast talk. This is beginning to suggest that in broadcast genres that focus on talk, the reception of that talk is registered and experienced as a communicative engagement whereby the viewer at home shares a *discursive* space with speakers in the studio.

Completing a "Turn Constructional Unit"

Completing a turn constructional unit is another way of showing active participation in talk. This can take on different forms, such as answering a question or finishing another speaker's utterance in face-to-face conversation.

ADJACENCY PAIRS.   One of the ways in which the viewer at home might complete a turn constructional unit within this shared floor is by engaging in "adjacency pairs." In conversation certain classes of utterances conventionally come in pairs, for instance, questions and answers or invitations and acceptances/declinations. Adjacency pairs establish both a normative framework for displaying sense making of each others' talk and also accomplish actions—e.g., sociable greetings, answering questions.

GREETINGS.   As discussed in chapter 3, the morning programs all open and close with traditional conversational greetings as though the presenter is co-present with the viewer at home—part of the personalization and sociability that makes the program ritually meaningful. In my data only one of the women actually takes up the position of responding with the appropriate second pair part.

Extract 11. Bette watching *The Time . . . The Place*, June 12, 1996, discussion program on "fathers' rights"

		Studio		Home
		[Opening of program introductory music and audience applause]		
1	John S	Thanks very much indeed, thank		
2		you [turns to direct address to		
3		camera] Hello:: good morning to		
4		you at home	Bette	No, thank you
5		well we all know in this country that		Good morning.
6		sadly one in three marriages end in divorce . . .		

In the extract above, Bette responds to John Stapleton's "thank you" for the applause, by saying, "no, thank *you*," notice the stress on "you." She then responds to the "good morning" greeting with the appropriate response that one might use in face-to-face communication. This did not occur in any of the other interviews but this should not be observed as a quantitative limitation in the data. The only way to interpret this is qualitatively, through my knowledge of "being there." It is obvious from the tape that here Bette is being sarcastic, playing with the conventions that she is aware exist within these programs of speaking to us "as though we are there." Bette is knowingly responding to the game. The fact that none of the other women do this is because they recognize that to talk to the television in such an obvious way might seem ridiculous, but Bette works around this by mocking the conversational invitation.

Questions and answers. However, all of the women, without exception, answer questions that are asked in the studio. For example:

Extract 12. Bette watching *The Time . . . The Place*, June 12, 1996, discussion program on "fathers' rights"

		Studio		Home
1	John S	That's a fair point isn't it Gillian if		
2		youngsters are subject to this		
3		emo:tional roller coaster it is		
4		arguable that they're better off with		
5		<u>one</u> stable parent, isn't it? Or with <u>a</u>		
6		stable relationship?	Bette	yeah!
7	Woman	I think, I think . . .		

Extract 13. Alice watching *Kilroy*, May 14, 1996, discussion program on "Should the elderly pay for their own care?"

		Studio		Home
1	Kilroy	But <u>is</u> compu:lsory insurance the		
2		way so that <u>e</u>:verybody has to take		
3		out insurance in the future?		
4	Man	No, <u>no</u> you've ins<u>er</u>ted the word		
5		compulsory at the moment and		
6		there's <u>no</u>thing in these proposals		
7		that talks about compulsory		
8		insurance.		
9	Kilroy	<u>Should</u> it be compulsory?		
10	Man	I personally think . . .	Alice	I:: think it should be.

Extract 14. Bette watching *The Time . . . The Place*, June 12, 1996, discussion program on "fathers' rights"

		Studio		Home
1	John S	Let's <u>just</u> go to the back row and		
2		make the point perhaps, in fai::rness		
3		to dads because it's <u>not</u> always the		
4		dads who are the disruptive figure		
5		you know I mean <u>mums</u> could be		
6		the disruptive figure too, yes?		
7	Man	That's right yeh,		
8		I've got <u>two</u>	Bette	N<u>o</u>, they ca::n't!
9		daughters she<u>'s</u> er nearly six and the		
10		other one's two . . .		

Often, answering a question involves more than simply agreeing or disagree-
ing with an utterance. The response is followed by the assertion of an opinion
that may indeed challenge the discussion as it occurs within the television
studio.

**Extract 15. Alice watching *Kilroy*, May 14, 1996, discussion program on "Should the
elderly pay for their own care?"**

		Studio		Home
1	Kilroy	Should we be helped to keep them		
2		at home?		
3	Woman	Well that's preferable absolutely but	Alice	Yes it <u>is</u> preferable really isn't it
4		on the other hand it's not always		you've still got your dignity
5		possible		

Alice answers Kilroy's questions as though she were taking part in the studio
debate and she also offers a subsequent justification for her answer, "you've
still got your dignity" (line 4).

**Extract 16. Cathy watching *Kilroy*, May 15, 1996, discussion program on "police
misconduct"**

		Studio		Home
1	Kilroy	Jonathon, <u>ar::e</u> the police racist?		
2	Jonathon	I think in <u>some</u> cases the police are		
3		<u>very</u> racist but like in other cases it	Cathy	<u>I:</u> think so. I don't think they're <u>all</u>
4		all sort of depends how you sort of		racist but I think <u>some</u> of them are.
5		ta::lk to the police. I think if you		
6		talk to the police with an attitude		

In the example above, despite Kilroy clearly having addressed his question to Jonathon (line 1), Cathy at home replies (line 3) even as Jonathon's
studio reply is in progress. Thus, across the medium of broadcasting a shared
floor can give the viewer at home space to formulate their own direct response to the conversational exchanges occurring in the studio. The issue
of "primary addressee" as usually established in Conversational Analysis is
complicated here since Cathy's response, within the conventions of the talk
genre, is equally valid. Here we see the "double articulation" of broadcasting
truly being utilized in both its attributes—as the studio addressee and the
home addressee respond simultaneously. This is suggestive of more than
"active listenership," rather, it is a clear indication of direct participation in
the televised debate.

Extract 17. Sandra watching *This Morning*, Jan. 16, 1996, discussion segment with Richard, Judy, and Prince Philip's biographer

		Studio			Home
1	Judy	Maybe the difference is the way			
2		the Queen rode <u>out</u> any suggestion of			
3		infidelity by Prince Philip—Is it			
4		because she was sure of his love in a			
5		way that Diana was <u>not</u> sure of			
6		Charles' love?			
7	Biog	It's a completely different situation			
8		isn't it? I mean it doesn't seem			
9		to me	Sandra	<u>No</u>, <u>I</u> don't think that's the case
10		that Prince Philip has ever been in			a:ll (.) <u>I</u>: think the Queen's know
11		<u>love</u> with anybody else except the			all along that he's been a bit of a
12		Queen and that he's (.) certainly			fly-by-night but you just <u>put</u> up a
13		nowadays given her his total loyalty			<u>shut</u> up in them days, you <u>don't</u>
14		his total support			<u>know</u>::w

In the example above, presenter Judy Finnegan is asking a question that implies that the Queen ignored suggestions of Prince Philip's infidelity because she was secure in his love for her, providing a conventional interpretation of events in terms of romantic love. Although the question is addressed to the biographer, at home Sandra ignores the response of the "expert" and provides her own reply (at line 9), which rejects both Judy's romantic interpretation and the biographer's acquiescence. Rather, she provides a potentially more sophisticated answer, where she suggests there have been changes in women's increased ability to speak out against male behavior in the patriarchal family setting. The biographer's answer and Sandra's clearly contrast with each other. What we are beginning to see here is that the opening up of a mediated conversational floor allows the challenging of the wisdoms discussed in the text. This becomes more visible in other viewer exchanges.

JOINTLY CONSTRUCTING A TURN.   The idea of a "collaborative floor" where turns are jointly owned and simultaneous speech is not interpreted as interruption was also evident when the women spoke together in the focus group. This is replicated in their experiences of television viewing as they use the strategy of joining in turns in the studio, not only by answering questions at the same time as studio participants, but also by jointly constructing and completing turns.

Extract 18. Alice watching *Kilroy*, May 14, 1996, discussion program on "Should the elderly pay for their own care?"

		Studio		Home
1	Woman	What I'd like to say very briefly is if		
2		the reward for a ca::ring daughter		
3		who sacrifices marriage and career		
4		is to find herself on the streets		
5		that's	Alice	Homeless
6		no encouragement for anybody . . .		

Extract 19. Emma watching *This Morning*, July 7, 1998, phone-in segment with Dr. Ruth Westheimer on sexual problems

		Studio		Home
1	Dr Ruth	. . . you already are say:ing we have		
2		a problem here (.) children, jo::b,		
3		a::ll of the pressures of li::fe you		
4		must make a priority by saying once		
5		a week we		
6		need some time together . . .	Emma	Wednesday morning ten thirty,
7				heh, heh, heh **[sarcastically]**

Extract 20. Angela watching *This Morning*, Jan. 18, 1996, discussion segment with fertility doctor

		Studio		Home
1	Judy	Still, the same statistics of er one in		
2		ten are still infertile?		
3	Doctor	well, as the		
4		er (.) information is	Angela	That's a lo:t in it
5		accumulating we believe that it is		
6		actually closer to one in six		
7		and er		.hh God!
8		there's been a lot recently on		
9		er pro-		I'm lucky then
10		-blems with men's sperm		
11		counts		men's men's, it is they're getting
12		falling and also some of the social		less.
13		changes . . .		

The examples above all show moments of joining in with the talk in the studio and completing a turn. An extension of extract 18 is included because thus far most of the examples have suggested that the women only produce occasional isolated utterances. All of the women make more extended exchanges throughout the duration of the program, and here, extract 18 displays an example more akin to conventional face-to-face conversation in which the viewer takes up a more sustained role in the interaction. By line 11 Angela jointly completes the turn occurring in the studio, "it is they're getting less."

In these examples the viewer at home takes the opportunity of a conversational turn in relation to the discourse occurring in the studio. Significantly, their inputs clearly respond to the sequencing of the interaction within the program. They also demonstrate an extension of the unitary speaker/hearer exchange that is usually at the core of Conversation Analysis. The nature of broadcast communication's double articulation means that it is possible for there to be more than one primary addressee and, as the speakers do not share the same physical location, broadcasting allows viewers to take turns simultaneously without either speaker losing a place in the interaction, or having to relinquish the floor. These rejoinders by viewers demonstrate a mediated conversational floor that allows simultaneous talk as a feature of the viewing practice.

Secondary Responses: Interrogating the Broadcast Text

Thus far, my analysis of para-social broadcast encounters has borrowed tools from Conversation Analysis and socio-linguistics. From the point of view of media studies, however, this analysis also provides some insights into how viewers make sense of the media text. Looking closely at these comments as communicative actions gives access to the very moment that the process of engaging with a text begins. When the viewers respond to questions we can see how they are interpreting suggestions in the studio, negotiating and often challenging them. The mediated conversation floor provides a picture of a text meeting its audience, as a "mutually constructed text," one that is dynamically produced with individual audience members.

If we acknowledge the establishment of a shared or "mutually constructed mediated floor" with this particular participation framework, we can also begin to think about other interjections from the women that do not necessarily fit clear conversational sequencing strategies. These are "formulations" and "argumentative interrogations."

Formulations

This second level of participation occurs when the audience member comments on the talk occurring in the studio and produces a "formulation" of what has been said. For example, in the case of news interviews such interactive "formulations" of interviewees' assertions are made by the interviewer for the benefit of the overhearing audience in order to "both advance the prior report by finding a point in the prior utterance and thus shifting its focus, redeveloping its gist, making something explicit that was previously implicit in the prior utterance, or by making inferences about its presuppositions or implications. They propose a direction for subsequent talk by inviting interviewee response to what is formulated" (Heritage and Greatbatch, 1991:104).

However, in these examples the viewers clearly make the formulation for themselves:

Extract 21. Sandra watching *This Morning*, Jan.16, 1996, segment on wrinkle treatment

		Studio		Home
1	Expert	. . . but certainly we, the wrinkles		
2		and the photo-damage are within		
3		our brief=		
4	Richard	=what on the National Health?		
5	Expert	er, no not usu [ally		
6	Richard	[no, I didn't think so		
7	Judy	[no, heh I mean		
8		sunbathin-		
9	Expert	can I just say one more problem that		
10		you have to watch out , which is	Sandra	Exactly, cos you can't get nothing
11		why you need a dermatologist is just		for vanity
12		that any (?) on the skin can end		(3)
13		up with what we call post		
14		inflammatory increase or decreased		Gotta be rich to get rid of wrinkles
15		pigmentation		

We can see here how the viewer at line 10 begins her formulation of what has just been said about the skin treatment not being available on the National Health Service. She shifts the focus to vanity as an unacceptable justification for health care, and then, at line 14, develops the point to suggest that you have to be rich to get rid of wrinkles. This example, while seemingly trivial, illustrates the discursive negotiation of meaning. As the viewer interacts with the discussion, she is also producing a commentary. That is, while she is encouraged as "Mrs. Daytime Home Consumer" to consider products and treatment (within the genre of the magazine program), Sandra's commentary points out that to look young is expensive and beyond the reach of most women who rely on free National Health Service medical treatment. Here is another example of how a viewer's reformulations illustrate a negotiation with the text:

Extract 22. Myra watching *The Time . . . The Place*, Jan. 20, 1996, discussion program on "female sterilization" (Gyn = gynecologist)

		Studio		Home
1	Gyn	. . . people think you can reverse it		
2		around and years later that if you		
3		meet another partner go and have		
4		your tubes put back together and		
5		have another baby and it's not that		
6		simple. So I would also call that a		
7		complication—it's the pain and the		
8		suffering years later to find out,		
9		new marriage, new partner		
10		no baby	Myra	because (.)
11	John S	which leads us to I suppose one of		if they have had it
12		the most controversial aspects of		done then because of
13		this. I mean there is a case for		post-natal depression or
14		actually saying, you can only be		something-
15		sterilized if, for example you're a		just decide, then say they
16		certain age or you'd had		split up and that's it
17		so many children . . .		

In this example, Myra provides a formulation of the gynecologist's warnings of the possibility of relationship breakdowns after the woman has decided to have a sterilization. However, she reformulates the discussion into a new point that has been neglected by the gynecologist. In lines 12–13 she suggests women might decide to be sterilized because of post-natal depression from previous pregnancies. Arguably Myra is inserting valuable information here that has not been discussed previously at any other point in the program. One might say that the male gynecologist is flippantly masking issues of women's psychology around motherhood in his argument about the difficulties of reversing sterilization. However, Myra in her capacity as lay speaker, and though she is not co-present, is able to engage with the text and provide her own insights into a "female-centered" problem.

Extract 23. Jana watching *Vanessa*, July 18, 1998, discussion program on "women door bouncers" (Bev = female bouncer, Maggie = sister)

		Studio	Home
1	Maggie	I had a taxi company for five years	
2		and I run that for five years and	
3		Kay actually worked with me and	
4		that got in my blood but I realized	
5		that I couldn't have a husband and	

		Studio			
6		children and do that job. <u>This</u> isn't			
7		the job for a married woman- wi-			
8		sorry **[to her sister who is not**			
9		**married]** for a divorcee			
10			with	Jana	what you're sayin' is that a <u>man's</u>
11		children to care about			life is more- is not as valuable as a
12	Bev	That's what I am=			woman's life
13	Maggie	=I'm ever so sorry			
14	Bev	I'm a single parent with a child			

In the extract above, Jana's formulation inscribes a new twist to the gist of Maggie's argument about the need for a mother to be in a "safe" job. Maggie is clearly presenting her position in terms of traditional patriarchal family relations (notice her misuse of the word "married" with regard to her single sister) whereby the wife/mother is constituted as primary child-carer who is most fundamental to her children's lives (later in this extract Bev, as a divorcee, talks about the pressures of being both the main parent and bread-winner). Jana's formulation, therefore, is about the value placed on the life of a woman in a dangerous job. The issue returns later in the same program:

Extract 24. Jana watching *Vanessa*, July 18, 1998, discussion program on "women bouncers" (Bev = female bouncer, Maggie = sister)

		Studio			Home
1	Maggie	You've gotta think of your kids,			
2		you're letting your kids down, you			
3		go home you can go home and you			
4		can't work ever again=			
5	Bev	=But you do a			
6		job to make a better <u>li::</u>fe for your			
7		kids			
8	Maggie	Yeh but there's other ways of		Jana	So, basically we shouldn't have
9		supporting your kids than (?)			female police women we shouldn't
10		come home injured			have female-

At home, Jana responds with her formulation of what Maggie's argument means to her—the studio argument relates to debates about women's employment in other potentially dangerous fields. Her reformulation of Maggie's argument as an equal opportunity issue displays a critical engagement with the conversation that exhibits active involvement in the talk over the duration of the show. In terms of the politics of the talk show, here Jana is also putting the personal discussion into a wider context concerned with social structure, rather than accepting the ideological problem as psychological dilemma; Peck (1995) argues that this is a key feature of the talk show's political function.

Reformulations in news interviews can work to be deliberately provocative. The interviewer, for example, might develop the interviewee's statements in a challenging manner in the interests of "good journalism" (Heritage 1985). But what is the investment for viewers' reformulations of the televised talk? The reformulations reveal particular moments that interrogate the broadcast discourse, thus confronting and sometimes contesting expert advice, institutional advice, and common sense. These challenges, however, unlike those offered by the detached professional persona of the news interviewer, offer highly personalized dynamic engagements with the positions thrown up by the text.

Argumentative Interrogations

The women were most vocal when they disagreed with discussion occurring in the studio. Many of the interjections described so far suggest that the women's responses occurred at appropriate moments in interactive turn-taking situations—agreeing, answering questions, finishing sentences, and so on. But at times when the women's feelings were most engaged with an argument in the studio, such invitations were not necessary. Arguably the women do not have to attend to the "face-needs" of speakers in the studio and their argument can afford to be more aggressive. In the next examples the women produce utterances that register direct challenges and interruptions in the text. For example, a viewer might directly ask questions about what is being said in the studio, even though there is no actual potential for reciprocal response:

Extract 25. Jenny watching *Good Morning,* Jan. 25, 1996, interview with mother and daughter after news story about a thirteen-year-old girl getting married to a Turkish waiter while on holiday. The daughter in the studio was apparently approached by the same man on holiday.

		Studio	Home
1	Nick	Now the news this week that	
2		thirteen-year-old schoolgirl Sarah	
3		Cook had married a Turkish waiter	
4		has shocked parents everywhere.	
5		Yesterday Sarah was made a ward	
6		of court by Essex Social Services.	
7		We'll have to wait to see if her	
8		mother's arrival in Turkey will now	
9		mean Sarah's return to the UK.	
10		without her husband. (.) Well our	
11		next guest is Corinne Haynes. Her	

12	own eleven-year-old daughter	Jenny	They've made her a ward of court,
13	Stacey was approached by the very		Essex (.) Social Services but she's
14	same man with an offer of marriage		in Turkey so how?
15	when they were on holiday in the		
16	country		

Or the viewer might directly question what is being said in the studio:

Extract 26. Alice watching *Kilroy*, May 14, 1996, discussion program on "Should the elderly pay for their own care?"

		Studio		Home
1	Man	It costs four hundred and twenty		
2		pounds a week of which we pay		
3		one hundred and twenty pounds and		
4		we expect to do that for the rest of		
5		his life (.) however long that may		
6		be and		
7		the problem nowadays is that	Alice	well, you're pretty wealthy to
8.		people are living a lot longer		afford a hundred and twenty
9	Woman	you're lucky		pounds and still be able to live
10	Man	We're not lucky to have that sort		
11		of- it's not a question of luck it's a		
12		question of responsibility		

This may be difficult to interpret from the transcript alone, but in the context of the studio discussion, a man is arguing that it is everyone's duty to care for their parents regardless of cost. However, Alice is annoyed because this disregards the fact that it is too expensive for most people. Alice's comment at home interrupts the man's turn but then is reinforced by a similar interjection in the studio from another woman, "you're lucky."

Cathy similarly challenges the direction of discussion in the next example:

Extract 27. Cathy watching *Kilroy*, May 15, 1996, discussion program on "police misconduct"

		Studio	Home
1	MP	You've got to remember that every	
2		police officer now according to the	
3		statistics will suffer from violence	
4		and assault every four years in his	
5		career. The police are being	
6		assaulted all the time-	
7	Kilroy	-sure	

8	MP	—now the	
9		way this program is going it seems	Cathy Yeh, but they know that when th
10		to be very one-sided that	go for the job.
11		the police seem to be going round	
12		beating up people	

In the example above, when the MP defends police actions in terms of the amount of attacks the police are subject to, thus attempting to shift the frame of the discussion to be more sympathetic to police, Cathy's aggressive challenge dismisses his utterance as she declares that the police already know the risks. Again, Sandra interjects in the next extract:

Extract 28. Sandra watching *This Morning* direct address link to advertisements where Judy Finnegan informs the viewer what is coming up after the break

		Studio	Home
1	Judy	Well, we're taking a short break for	
2		the news and coming up later this	
3		morning an interview with the	
4		controversial royal biographer	
5		who's reportedly deeply upset the	
6		Queen with her new book called	
7		Simply Elizabeth. It seems that she	
8		and Prince Philip are now in for the	
9		same tabloid treatment as Charles	Sandra Good serves em right (.)
10		and Diana—the author talks for the	Poor Diana gets all the flack!
11		first time on television.	

Judy's suggestion is one of regret that the Queen and Prince Philip are coming under such scrutiny; however, Sandra clearly challenges this and turns it completely around in support of Diana. In doing so, she rejects the issue as it is formulated by the presenter in the studio and interrupts Judy with a direct rejection of her statement. In the next example the viewer's own lay knowledge directly challenges that of the expert:

Extract 29. Angela watching *This Morning,* Jan.18, 1996, phone-in segment on fertility

		Studio	Home
1	Caller	Hello	
2	Richard	Hello, now how long have	
3		you been	Angela You've told us now
4		trying to get pregnant?	
5	Caller	erm, about eighteen months now	
6		erm	

```
 7   Richard   Right go on                              Angela   (        ?         )
 8   Caller    I don't have regular periods, so I
 9             erm obviously don't know when
10             I'm about to ovulate-
11   Richard                       -arrh
12   Caller                          —erm I see my
13             doctor but he says to give it
14             two years before he's willing to go
15             any fur- [any further                             t.hh. it should be a year hh.
16   Richard            [so-
17   Judy              [so, so another six months
18             basically
19   Richard   So, you and your partner have not
20             had specific tests at all then, I mean
21             he hasn't had his sperm count
22             checked or anything like that
23   Caller    No
24   Richard   So, you're just trying=                           Blame him !
25   Caller                    =I mean my partner                heh, heh, heh
26             does smoke and I don't
27             know if that has anything to do
28             with it but the main problem is that
29             I am=
30   Richard      =irregular=
31   Caller                =I have irregular
32             periods
```

Here, Angela comments on the talk with the second-person pronoun—"you've told us now"—but continues her involvement in this conversation with an inaudible utterance at line 7, followed clearly by a direct challenge to a doctor's advice, as presented by the caller. The caller reports that her doctor will take no further action until after two years of trying for a baby. Angela is convinced that she knows better, as she says, "it should be a year" (line 15). She then continues with the direction "blame him!" (line 24). This indicates that the viewer is able to make direct challenges to pieces of information. Although she is not questioning the woman caller, she *is* questioning the advice given to her by her doctor. Angela's personal knowledge as a woman with children overrules the account given by the caller and signals her direct participation in the discussion.

What is beginning to emerge is that participating in the discussion and offering argumentative interjections is often substantiated by the evocation of subjective points of view, echoing the privileging of lay knowledge by the talk show genre (Livingstone and Lunt, 1994), as we can see clearly in the next extract:

Extract 30. Alice watching *The Time . . . The Place*, May 14, 1996, discussion program on "Should the elderly pay for their own care?"

		Studio			Home
1	Kilroy	Is Alf right then? Should the			
2		children be inheriting? Do children			
3		have the right to inherit?			
4	Woman	yes, yes they do. My mother and			
5		father worked all their lives, they	Alice	Well, perhaps they ought to put
6		paid their dues why shouldn't they			amount, state an amount, if your
7		have the house? I'm struggling to			home's—see somebody said
8		look after my mum.			although your home's taken into
9	Kilroy	I, I'm a le-, I, I work in Victoria			account, a lot of people invest th
10		Station cleaning out the lavatories			money in valuables. Now I
11		and I have to work hard all week			wouldn't have thought of that yo
12		and I earn just enough to keep my			know so that's the way of getting
13		family . . .			around it.

Alice is clearly working through her own argument in relation to the discussion occurring in the studio. In response to the question about whether children should inherit their parents' homes, rather than use the money to pay for their care, Alice begins to form an argument about that depending on the value of the home in question (line 5), that they should "state an amount." However, she then begins to rethink this argument as she remembers a contribution from earlier in the discussion—that "some people invest money in valuables" as a means of bypassing a property means test, which is something that had not occurred to her. This demonstrates that in thinking (and talking) about an issue, an involved viewer begins to work around a number of ideas and relate them to their own subjective thoughts and points of view—"I would never have thought of that." This begins to open up the way in which positions can be transitory and constituted through *processes* of negotiation as the discursive encounter evolves.

Tertiary Responses: Invoking Personal Experience

The women's contributions to the discourse in terms of their own personal experience often took a form that echoes the genre's focus on individual stories, suggesting that they feel incorporated into the intimate forum. This is one of the main ways in which the women in the study "interactively" make sense of the morning program discussion. In the next extract, Cathy is watching a discussion on *Kilroy* about police misconduct but is able to formulate an opinion through vocalizing something of her relationship with her son:

Extract 31. Cathy watching *Kilroy*, May 15, 1996, discussion program on "police misconduct" (MP = John Townsend, Conservative MP for Bridlington)

		Studio	Home
1	MP	I think it's society's problem as well	
2		particularly as far as young people	
3		are concerned. Society in particular	
4		the (chattering) classes have set	
5		their minds against physical	
6		punishment and I've got a lot of	
7		sympathy for the police erm I	
8		actually do believe we are suffering	
9		from the demise of the old-	
10		fashioned good hiding. We've done	
11		away with the cane in schools	
12		so what do we do with young	Cathy I think there's too many do-
13		bullies like ↑these- you exclude	gooders around
14		them from the school and they end	(3)
15		up on the street causing trouble and	
16		until we bring back some form of	the do-gooders where the- the
17		corporal punishment and we get	things should be sorted out like
18		parents to take on more	you've got people jumpin in and
19		responsibility we won't get	saying ooh you shouldn't be
20		anywhere. In the old days when I	allowed to do this like smacking
21		was a young boy the policeman	children people are telling you
22		could clip 'em around the ear and	you can't smack your children now
23		now as the gentleman just said	well they're your children you
24		now he would lose his job. We've	discipline them. I mean you have
25		got to give the police more powers,	gotta battle other people (.)
26		so we don't want real violence but	I mean if I come to discipline
27		clip them over the ear would be	[Andrew] now he tells me "I'll
28		quite, quite (the thing)	phone Childline" heh, heh, I mean
29		the old days you'd get a cuff across	that's how bad it's got
30		the ear as you said, which is quite	
31		right.	

In the extract above, the MP is clearly articulating a very conservative line concerning discipline and police power. Cathy, however, ignores his speech and rearticulates his argument in terms of her own experience as a mother, not in terms of policing powers. It seems that she is talking about a perceived broader liberal perspective against physical discipline that exists within contemporary culture. Moreover, she refers to people who hold such beliefs in her own phrase as "do-gooders" and then goes on to tell an anecdote about her own son Andrew's ability to use his knowledge of well-publicized help lines for children whenever she comes to discipline him. She then evaluates this in terms of the studio debate, "I mean that's how bad it's got" (lines 28–29).

This extract is interesting because the MP's argument is about the police, the main topic of the studio debate, while Cathy finds common ground in terms of her own experience of disciplining her son as a single mother. She rearticulates the discussion in terms of her own subjectivity and experience as a mother, even though it does not exactly address the issue authoritatively presented by the MP, as she vicariously participates in the studio discussion. The grounds of participation are not necessarily dependent upon knowledge, even personal or common knowledge of the particular issue, but rather depend upon the ability to discursively mobilize some experiential connection that can be relatively easily folded into the flow of the mediated conversation.

In the following extract we can see how in the conversational flow the negotiation of the text in relation to personal experience sees the viewer discursively shift her position in relation to the topic at hand:

Extract 32. Alice watching *Kilroy,* May 14, 1996, discussion program on "Should the elderly pay for their own care?"

		Studio		Home
1	Kilroy	. . . Let us say it was me and I've		
2		got this expensive house and I now		
3		need nursing care—not National		
4		Health Service treatment but		
5		nursing care. I have to sell my		
6		house in order to get that care. I		
7		have to sell my house in order to		
8		pay for it .hh Are you saying that I		
9		shouldn't have to sell my expensive		
10		house, that I should be able to give		
11		it to my children and your low-paid		
12		constituents who are in work now		
13		paying taxes should pay to keep me		
14		in care while I give my expensive		
15		house to my children? Is that fair?	Alice	That's the other side of the
16	Expert	Hang on		argument, of course.
17		**[audience noise]**		
18	Woman	He is not saying that at all		When you put it like that yes, yes
	Expert	Can I just-		
19	Audience	heh, heh, heh, heh		
20	Woman	No, he is NOT		
21	Kilroy	I'm asking HIM		
22	Woman	Go on then		

23	Kilroy	Go on then she said, go on then Alf		Alice	But, you see a modest home
24	Expert	Right, now I'm saying a number of			wouldn't last very long would it?
25		things. I'm saying that it was not			I'm on about our sort of **[gestures**
26		their expectation that they would			**around the room]**
27		have to dispossess er mainly			
28		daughters, caring relatives, many			
29		who have given up the prospect of			
30		marriage, of a career to look after			
31		an elderly mother or father or both			I'm more concerned that there's
32		and whose reward for that is now to			always a home here to come to if
33		be told that they've lost the home			things go wrong that was my
34		they expected to inherit.			concern.

Alice begins to take on Kilroy's point about the ethics of the ordinary tax-payer paying for care while the children of elderly parents inherit their property. She formulates it as "the other side of the argument" and to some extent agrees with Kilroy, directly addressing him, "when you put it like that" using the second-person pronoun. As the discussion continues, however, she thinks about her own situation and the possibility of selling her own home—"but you see a modest home wouldn't last very long" (lines 23–24) as she gestures to her surroundings. The "you see" here is clearly addressed to me, as I become the primary recipient of her discourse as she embarks upon a description of her own personal circumstances. After considering this she finally articulates her own immediate concern as a mother, which begins at line 31, where she is more concerned "that there's always a home to come to." After thinking about Kilroy's suggestion that the parental home should provide the capital for care for the elderly, Alice draws upon her own position as a mother of four children who all presently live at home. Her primary concern is that there is somewhere for them to live, and she ultimately rejects Kilroy's suggestion through working through her personal stance in terms of her subjective *lived* experience of motherhood with a relatively modest income.

Clearly then, by using this methodology we are able to see the shifting positions that one might occupy over the duration of the viewing experience, rather than attempting to fix viewing positions in terms of their reading after the event. In previous chapters I have made a case for considering the dynamism of speech as a crucial part of the communicative framework in which broadcasting is embedded into the routines of daily life. Understanding text-reader relations as a straightforward transmission model of communication has traditionally been complicated; for example, in Hall's encoding/decoding model he recognizes the potential asymmetry between the encoding and decoding process, depending upon the social location of viewers. He draws upon

Volosinov's concept of "multi-accentuality"—the idea that the sign may have more than one meaning as it comes into play in social life—to account for the struggles over meaning at the connotative level. Here, however, a return to Volosinov/Bakhtin enables us to unpack the complex nature of the viewing process and explore "multi-accentuality" not just *between* reading communities, where positions are fixed in the interpretation of particular reception communities (via the interview or focus groups discussion), but also *within* the dialogic interactions of individual viewers with broadcast texts. This opens out a significant dimension to television viewing that has traditionally been locked out by the prominence of the text-reader model of inquiry.

Telling Stories

"Story-telling plays a central role in friendly conversation between women" (Coates, 1996:94). The form of personal narrative is one of the key features of talk show and magazine program discourse. It is hardly surprising then that the women often produce their own narratives as they interact with the program. Using narrative involves an extended turn whereby the routines of conversational turn taking are suspended. Interestingly here, however, in *moments* of viewing, the use of narrative can provide a stage for the viewer, relegating the discourse produced in the studio to the background. In capturing a "mutually constructed text" there are moments where the viewers' contributions take precedence, through the staging of personal narrative events that can only be made visible in this way if we accept the dynamic nature of broadcasting. The blurring of the traditional conceptualization of text/reader relations is most pertinent here. The viewers' ability to interact allows them the space to produce their own text such that the power of the televised text becomes only part of the reception process. The viewer therefore is not simply "receiver" but at crucial moments is also "producer" in various viewing moments. In non-mediated conversation, although a narrative account suggests an extended turn of monologue, it does not mean that the narrative stands outside of the conversational exchange.

Sacks reminds us that narratives are "carefully and appropriately situated" by their tellers in sequences of talk (1978:261). Most stories get told with a three-part sequence: a story preface that announces the availability of a story, a response whereby other participants align themselves as hearers of the story, and ultimately the third turn that is the production of the story. For example:

BARBARA: My aunt died
MARTHA: Died, what happened
BARBARA: ((tells story)) (Goodwin, 1990)

Labov (1972) claims that the subsequent narrative can be organized into six elements:

> Abstract: summarizes the central action and main point of the narrative. A story-teller uses this to preface the story.
> Orientation: sets the scene.
> Complicating action: central part of the story proper.
> Evaluation: addresses the point of the narrative. These often appear in "free clauses," as such they are not actually part of the narrative.
> Resolution: final conclusion to sequence of events.
> Coda: wraps up the action.[5]

These elements would usually occur in order, apart from evaluations that can occur dispersed through other elements. Here is how a viewer inserts her own narrative into the context of viewing the televised discussion:

Extract 33. Angela watching *This Morning*, Jan.18, 1996, segment on fertility (Gyn = gynecologist)

		Studio	Home
1	Gyn	. . . there are some tests that you	
2		can	Mhm
3		get over the counter through the	
4		chemists to er identify the	Take your
5		fertile	temperature it goes up!
6		time of the cycle but the biggest	
7		difficulty really with this situation	(1)
8		is obviously you're potentially only	
9		fertile once in every four months so	That's how I got caught with mine
10		chances are obviously reduced	(.)
11		Mhm	I took my temperature—when it
12		certainly in these kind of situations	rises you have it (.)
13		we could try and step into the	Got [Candy] the first time and
14		investigation half way and see if we	[Amy] the second time
15		can actually give you something to	so it worked.
16		get the ovulation more regular. And	It's a bit spontaneous—it's like
17		I think you should probably press your GP.	COME HOME

In this example, Angela displays active listenership (line 2) and she offers her own advice for how to identify "the fertile time of the cycle" with the direction at line 4. Angela, in keeping with experiential validation we have seen before, supports the accuracy of her statement by stating that that's how she got pregnant (line 9). One could see the utterance, "that's how I got caught with mine" as a story preface that invites a second turn response of, "how did you get caught with yours?" (I might be expected to provide this turn). This turn is not taken and Angela pauses before she begins her own narrative at line 11. Therefore, before embarking upon her narrative account Angela engages in the conversational norms that usually apply in face-to-face conversation.

In terms of Labov's structure, the opening line "that's how I got caught with mine" could be seen as the *abstract* that summarizes the main point of the narrative and invites questions. There appears to be no *orientation* but there are the narrative clauses that appear temporally sequenced—the *complicating action,* "I took my temperature" (line 11), and the *resolutions,* "Got [Candy] the first time and [Amy] the second time" (lines 13–14). Then follows her *evaluation,* "so it worked" (line 15), and the *coda* could be, "it's a bit spontaneous it's like COME HOME" (lines 16–17), which returns the discourse to the present tense. However, analyzing the narrative in terms of Labov's structure does not necessarily tell us about the specificity of narratives produced in this particular setting. While broadcast talk creates new kinds of discursive forms and genres specific to the context in which they are produced, it is also clear here that new discursive forms are also produced in their daily iteration across the medium of broadcasting in the everyday lives of viewers at home.

When Thornborrow refers to the narrative functions deployed in talk shows, she suggests that "stories are a key resource within the talk show discourse in so far as they are used by speakers to accomplish a variety of actions—not just to tell of their own experiences, but to construct their position within the situated context of the talk as they engage in the dynamic interactive business of 'having their say'" (1997:259). Here, the data show that "having their say" is a mechanism through which the women orient themselves to the broadcast discourse.

Extract 34. Jana watching *Vanessa*, July 8, 1998, discussion program on female bouncers (Kay = female bouncer with children, Maggie = Kay's sister, Bev = another female bouncer)

		Studio		Home
1	Kay	I've done it for four years I must be		
2		good to be able to—t'have stayed in		
3		The job con [tinuously		
4	Bev	[I'm not		
5		questioning	Jana	We had er a run-in in Stones
6		whether you're good or bad at the		a couple of weeks ago where the
7		job what I am questioning is your		manager <u>hit</u> one of my friends-
8	Kay	mhm		ma:le there's absolutely no reason

9		logic in that it is the o:nly way you	like really swung at 'im right across
10		can provide for your kids	my face (.) it came right
11	Vanessa	Kay, it's quite interesting, interesting	across my face and Adam- it
12		because Steve and Maggie have	knocked Adam out- I got inside
13		formed a sort of alliance the most	after all the (.) his brother's a
14		unlikely pair but they're both saying	marine and all his marine friends
15		virtually the same thing to you,	were down outside going mad at
16		they're both looking at you- they're	the doorman and everything
17		both looking at you [they're both	whereas if these doormen had been
18	Bev	[the only	female the females would have
19		difference is warning you and	been able to calm them down
20		(.) and that Maggie's saying that	and say the manager was wrong we
21		doormen are thick	know that and been able to talk
22	Maggie	No	to them there'd have been half as
23	Vanessa	Well they're both- she didn't say they	much trouble
24		are thick	
25	Bev	You did say that you did say that	

Here, Jana takes an extended turn to tell her narrative. She begins with her "story preface" at line 5—"we had a run-in in Stones" [a local bar]—and some orientation ("a couple of weeks ago," "where the manager hit one of my friends," lines 6–7). There is an evaluation in line 8—"there's absolutely no reason"—and then she continues with narrative clauses that are chronological. At line 17, however, Jana reveals the evaluative point of the story, which positions the narrative in terms of the studio debate about female bouncers. Jana's narrative helps her to skilfully construct her position by suggesting that had the bouncers been female, they would have talked to the marines and "there'd have been half as much trouble" (lines 22–23). In so doing, the viewer is making a critical comment on the nature of an all-male confrontation that she suggests female bouncers would have been better equipped to diffuse, ironically, through "talk."

Evaluations within talk shows "function as contentious statements which may then be taken up and responded to by other participants" (Thornborrow, 1997:257). In the case of the viewer at home, they cannot be used to sustain the dynamic of studio talk or to affect its direction, as the participants are not co-present. Arguably then, the viewer is positioning herself in order to display her alignment to the discourse to me, the other "silent" viewer. In this scenario the narrative and the consistent production of the evaluation has another crucial function. At home the woman is positioned as the "viewer" and a "participator" in the audience. As such she must make sense of the text that flows into *her* home. Personal subjectivities are induced as the publicly mediated talk meets the private domestic space of the home. In this collision, encouraged by the genre's emphasis on personal experience, the women are encouraged to "have their say" too, but their contributions are often more complicated, they are also about the active relational performance of "what this means for me."

Extract 35. Jenny watching *Good Morning*, Jan. 25, 1996, segment on children who got their parents to give up smoking

		Studio		Home
1	Mother	When Catherine came home that		
2		day and actually said I was so upset		
3		like I said in the video that erm that		
4		I decided to stop and that erm the		
5		only way to erm stop is just to		
6		I didn't throw my cigarettes away		
7		but I put them in a draw	Jenny	The thing is though
8		and then		she's been smoking
9		about six months later I threw them		all the time that child's been
10		away.		growing up right
11	Nick	And have you fully		from a baby
12		stopped now=		I er I was workin in
13	Mother	=two years now		the pub the other
14	Nick	and have you definitely, definitely		day and er a
15		stopped		couple came
16	Mother	two years		in they had two young
17	Nick	Because you went ten years=		girls, I'm talking like maybe abou
18	Mother	=I went		er oh two and the
19		ten years when I was having my		other one was about
20		children and then I started smoking		three and they
21		again n' thinking-		were having a meal
22	Nick	—when the pressure		both of them were smokin'
23		was on in your life and		by (.) like (.)
24		things were a bit difficult		like they'd do it one at a time
25	Mother	and I thought it would		and one'd go out and
26		make me lose weight and in fact I		stand in the corner
27		put two stones on smo[king		but it's still gonna travel
28	Nick	[God		I mean it was like
29	Mother	and (.) when I stopped smoking I		from the fire **[points]** to
30		lost two stone as well. So people		there **[points]** and I
31		who think they'll lose weight by		felt like sayin'
32		smoking they don't		but it travels
33	Nick	So what has been the strongest		(2)
34		factor in you being able to give up		I mean I come
35		Is it willpower?		home from work
36	Mother	willpower and Catherine sayin'		and I mean everyday
37		that and also now I realize that it		I have to wash my

38		does smell awful but you don't		hair and change
39		realize it when you are a smoker		my clothes
40		it's only when you stop	Helen	Yeh
41	Nick	Do you smell better now Catherine?		
42		Does she smell better? Are you		(.)
43		really happy about that?		Because of the
44		[Catherine nods]		smell on me
45		We- were you really upset with		and I'm behind the bar
46		what happened at school that day?		

This, like many of the women's personal stories, has quite a complicated structure. The narrative is placed within the context of the program segment that is about parents who smoke, and includes a talk with a girl who was bullied because she smelt of cigarettes. Jenny's opening statement (line 7) does not look like the usual "story preface" that invites a story. Without a host to elicit the story, Jenny seems to be linking her narrative to the events detailed in the studio herself. However, she then embarks on a series of narrative clauses that relate to the events she witnessed while working in the pub—she makes the evaluation "but it's still gonna travel" (line 27), declaring how pointless it is to simply smoke away from the children in the same room, which is directly related to the studio-based discussion. However, this leads to another small narrative about herself, "I come home from work . . . " (line 34), the evaluation of which leads to a "coda"—the clause that wraps up the action like "and that was that"—which is "and *I'm* behind the bar" (line 45).

What is evident in this extract is the fact that the story provides a space to evaluate "what this means for me." Jenny, in telling the story about the couple with two children smoking in the bar in which she works, is led to consider her own job. The viewer's evaluations serve to position them in order to take up the personal significance of the issue. However, as the women "stage" their own experience another phenomenon in the "mediated conversational floor" emerges from the context of the viewing environment. It is apparent from the constructions of the narrative that at this point they are told for my benefit.

Jenny uses the third-person pronoun "she" (line 8) and my place as listener is marked by my own "active listenership," "yeh" (line 40). This is visible in some of the other narratives and extended turns that the women produce. This does not necessarily invalidate what has gone before, but represents a more complicated phenomenon produced in relation to my presence. Here, then, the TV text becomes a pretext, a reference point whereby the women elucidate subjective accounts occasioned by the "textuality" of the program. The text here is stimulating memories that may have been recalled, if not vocalized, had I not been present. The benefit of this kind of research is that it takes us to precise locations in the text that are meaningful to the women's personal identities, points that could not be accessed through the interview or focus group, giving more specific insights into the way textuality and subjectivity are mobilized together, which will be explored further in the next chapter.

Conclusion: The Mutually Produced Text

The argument here is not to imply that these exchanges of electronic sociality are the same as face-to-face interaction; it is obvious that the studio cannot respond to the viewer at home and neither can the audience responses influence the direction of the broadcast. Nor does my research necessarily provide evidence of increased "powers of resistance" in the interpretative frame that much audience research has followed. But I am suggesting that through these para-social encounters there clearly exists a conversation floor that is specific to the conditions of broadcasting: a "mediated conversational floor." Through broadcast communication, in morning talk television at least, viewers' experiences of the discussion can be influenced as much by their own speech production as by that produced in the studio, thus producing a "mutually constructed text." This is an alternative dimension to television reception related to the mechanics of television dynamically taking place *in time* that is not normally documented. It is possible that such mediated communicative practices precipitate new ways of constructing and articulating contemporary identities in relation to television and broadcasting, a possibility I address further in the next chapter.

A key dimension here is the way in which a particular *feminine* subjectivity appears in these mediated intimate forms of expression. Gendered articulations are not tied directly to assumptions about women's talk such as "women are more cooperative," but they are located within the interactive appeal of the specific programs. Arguably, and this remains to be tested by other research into the correspondence between speech genres and media genres, this is a feminine communicative competence necessary for taking pleasure in daytime television talk, in the same way that Brunsdon (1981) argued about the cultural competences required for appreciating soap opera. Recall how in the previous chapter the women suggested that the relating of personal, private experience had turned their male partners off from the genre.

But this methodology is also revealing the way in which this takes place. The actual content of the show alone does not help us to determine what the women's responses might be, but the pragmatic way in which the discourse encourages the mobilization of their subjectivity *performs* its meaning. The women therefore play out their own subjectivity in relation to the televised discourses through the validation of their "ordinary" roles as women. Therefore, regardless of the content of the discourse, the women are encouraged to take up a reflexive position about how they are implicated in the discussion, and in doing so they perform the roles of mother, carer, worker, and so on, through their lay expertise. Gender performativity is mapped into mediated relationships, here through the daily discursive mechanics of sociability and self-reflexivity. This takes place in the sustained working through of discursive positions made visible by using an audience research approach influenced by discourse analysis, capturing moments of viewing and allowing us to see the *text-in-action*. We can see this more fully in the next chapter as we take a closer look at some more sustained and intimate moments of talk produced by the women. These begin to unravel the discursive mechanics of the relations between textuality and subjectivity, urging us to think through the mediation of self-reflexivity in the contemporary era.

7. Texts, Subjects, and Modern Self-Reflexivity

Introduction

Accounting for the interactive potential available to viewers in watching talk shows has begun to give us closer insights into the relationship between textuality and subjectivity. The methodology used here can more accurately identify particular moments from texts that are salient to personal experience, and thus begin to unravel the workings of those experiences as mediated encounters. This chapter works with two further and more sustained examples of the women in the study talking during the programs. This type of research can take us beyond the usual assumptions made about women's "referential" TV viewing patterns, which assume a normative relation between women as gendered and the appreciation of gendered genres. Established explanations of women's television consumption do not entirely account for the dialogic nature of these encounters; in contrast, this book offers a closer inspection of how viewing unfolds in the process of "doing" gender, following the directions made by Butler (1990) on gender performativity. Here we see how the women's responses can be explored through contemporary arguments about the performance of modern self-reflexivity, locating these empirical findings within the numerous accounts in current social theory that are concerned with how identity is now made through a constant push to narrativize and psychologize one's own life. The search for individuality through consumer and commercial culture is accompanied by various regimes of self-government and self-inspection. These newer forms of the making of contemporary subjectivity are explored here as intricate mappings between text and subject that are discursively *accomplished* through pragmatic actions.

Feminism, Television, and Subjectivity

Questions of subjectivity have always been central to the feminist contribution to understanding the role of television in the lives of women. They have often been evoked to take issue with popular, and sometimes academic, derisions of feminine pursuits seen in the light of the larger "mass culture as feminine" debate discussed in chapter 1. Feminist researchers have attempted to "rescue" denigrated genres in keeping with feminist imperatives to document and validate women's cultural pleasures, however looked down upon by mainstream elitists. This chapter continues this vector of debate but argues that female practices of viewing should not only be dignified but also be seen as a crude lever in shifting the balance between the public and the private, exploiting the possibilities of TV to make new kinds of bridges between the two.

Reception analyses of feminine genres pivot around a common question: "How does audience reception interact with the construction of gender at the level of identity formation, subjectivity and discourse?" (Van Zoonen, 1994:108). Research on television preferences have suggested that women have a tendency towards "soft" genres, based upon emotion, melodrama and so on, while men have preferred "hard" genres related to factual programming. (Morley, 1986; Gray, 1992). This has made work on soap opera "representative of, or typical of, the Western second-wave feminist engagement with the media and popular culture generally" (Brunsdon, 2000:19). As we have seen, it was Brunsdon's early textual work on *Crossroads* that suggested that the gendering of soap opera is related to the text's dramatization of the "cultural competences" that women inhabit in everyday life by deploying "cultural knowledge of the socially accepted codes and conventions for the conduct of personal life" (1981:10). Since then, there have been a number of audience studies that have argued that it is this connection with the personal and private world that has dominated women's attachments to popular media. For example, Janice Radway's (1984) work suggested that reading the romance was connected to the negotiation of daily experience in relation to familial and marital relationships within a patriarchal order. Ien Ang's (1985) research asserts that watching *Dallas* offered an "emotional realism," whereby the emotional predicaments of characters resonated with the subjective experiences of women viewers: "What is recognized as real is not knowledge of the world, but a subjective experience of the world: a 'structure of feeling'" (1985:45). Similarly, Dorothy Hobson (1991) argued that soap operas function for women as a vehicle to talk about their own lives in what Liebes and Katz (1990) call a "referential mode" of viewing whereby the personal is integrated into the viewing experience with comments like, "that man is like my boss" or "I would never behave like Pamela." They suggest that "viewers related to characters as real people and in turn relate these real people to their own real worlds" (1990:100). Other nuances in this work suggested that this "relational" viewing style was more likely to belong to working-class female viewers, while middle-class women were more like likely to adopt a critically distanced viewing strategy (Press, 1991). On the whole, however, studies recurrently found that working-class women tended to project the television series onto their own lives.

If the focus on television and subjectivity was initiated with research into the soap opera in the late 1980s and early 1990s, then the next generation of programming to take on this baton is the talk show. For Hobson, the soap opera offered a space for female audiences to talk about their personal lives, while the talk show simply cut out the expensive cast bill and elevated the audience to the stage. As we have seen in chapter 1, talk show critiques take highly polarized positions. On the one hand, talk shows are holy: a democratic forum bringing the private world into public discourse (Carpignano et al., 1990; Squire 1994). On the other hand, they are seen as unholy: ideologically repositioning social issues as personal dilemmas (McLaughlin, 1993; Peck, 1995). There is a remarkable resemblance between reception analyses of soap operas and talk shows. For instance, Engel Manga's (2003) work with women viewers of talk shows suggests that some shows are seen to offer "legitimate" discourses that strike chords with everyday experiences whereby the women encounter these shows as "*enacting* discourse" about relevant issues with which they can identify.

As outlined in chapter 5, Livingstone proffers that studying the gendered differences of audience responses to talk shows "allows for the grounding of these arguments [about the public sphere, the media, and feminist theory] in the actual practices of everyday life" (1994:433). In her study of male and female audience interpretations of talk shows, she concludes that the women's more favorable appreciation of the genre is a response to their modes of reasoning, which are contextually founded, rather than the abstract moral judgments that belong to traditionally masculine forms of rational debate and that condition men's more negative responses to the genre. While the men in her research were generally seeking consensus and abstracted solutions to the problems laid out in talk shows, women tended to appreciate the personal and situational narratives being expressed. Livingstone begins to open up the relationship between television and the way in which the self is articulated in contemporary culture. Employing Benhabib's (1992) critique of postmodern ethics, she argues that in this process of empathizing with positions put forward, women viewers are engaging in processes of "position-ing the self." This is an interesting development, but it still barely tells us of the precise forms (stories, narratives, discourses) of "positioning" that the women evoke in their appreciation of the text. This chapter aims to supply the detail of the interplay between text and local experience. By focusing intently on the dynamic emergence of the text/subject relationship, it takes a fresh look at the relationship between television programming and its role in the formation of subjectivities of women viewers.

Reflexive Subjects

The increasing proliferation of contemporary media means that they offer, normatively and daily, points of comparison for the making of the self in its private/public interface. In relation to television in particular, John Ellis has suggested that our involvement in television as an audience is one of continu-ously "working through": "Yet even for the most isolated viewer, broadcast television's sense of being-together [while being apart] is the basis of working through, the open process of turning over social meanings which has become such a feature of the everyday programming of the age of availability, from daytime talk to infotainment to docu-soap" (2002:177).

Helen Wheatley suggests that a similar process is encouraged in the gen-dered address of gothic drama, in which the unheimlich juxtaposition of fear and the home asks the female viewer to "worry at" their possible resonances with the image (Wheatley, 2006). What might this "working through" (or "worrying at"), which Ellis describes as simultaneously an individual and collective process, have to tell us about the *ways* in which the media has a role in the contemporary formation of self? Ellis's description of "working *through*" tends to imply that an end point may be found, while Wheatley's phrase implies an ongoing set of relations that fits better with continually regenerative processes of self-reflexivity in contemporary social thought. Recent literature points to modernity as an age in which the "reflexive project of the self" is part of encroaching and continuous processes of individualiza-tion as the direct result of changes in social relations (Giddens, 1991a, 1991b; Beck, 1992). Much work in sociology describes identity as therefore "in crisis," "fragmented," "narcissistic," "situated," or "saturated." Plummer usefully pulls these various terms together, explaining the collective gist of this movement: "What lies at the heart of this enormous outpouring of writing about 'the modern human being' is the idea that a highly individuated, self-conscious and unstable identity is replacing the old, stable, unitary self of traditional communities. These new selves are 'constructed' through shifts and changes in the modern world, and partly create a new sense of permanent identity crisis. The search for 'understanding' and making sense of the self has become a key feature of the modern world" (2001:83).

This process is accompanying, and is partly produced through, the shift of cultural practices from the sphere of work to the realm of consumption. Leisure pursuits, life-styling processes, and therefore *media consumption,* are becoming more central to the processes of constructing and negotiating identity than in older, context-bound forms of social organization.[1] The key thinkers of this "individualization thesis" suggest that this process takes place through the re-negotiation of "expert systems,"[2] contemporary mediators that reinforce a conceptualization of the subject as a reflexive individual rather than as part of a collective social organism. For Lash and Urry, aspects of the media are powerful in the "re-subjectivization of space": "What we want to add to this is the importance of *aesthetic* 'expert systems' of the use of film, quality television, poetry, travel and painting as mediators in the reflexive regulation of everyday life" (1994:54, my emphasis).

Despite the proliferation of these arguments in sociological thought, the literature on television's relationship with its audiences rarely seeks to locate findings about self-referentiality within these broader social shifts. I want to identify particular mechanisms of the dialectical interplay between text and subject to argue that the relationship between television viewing and subjectivity might not only be related to particularly gendered forms of referential viewing, but may also be transformed by broader processes at work in the (post)modern project of selfhood.

The ubiquity of mediated culture must make it significant to any fully comprehensive understanding of modern subjectivity. But television use is incorporated into arguments about consumption and identity as though it were any other manufactured product. Indeed, in media reception analysis there has been, for some, a shift from describing viewers as "readers" of texts to "consumers" of products (Morley and Silverstone, 1990). This might involve making a semiotic choice about a wide-screen, silver, or black television as a statement of who you are or aspire to be as a marker of your lifestyle choices in "the aestheticisation of everyday life" (Featherstone, 1991). Or, consumer decisions involving aesthetic judgments between what Lash and Urry (1994) call "quality television"—between *ER*[3] and *Brideshead Revisited,* perhaps— might also offer significant cultural symbolic resources (and capital) to the negotiations of selfhood.

Useful as this may be, I wish to pursue a different track. It is not difficult to see that making choices about television as an object, or between programs as products, are different processes from those at work when actually watching televisual events. Much of the work in the feminist tradition that I described earlier maintains a notion of televised communication as "text," and not "product," in order to analyze the "text-reader" relationship. While the dialectic of "text-reader" still has its limitations of the kind I have described in earlier chapters,[4] regarding reception as "consumption" in the ways described above inevitably bypasses observations of media texts' more specific intervention in negotiations of subjectivity. I want to examine much more closely how connections between textual products and subjectivities are made and reproduced. Are television texts simply mirrors that consumers/readers hold up to reflect their daily selves? How does that work? How might we as researchers tap into the ways in which television texts, in this instance, hook into daily life and experience? Which forms and what textual strategies connect with which people about what moments of their subjective experience? How is this taken up in the performance of their identities?

Recall that during the interviews the women produced much the same kinds of referential statements that previous studies of women's television consumption have offered. For example:

HELEN: Do you think people like listening to other people's problems?
JENNY: erm yeh because they can relate to them ca::n't they really and think oh yeh I'm in that situation or I know someone in that situation a:nd if you have got a problem of your own and you're sitting there listening to it and you think o:h perhaps I'm not *so* bad after all you know.

Jenny here is clearly expressing the ways in which television discourses about other people's problems can be used to position oneself more favorably against "others'" experiences. Ideologically this might have the effect of masking women's "real" position within society, placating dissatisfaction that might otherwise be related to stratified inequality. But in terms of the self, it also offers a space within which to articulate oneself and, to some extent, possibly realize a version of self where one might not have been visible. For example, in the next extract recall that Angela clearly feels a point of contact with another woman represented in the program, whose child won't stop crying:

HELEN: How do you feel when people get upset?
ANGELA: That one the other day upset me. That woman who aborted the baby ten years ago (3) and there was one not long back on cry babies and *she's* a cry baby [**gestures to her youngest daughter in the room**] and they'd got this baby on that was really, re:::ally crying and that upset me 'cos I got reminded me what she: was like and I nearly rang in then cos that—to say to that woman if she need someone to talk to (.) but I didn't.

The difference between this extract and the first is that Angela locates a specific instance, a *moment* in which her own experience became publicly realized as shared in a curious public/private context as "real." It is the kind of articulation that can easily be mapped onto the formulation of the "referential mode" of viewing. In this book such moments are significant, because they indicate particular resonances, points of action, produced through the relationship with the broadcast text at the time of viewing. Here I want to take a detailed look at how this relationship is specifically produced.

The Life of the Text in the Life of the Home

As we have seen in the previous chapter, all of the women in the study talked throughout the programs and made many comments that related to their personal and everyday experiences in ways that approximate a face-to-face conversational imperative. Interestingly, as well as interjections and utterances, the women produced their own stories and explanations of experiences invoked by the studio discussion. According to Plummer, the start of the twentieth century was characterized by an unprecedented proliferation in the telling, witnessing, and, importantly, recording of life stories. It has "become such a voluminous business that we could even start to talk of something like an 'auto/biographical society': life stories are everywhere" (2001:78). He goes on to locate the proliferation of life narratives within those historical shifts brought about through accelerated industrialization. The realization of a "possessed" individual, in a movement away from other structures of organization and government, means that such personal narratives take on new meaning. In offering an interpretation of one of the contemporary ways in which the media is directly involved in the production of selfhood, here two of the richest and most interesting examples from my data are analyzed. The extracts below are example of "moments of television" in which the viewing experience produces extraordinary accounts of subjectivity.

Extract 1. Alice watching *Kilroy*, May 14, 1996, discussion program on "Should the elderly pay for their own care?"

		Studio		Home
1	Valerie	. . . what is happening is very sick		
2		people are being discharged from		
3		hospital forcibly when they have no		
4		statutory rights to do that into		
5		residential homes. Social services	Alice	that's what happened
6		have no statutory rights, no lawful		to my dad
7		rights to do that		they wanted to send
8	Kilroy	But that's Valerie that may or may		'im home from hospital
9		not be happening but I thought the		and we refused to

10		argument, I thought-
11	Valerie	but it is happening
12		**[audience noise]**
13	Kilroy	I know, I know but we also know
14		Valerie as a fact that there are a lot
15		of elderly people in hospital
16		blocking up beds who don't need
17		medical care
18	Valerie	There are NOT!
19	Kilroy	Well there are [Valerie
20	Valerie	[In my ca[se-
21	Kilroy	[But that's
22		not what we're arguing about is it
23		now?
24	Valerie	(?)
25	Kilroy	What we're arguing about is
26		whether or not those who have
27		the means should be expected to
28		pay for their own care
29	Expert	Their answer as you've heard
30		**[audience noise]**—not for health—
31		we're talking about care
32	Expert	Their answer as you've heard is
33		that they have been paying. We're
34		not talking about people with the
35		most expensive homes. Many of
36		them are looking after themselves
37		now, without resorting to nursing
38		homes. My starting point is that
39		both sides of parliament have now
40		accepted that the present
41		arrangements are wrong .hhh my
42		concern is that there are victims
43		of the present arrangement over
44		forty thousand of [them elderly
45	Valerie	[YES
46	Expert	People all .hh had their homes sold
47		Above their heads
48	Valerie	Last year and again
49		tens of thousands=
50	Kilroy	=so what should
51		have happened? What should, so
52		hang on Alf, what should have
53		have happened?
54		These people who-

take him home
it was awful but
I mean I sort
of live twenty
miles away from mom
I've got a car
to keep popping
over, he couldn't
get up and down
the stairs, he kept
leaving the taps
on, the cooker
on, he's burnt
all the carpets
you know well
Mom just couldn't
cope so-
but the doctor was
clearly under pressure
in hospital to vacate
the bed as soon as he
got a little better
physically, you know
they wanted him out.
No, but we thought if
he goes home we could see
mom dying first when really
she's well to a certain degree
but she's frail, she's eighty-three
and she's gone quite frail.
She couldn't pick him up when
he fell. He wouldn't let
a neighbor come round
and pick him up it
had to be a member of the
family .hhhh
My sister-in-law happens
to live close before
now has had to get the
kids out of bed because my brother
wasn't there, put them
in the car to drive down
'cos mom just couldn't pick
him up and he went mad when
mum tried to get the

55	let's say it was me and I've got this	neighbors in. So it was going
56	expensive house and I now need	from bad to worse so I really
57	nursing care—not National Health	sympathize with some of these
58	Service treatment but nursing care.	people
59	. . .	

Alice is watching an episode of *Kilroy* about the cost and responsibility of caring for the elderly, a program that resonates quite strongly with her current situation as she has an elderly father who needs professional care, but her family does not have the means for a private residential home. When a speaker discusses the problems about the elderly being discharged from hospital, Alice recognizes a similar experience in her own life. She opens with the preface "that's what happened to my dad" (line 5), which allows her to begin her own story. The subsequent extract represents an intricate weaving of both personal experience and validation of the point of her story in relation to the televised discourse. The subjective account is dynamically evoked through the experience of the broadcast.

While the host, Robert Kilroy-Silk, at line 8 is questioning whether or not discharging the elderly from hospital "may or may be not be happening," Alice is embarking upon *her* story that supports the validity of the studio speaker's (Valerie's) point, by offering her own personal evidence. Between lines 7 and 10 Alice produces an abstract of the story, "they wanted to send him home from hospital . . .," which clearly relates to the development of the studio debate. Alice stresses how "awful" it was as the studio speaker attempts to reinforce that "it *is* happening." Here Alice is announcing the difficulties of her real experience and locates it within broader suggestions from the studio that this might be a shared experience. She is establishing the primacy of her subjectively "lived" experience as part of her experience of watching the program.

When Kilroy again at lines 15–16 argues that elderly patients are "block-ing up beds," Alice tells the story of the dangers of her father being at home (lines 12–26). She acknowledges Kilroy's point about the pressure on National Health Service hospital beds, " but the doctor was clearly under pressure . . ." (line 27), negotiating the position put forward in the text, and then returns to her explanation of her parent's situation and her ongoing concern for the health of both of them. This announces the broader picture about the health and well being of other family members in relation to the doctor's diagnosis of her father. There is another story embedded here about her sister-in-law getting called out to her parents' house during the night, beginning at line 46. Here Alice is comparing her role with that of her sister-in-law. She is work-ing through her gendered identity as a caregiver for her elderly father; note how she discusses her sister-in-law's actions and not her brother's. Finally, she produces an evaluation of the situation, "it was going from bad to worse" (lines 55–56) and then ultimately her personal coda, "so I really sympathize with some of these people" (lines 56–58), whereby she connects herself to other members of the studio audience. Here, and elsewhere while watching the program, she evaluates her own position on the studio topic in terms of her own personal experience.

To suggest that Alice is "deconstructing" the meaning of the text in the conventional terms of reception research rather eludes the dynamism at work here. Neither the text's discourse nor that produced by Alice are stable entities. Relating one's own subjective experience to the discourse produced in the studio occurs here through a negotiated series of pragmatic moves and it appears more like a series of "acts" in a dialogic encounter than in the encoding and decoding of meaning. In this dialogic interplay, the self is induced into these extraordinary discursive moments. Nikolas Rose (1989), in *Governing the Soul*, has argued that we have become "intensely subjective beings" shaped by a number of forces in Western culture that have institutionally and organizationally conditioned practices of self-inspection, reflection, and self-government. Drawing on Foucault, he claims that "technologies of the self" are invested historically through, for example, national roles produced by government during wartime, organizational structures of working, strategies in management and workplace communication, and psychological interventions into childhood and family life. While Rose's work insists on a governmental approach that is not necessarily intended to inform empirical work on the ways in which this powerful discursive practice might be embodied, it is possible to take from his work the phenomenological suggestion that these new formations of subjectivity are also produced through greater emphases on "intersubjective" relations. In discussing psychology's contribution to the greater regulatory interventions into family life, he suggests that "personal desires have been caught up in social networks of power and control, shaped and organized through images and criteria provided by professional technicians of subjectivity and intersubjectivity" (1989:151). He suggests that influences from psychology upon modern family life have forced a greater inspection of our selves in terms of our relationships and interactions with others, referencing the dominance of therapy in popular culture as contributing to this phenomenon. In the talk show domain, "experts" advise on what one should "normally" feel in any given situation and as a result of these interventions into our "selves," Rose says that we have become, "educated in therapeutic discourses of the emotions, one that, we can use to turn our own 'cases' into stories . . . we learn a language and a technique, a

way of selecting, mapping and interpreting certain modes of interchange . . .
we learn to make ourselves manageable . . . through our identifications with
a narrative of the emotions . . . hence obtaining the capacity to construct our
own endings to the soap operas of our lives" (1989:253).

It is possible to see these relational experiences of television viewing as
operating in this way. Alice employs a mode of mapping her experience
onto the discussion occurring in the studio. She negotiates her experience
intersubjectively through a number of discursive moves: firstly with Valerie,
whose particular points she supports; secondly against Kilroy, who questions
their position; thirdly, with the institutional face of the National Health Service; fourthly, as a daughter whose gendered duty it is to care for her parents;
fifthly, sharing experiences with her sister-in-law as another female caregiver;
and then finally in her coda with those in the studio who also cannot afford
care, arguably her mediated working-class counterparts.

What is specific here, and why critics have been so concerned with issues
of the talk show and the public sphere, is that these intersubjective negotiations are produced in a domestic space that is particular to daily broadcasting, rather than the more rare opportunity at a co-present public event. One
might argue, though, that this example works particularly well because the
viewer fortuitously, for the researcher, has a personal insight into the studio
discussion taking place. This could never be built into the research design, as
the contents of talk shows, due to their daily repetition, are never published.
The resonances that this program and others may have had with the subjects
of my study are mostly due to the gendering of the genre, its mode of address, and sometimes the choice of topic in production stages that mirror
contemporaneous issues, often taken from the news. However, in extract 2,
arguably a more complex negotiation of subjectivity takes place where the
topic of discussion produces the configuration of the subjective identity of
the viewer in a more convoluted way.

**Extract 2. Bette watching *The Time . . . The Place*, June 12, 1996, discussion program
on "fathers' rights"**

		Studio	Home
1	John S	. . . say for example the parent, and	
2		it's not the case with this chap, say	
3		say for example that the parent had	
4		beaten the mother, you're still	
5		saying that the child should see that	
6		father?	
7	Woman 1	Yes I am yes	
8	John S	Yes	

#				
9	Woman 2	Why?		
10	Woman 1	Because I think it's important for the children—		
11		the mother		
12		and father	Bette	I've gorra butt in 'ere I mean
13		should keep their differences away		I have
14		from it all		
15	Woman 2	I agree with that completely that the		
16		parents erm agendas should not		
17		come into it that it should only be		
18		based on the child's welfare		
19	John S	Mary, you, you work [in this field		
20	Man 1	[yeh, yeh I—		
21	John S	sorry		
22		I'm going to Mary first.		
23	Mary	Yes I'm president of the Network of		
24		Access and Child Contact		
25		Centres and I would echo		
26		what you say	Bette	[looks out of her window onto
27		because often the problem		the street]
28		between two parents, not between the parent		we've got, we've got
29		and child and in contact centres		er two, three, four
30		we can actually keep the		we've got five
31		parents apart and I've seen a family		families in exactly
32		where they've come for years		the same situation
33	John S	[to woman 2] Would you consider		here exactly (.) Diane's
34		that?		husband is a
35	Woman 2	er my ex-partner and I have no		drunken alcoholic
36		problems with each other what-so-		drug-taking person
37		ever		Sally's husband is
38	John S	He's happy with the arrangement?		er—he's got married
39	Woman 2	Well he understands it and accepts it		again—nice guy
40		and he is also aware of how		he just decided
41		damaging his behavior is		he wasn't avin
42	John S	But do you think Samuel will thank		anymore he just
43		you both- [both of you because you		decided one day
45	Woman 2	[erm we come to the same		well he was
46	John S	You're both		very much in
47	Woman 2	decision erm that's one of the reasons		the minority ere
48		why I wanted to do this		because he's black
49		program because as I said to (?)		but 'e's a lovely
50		this is a very lonely decision and I can		man- 'e bent
51		only do what I feel in my heart		over backwards to
52		is best for my child I don't know.		welcome us into
53	John S	But you're doing what you think is		the avenue but
54		right.		he was so

55 Woman 2 I'm doing what I [think's right
56 John S   L[ady there and then the
57   gentleman here, yes
58 Woman 3 Yes, you say that it's the <u>right</u> of a
59   father to see a child well I don't
60   believe being a parent is a right I think
61   it's a role that we have to play;
62   It's not a right we have to that child we
63   it's a role we have a huge
64   responsibility. It's the most vital role
65   we will play in life and erm being
66   parent and giving a child
67   everything that they need, not what
68   they want, what they need, should
69   come naturally as should the ability to
70   always put your child first
71   because children are so
72   impressionable, they need to feel
73   secure, loved, wanted they need
74   emotional stability and most of all
75   they need love=
76 John S   = Does your child see
77   his or her father?
78 Woman 3   No, no now that's through his
79   choice he hasn't made contact
80   he's only ten months
81 John S   Your partner's choice?
82 Woman 4 yes to me that proves he's not a father
83   because as a father or a mother .hh
84   you have your child's
85   best interests at heart and if he loved
86   her and cared for her he
87   would be there if there's anything my daughter
88   needs he would be
89   part of her life
90 John S   You would like her to see him would
91   you?
92 Woman 4 Well, erm now, now he's been away
93   for so long I mean he has two
94   teenage children whose lives he's
95   walked in and out and in and out of
96   and those children- I mean the
97   emotional damage irrepair-
98   unrepairable. You never get over
99   things like that.

isolated you know
away from all
his—he came
from [Westhampton]
from a black area
to Forest Avenue
where there are
few black people
in [Chinnock] you
know and I
thought "God how
nice" cos I'm
not a bit racist
at all you know
I mean people
are all the same
no matter
what color
they are (.)
Take that woman [woman 3]
for instance
why:: if the
dad's gone and
pissed off and
left her- you've
gotta fill the
place of a father
you know could
you see 'er
goin' playin' football
or takin' them
to the baths er er
on the pure
assumption of
just lookin' at
'er (.) Do you
see what I'm
gettin at? You
know you can
fill the father's place.
Sally plays
out with the
kids she plays
kickin' the football
and takes them everywhere

100	John S	So, are you saying that your, your	which is the way I'd have
101		child can do without this particular	had it you know.
102		dad?	Men I would
103	Woman 4	What I'm saying- I'm not saying a	(?)
104		child doesn't need a father if a man	That's because I'm
105		knows how to be a good father and	gay I mean I've
106		puts the child before himself and gives	gotta get that
107		the child what she or he	over to you
108		needs then a child should have a father	I don't know if
109		but until Adrienne's father	Julie told ya
110		is capable of giving her what she	I can see things
111		needs, putting her before himself,	different that's
112		giving ti- being available	why if these women
113		whether it's	they- I mean I love
114		six hundred mile away or in the	kids- but I can
115		same house until he's capable of doing	see:: where they're
116		that erm I don't want him to	goin' wrong
117		the damage to her that he's done to	(2)
118		his other two children	
119			Exactly!

In this example, Bette is watching a talk show program about fathers' rights to get access to children. At line 12 she suggests that she has to "butt-in," which marks her opinion upon the discussion taking place as important—it suggests that she is experiencing watching the program like a conversation. There is a pause here before Bette begins to articulate the relevance of the experience to her own life. At line 25, sitting near the window, she looks out on the street in which she lives. It is a small cul-de-sac on a council housing estate in "Chinnock" in the Midlands of England.

Bette begins to put forward her reflexive account of viewing through other "local" relationships by discussing the families on her street whose situations compare to the personal dilemmas being related in the studio. We begin to see the blurring of the televised text and her local life. She moves through a number of families and the social dysfunctions of Diane's husband (lines 33–34) but then extends sympathy to another absent father (Sally's husband, lines 37–50). This is significant to Bette's construction of her own subjectivity. She talks about her relationship with Sally's husband and how he "bent over backward to welcome us into the avenue" (lines 50–53). She discusses his isolation as a black man coming from a nearby city with a large black population into a predominantly white area. She then positions herself politically as not a racist (line 67) and then moves back to the broadcast text and to discussing a woman in the studio. Bette is suggesting that the woman should take on activities that are usually gendered and associated with fathers, like playing football or "takin' them to the [swimming] baths" (line 86) . . . "you can fill the father's place." Bette's implication is that by looking at the traditional feminine appearance of woman 3, who is talking about her child's father having no contact with her child, she may not be able to take on some of those activities that are "normally" fulfilled by a father. Bette then shifts back to her local life and to discussing Sally in her street, who she suggests does take on this role. This is significant because Bette then makes the subjective comparison, "which is the way I'd have had it you know" (lines 100–101), that is the kind of parent that she would have been.

These accounts of other people in the street and those in the studio are intersubjective moves whereby Bette is directly positioning herself. This is revealed in the moment in her account when these contexts fall into place and Bette reveals "that's because I'm gay" (line 105). We can now see her subjective position being built up through a series of discursive moves, negotiated though her relationships both locally and textually. She talks about her neighbors in the street because as a gay woman in her sixties, living with her same-sex partner and not having children, the topic of fathers' rights to see their children is not directly subjectively located within her immediate experience. These are not straightforward "referential" comparisons to her own life in the same way that previous authors have concluded about gendered programming. Bette here can still articulate her sense of self through her intersubjective relations with others. Through identifying Sally's black husband, who welcomes her and her partner into the street, she discursively creates a marker of affiliation, both realizing a marginalized position within a street that is mostly occupied by white heterosexual families. She is politically aware of this position as she makes clear her liberal attitude to difference. Then again, Bette articulates herself in relationship to woman 3 in the studio, whose point is that fathers *should* be involved with the rearing of their children. Bette is concerned that this might be supporting the gendering of roles that are traditionally expected of parents, a position that Bette, in her performance of herself as a gay woman, does not accept. Her identification of Sally as a good parent because she fills the role of the father is significant, as Bette compares her to the kind of parent that Bette would have been—one that can take on the attributes of both parents. Therefore, in relation to the program discussion about the expectations of the nuclear family, Bette constructs herself outside of culturally conceived conventions of family life and suggests that "she can see things different" (line 110) and can "see where they're going wrong" (line 116). Looking between her television screen and out of the window onto her street, Bette's gay identity makes her a knowing onlooker who can finally endorse woman 4 in the studio, who is concerned about the damaging effect of some fathers in the lives of their children, "Exactly!" she declares that someone has finally got it right.

Despite the personal framework of the program not directly encompassing Bette's actual personal experience in her own familial relationships, the text and the negotiation of subjectivity are complexly imbricated. Bette is able to deploy discursive techniques whereby she intricately negotiates her position intersubjectively between her experiences of both the textual and the local. The relationship in this particular example goes beyond simple "referential" mapping; rather, it is a modern self-reflexive production of subjectivity produced through these particular conditions of broadcasting.

Television Viewing and Self-Reflexivity

Since I argue that these research findings cannot wholly be explained by traditional recourse to the gendering of "referentiality" in viewing experience, I suggest their relevance to contemporary debates on modern self-reflexivity and gender performativity. My examples are reminiscent of Livingstone's (1994) observation that in watching talk shows women produce lengthy attempts at positioning the self, but more specifically these examples are dialectical products of the particular space offered by moments of television broadcasting. As we have seen in chapter 2, Giddens (1991a) argues that the modern environment, out of which the emphasis on self-reflexivity emerges, is affected by changes in the organization of space and time. We experience "empty time" where time and space are not bound together in the more stable arrangements of the pre-modern era. He refers to "time-space distanciation" as the dislocation of time from space wherein social systems are torn from their immediate and local contexts and redistributed: "By disembedding I mean the 'lifting out' of social relations from local contexts of interaction and their restructuring across indefinite spans of time and space" (1991a:21). Social relations are no longer confined to the local, as we can engage in interaction with distanced and absent speakers where co-present and co-spatial arrangements are no longer required. Although Giddens does not talk about the media specifically, he does point to what he calls the increased "mediation" of experience as our intimate forms of life are transmuted through global processes. His phrase "intimacy at a distance" might indeed begin to capture broadcasting's "reach" in these particular emotive encounters brought about by the technology of broadcasting. The concept of re-embedding is therefore useful to describe mediated encounters (Moores, 1995, 2000). It is "the reappropriation or recasting of disembedded social relations so as to pin them down . . . to local conditions of time and space" (Giddens, 1991a:79–80). What is at work here in these extracts is empirical evidence of the bringing about of reflexive subjectivity through the broadcast encounter. The women in my study are making use of the text as they view, "lifting out" the examples from the studio discussion and "recasting" them so as to "pin them down" to their local conditions of time (here, now) and space (my home, my street). They do this through negotiating intersubjective relations that are arguably encouraged through contemporary governmental discourses in popular genres such as "therapy" and "talk shows" (Rose, 1989), which are here evoked in the specific arrangements of time and space created by broadcast television viewing.

Conclusion

Seeing "texts in action" enables us to build a much more precise account of the mechanical relations between textuality and subjectivity in particular contexts. Doing so, in this instance, demands that we reconfigure what is occurring when women viewers make recourse to the personal in their appreciation of certain genres. Reflexive arrangements are not *only* produced out of competences that are culturally constructed as "womanly" because the women *are* women but the women are able to do gender as part of wider pressure where mediated selves are "positioned" through the "re"-grounding of traditional social arrangements as they have become detached from their local contexts. In this way the mediation of experience assists in the performance of gender identity.

Media reception needs to be further explored in relation to social change and modern processes of self-reflexivity, but this is not pursued through a focus on "aesthetics" (Lash and Urry, 1994) that might lead to a paradigmatic closure on the value and pleasures of women's practices. (Work on romance, soap opera, and talk shows emphasizes an "emotional realism" rather than an aesthetic one.) Soap operas, talk shows, and possibly now reality TV are forms that are popularly conceived as attractive to those with gendered "feminine"—not aesthetically valuable—tastes, and are therefore often omitted from an aesthetic framework. I focus rather on the ways in which broadcasting phenomenologically engages in the real time and space of viewers, where they pragmatically take part in the reflexive production of self. Subjectivity in these instances is therefore *accomplished* through a series of discursive actions occurring while the broadcast text is alive, not through aesthetic choices that are flatly appropriated. When Plummer argues that the life story has become increasingly represented and mediated through chat rooms, television, and film, he argues that, "In all this, the boundaries between life, media and the story of a life are seriously changing" (2001:98), and here we can see the boundary between the text/subject interface dissolving in a re-inflection of women's viewing behaviors as modern *acts* of self-reflexivity.

If particular relationships between texts and audiences are achieved through communicative acts, then this potentially opens up new questions about the dynamic way in which media forms are active in contemporary identity formation. The women's voices perform certain mediated communicative functions across broadcasting: questioning, reformulating, positioning. The nature of the genre constantly reiterates a hetero-normative frame where the women speak their roles as women, like the genre of gossip, which provides the *form* in which they respond. For Bette, a gay woman, she must complexly work out her relationship to the issue of absent fathers by outlining herself in relation to that hetero-normativity. Her performance of her identity is what ultimately makes sense of the position that she takes in relation to the text. This suggests that the discursive apparatus of daytime television, in this instance, works to encourage the women to practice and rehearse their gendered temporality alongside the temporality of broadcasting. This may offer moments of realization *and* capitulation to dominant norms as gender is more tenuously articulated. These findings are redolent of a more dynamic process at work in the interplay between media and identity than has previously been documented, and the conclusion of this book picks up the implications of this data for contemporary debates in media studies. I outline how these findings, which represent a type of mediated interactivity, begin to challenge some of the basic assumptions made in new media theory, and how feminist accounts of the politics of self-reflexivity begin to challenge some of the tenets of the individualization thesis. Finally, I suggest that it might be possible to use the metaphor of *mechanics* deployed here in order to unpack further the mediation of identities in the modern age.

Conclusion:
Media, Mechanics, and the
Politics of Self-Reflexivity

This conclusion speculatively draws together some of the implications of this research for media and cultural studies and feminism. Earlier chapters identified how a literary text-reader model applied to media research ultimately marginalizes a concern with the pragmatics of communication and fails to locate mediated communication within the broadest contexts of communication per se. This book has painted an alternative picture of the way in which broadcasting, and here in particular talk-based television, contributes to the gendering of the socio-communicative sphere of everyday life. It offers empirical evidence of the ways in which gender performativity can be mediated.

In a similar fashion, transitions to "new" media mean that academics are calling for shifts in our thinking in order to analyze forms of "connectivity," rather than analyzing systems of representation that are associated with "old" media. Within these positions there are radical suggestions that identity is being reproduced through an entirely different set of relations between the subject and new media than those that existed in the mass media era. However, there are some dangers inherent in the way those proposals are being made to separate out "old" and "new" media. I suggest that these arguments are grounded in techno-centrism and driven by some of the dominant narratives of media studies. This book has tried to account for an alternative approach to the communicative aspects of mediated interaction, but it is also important to assert that the analysis of media as "ritual" forms of communication does not necessarily lead us back to a simply functionalist description of how the media meets certain human needs. This conclusion argues that establishing the communicative *mechanics* of how broadcasting works, in these findings through gendered processes of sociability and self-reflexivity, illuminates important questions about the politics of mediated communication that might be applicable to other media and other audiences.

New media scholars are suggesting a need to move beyond the analysis of semiotic meaning systems to account for changes in the relationship between media and audiences. These observations come to light through accounts of seismic shifts brought by new media technologies that necessitate a re-ordering of the concerns from the "old" media era, to the "new" media era. Mark Poster (1995), for example, announces a "second media age" in which the distributive capacities of new media fundamentally force new ways of thinking. For example, the "one-to-many" communication principle of the mass media (broadcast) era is arguably being replaced by the "many-to-many" model of the digital (Internet) era. Such a position is characterized by Kapor, who suggests that the crucial political question is "Who controls the switches?" "There are two extreme choices. Users may have indirect or limited control over when, what, why and from whom they get information and to whom they send it. That's the broadcast model today, and it seems to breed consumerism, passivity, crassness, and mediocrity. Or users may have decentralized, distributed, direct control over when, what why and with whom they exchange information. That's the Internet model today, and it seems to breed critical thinking, activism, democracy, and quality. We have an opportunity to choose now" (1993:5, cited in Poster, 1995). There are, of course, numerous optimistic accounts of the new media era that herald its democratic potential. These suggest non-linear models of new communications technologies, decentering the founding ideas surrounding the "mass media" and its ideological power. This is mostly because there is new potential for "users" (and not readers) to become message makers too in the re-distributive "network" of production. Some commentators, like Scott Lash (2002), even suggest that we need to reorient our thinking around "information flows" in the new networked era, where we have moved into a technological culture. Whereas, in the older era of representation there is clear distance between the cultural representation, the object it represents, and the subject (the audience) setting up a particular set of relations, the information order is characterized by immanence where subjects become interfaces *within* the network of communication. Users are therefore positioned in relationship to their connectivity, rather than subject to texts' subject positionings that are relatively fixed. In this sense, the Internet age is characterized by a new relationship to proximity wherein subjects are implicated in the making of communication flows so that they no longer have any distance with which to reflect upon the "meaning" of particular types of information. In the contemporary age, the logic of information "flow" produces instability in any structure of meaning, thereby dissolving any systematic relationship between the signifier and signified, rendering semiotics rather redundant in the analysis of the politics of the (new) media. Thus Lash asks, "But what happens when speaking disengages from the organic being of language, and re-engages in a logic of flow? What happens when speaking becomes *parole* without *langue,* becomes performance in the absence of competence? What happens with a new hegemony of flow, of flows of utterances? We then ask less what words mean but instead what they do. How they perform" (Lash, 2002:216).

In his call for a technological phenomenology, Lash asks us to think about *action* rather than meaning. Similarly, in her plea for a mathematics of communication in the information era, Terranova suggests that information must be seen as having a physical and material force, arguing that the "*dynamics* of information take precedence over those of signification" (2004:55, my emphasis). But the problem here is that these arguments suggest a move "beyond" meaning, and if we accept them we are in grave danger of losing our purchase on "meaning" altogether. This seems absurd, since meaning is *also* generated in *action*. Elsewhere in this book we have discussed how understanding the pragmatics of communication enables an account not just of the semantics of *what* is said, but also an appreciation of how meaning is generated in specific contexts. Terranova suggests that we need to comprehend what she calls *tactics* of information: these might be force, timbre, repetition, and so on, and their various modes of distribution. These are features that may well be exaggerated in a more convoluted web of distributive systems in the new media environment, but that have resonance with the normative pragmatics of *any* type of communication.

My point here is to question why these observations have come to light only in the apparent retrospective accounts forced by the shiny "new" media. They suggest that we need brand new theoretical tools for newfangled technological capabilities. Freedman (2006) points to the deterministic nature of many of these accounts of new media, which read off actual uses of media technologies from their technical capacities. Perhaps this is partly because the aptitudes of new technology are quickly labelled, but other authors are beginning to account for the consistencies that new media maintain with the "old." For instance, Bolter and Grusin (2000) point to the ways in which apparent characteristics of the Internet and digital era have their precedents in older media forms of art, photography, and video. Key buzzwords such as *immediacy* and *interactivity* are bandied about as part of the new trappings of the digital era in which communication becomes instantaneous and dialogic. However, these terms have been key tropes throughout my audience research on broadcasting. Consider Paddy Scannell's (1996) historical account of similar features of early broadcasting, implying that broadcasting's intimate relationship with its audiences suggests the end, rather than the beginning, of the mass media era. It is clearly not simply the technology that suggests we re-route some of our media analysis into the politics and possibilities of performative action, although perhaps it may suggest we now need to ac-celerate our pace. New media change might put a new spin upon the ritual relationships with media that have *always* existed. It may be that all this time we have missed an opportunity to make ourselves better able to monitor how technological change impacts upon how meaning is made in forms of everyday communication in the first place, partly because we separated out forms of communication into distinct modes of inquiry.

Earlier chapters have argued that there is something to be learned from understanding the relationship *between* interpersonal communication and mediated communication as forms of communication in the broadest sense. Chapter 2 charted how media studies, particularly in the UK, was so in-fluenced by Marxist accounts of ideology and hegemony, based in a class politics of trying to understand processes of persuasion, that a concern for content and a demystifying of the media's messages was such a potent ana-lytical approach. This approach began by assuming that "mass reception" meant mass persuasion, while most work in reception studies has compli-cated such a broad assumption. Let us not disregard these important stages in the knowledge factory of our subject area, but it is important to argue that in the primary separating out of the distinction between langue and parole by Saussure, which led to the heralding of semiotics as our primary tool of analysis, we missed the opportunity to build another vital spine to media studies that had the ability to connect forms of mediated communication to everyday life and interaction—the relationship between the media and forms of "parole," as it were. So, when Lash asks those perplexed questions about what we do in a world of utterances wrenched out of stable meaning systems, the answer would have been more readily available had a complete body of knowledge on the pragmatics of mediated communication been available. It was not the technology that tripped us up in our analytical progress, but rather our theoretical legacies.

Of course, there are indeed significant shifts in terms of the dynamics that operate around the progression from print to broadcast and to Internet eras, but those shifts might be seen in terms of a series of continuities if we can be-gin to understand their place in the socio-communicative sphere. And clearly each shift does not eclipse the former entirely, despite the apocalyptic claims that were first made about the Internet (Freedman, 2006). Since our primary mode of communication is language, then different media are *also* merely ways of intervening in and potentially transforming its distribution, and of course that mediation is further complicated by the media's roles as institutions of power, just as power (institutional or otherwise) is normatively invested in *all* processes of communication. (Different media also offer us different types of involvement and action that need to be incorporated into the politics of pragmatics, whereas in this book I have focused mainly on speech.)

However, it is curious that in the history of media analysis there has always been an idealistic recourse to a primary model of communication based on face-to-face communication and interaction. As discussed above, major fears about the "mass media" were concerned about lack of reciprocity and its use as a one-way transmission mechanism. These concerns were therefore united with the idea that a truly democratic model of the media could only be based upon the authentic and primary model of conversation. As Durham Peters observes, Adorno, Brecht, Williams, Bourdieu, and Habermas are just some of the founding scholars who have called for mass media to become a "means of interactive public access" in the interests of "dialogic democracy" (Durham Peters, 2006:115). Similarly, those who herald the potential of digital media often do so because of its technical capacity for forms of interactivity. With classic humanist nostalgia, face-to-face communication is assumed as the primary, egalitarian model against which surrogate mediated communication is found wanting.

But it seems clear that these arguments claim too much for conversation itself, as though all that is needed is interactivity to gain democracy. One only needs to look at the huge bodies of literature in areas such as socio-linguistics and discourse analysis, some of which have been accounted for in this book, to understand that interaction of any sort is rarely without its own contextual power dynamics. While "talking back," according to bell hooks (1991), might well have offered a route outwards for black political action, let's remind ourselves of the discussion in chapter 1 of gossip, where talking at all for women might be characterized as "an index of their powerlessness" (McRobbie, 1982/1991).

In this light, the relationship between mediated communication and its face-to-face conversational ancestor needs considerable thought. It is clearly the case, as Durham Peters (2006) recounts, that the mass media has become increasingly conversational, and conversation itself has become increasingly mediated.[1] For some, the conversationalization of the media may be the antithesis of increased democracy, actually recruiting subjects to a dominant ideological agenda and in fact closing off the possibility of open debate (Fairclough, 1992, 1995). Indeed, the media's engagements in conversational styles are often also blamed for an apparent decline in "purer" daily conversation between individuals; recall the discussion in chapter 1 about how more talk on television was seen to be engulfing and eroding "true" debate. And in terms of the empirical research in this book we might be all too quick to assume that the conversations with television recorded here are sad, parodied substitutes for *real* discussion. The women's utterances are still contained in the domestic sphere, while they are given a feeling of participating in debate. This could be interpreted as phantom participation through which the women are ideologically repositioned as the silent masses, implying the pathology of this female audience caught up in a fake world of sociality. However, this does not entirely account for the complexity of the women's practices or give any credence to their discursive competences. Like Scannell, I would argue for the authenticity of these relationships. (Although "authenticity" is a troubled and politicized term in relation to feminized and classed forms of speech, a term that needs to be unpacked further in relation to media discourse.) But here let us recognize that in the contemporary era media technologies must force us to stretch our conceptualization of what we accept as conversation.

In earlier chapters, Goffman (1981) reminded us of the fact that everyday face-to-face conversation is rarely a straightforwardly dyadic relationship between speaker and hearer. Durham Peters reinforces this point: "Theorists who lament the decline of conversation are often too strictly normative in what they accept. Para-social interaction for instance should be relieved of its stigma as a psychic disturbance, however mild, which afflicts fans and immature people. Why is it a sign of mental illness to converse with entities that cannot quite reply—walls, books, oneself, or TV sets[?] . . . The concept of para-social interaction, in showing that people simulate conversation in imagined relationships, reveals something relevant for all social relationships, not just mediated ones. . . . Para-social interaction is only the tip of the iceberg—the ways in which we live amid exploded conversations, turns that never quite connect" (Durham Peters, 2006:120).

This book, therefore, represents, to my knowledge, the first research that actually documents para-social interaction with television as an empirical reality, while chapters 6 and 7 account for a broader communicative participation framework that establishes a "mediated conversation floor." However, it cannot be the case that *all* types of mediated conversation look this way. This is a particular type of programming and a very particular white, working-class, female audience. The rather loose discussion between whether these conversations are fake or authentic does not quite capture the potential for research here. The tip of the iceberg, so to speak, is to recognize para-social encounters as lived communication and part of social experience; the rest is to begin to document the myriad of ways, with different types of media, different genres, and with different groups of people, that these electronic interactions may take place.

However, this is not to suggest that what we will uncover in our efforts is a map of experiences that confirms a relative, if rich, tapestry of authentic mediated communication. Carey's (1989) distinction between "ritual" and "transmission" modes of communication, though it has been helpful here, is too simplified if we insist on those categories being mutually exclusive. Ritual forms of communication do communicate things in particular; it is just that one needs some knowledge of their *performative* functions in order to be able to grasp the complete meaning—in order to "get it." As linguists remind us, the semantics of language, what things come to *mean,* can only be documented descriptively and not prescriptively, precisely because of the dynamics of language in social change. Meanings dynamically evolve because of how they are deployed performatively, alive, in lived social relations. Volosinov clearly registered the relationship between the *action* of communication and its political force as diachronic (dynamic over time), rather than synchronic (stable over time). Recall the discussion in chapter 2, which cited his description of how *all* ideological phenomena "cannot be entirely segregated and divorced from the element of speech" (1973:15). In relation to media research, we might then be able to adopt more of his way of thinking if we try to understand why some people "get" certain media products and not others, if we think of the communication as "in motion," functioning diachronically *in time.*

Let us now briefly return to one of the observations made about the "new" information order. Terranova suggests that we have to think about the material and physical force of information, what she refers to as "tactics." This might be an interesting metaphor, but it is not necessary to call for this only on the basis of a move to a new technological information order, that is unless you saw the "old" information order as only an assemblage of texts. In language, *all* communication *always* maintains material and physical force as it is played out. The mediation of communication therefore *also* maintains a dynamic and material energy. In chapter 4 I called for an audience research methodology that could more accurately embrace the fact that broadcasting takes places, happens, physically *in time* by recording the experiential phenomena of "texts-in-action."

Therefore, further research needs to consider how different media establish their own particular spatial and temporal dynamics, which are rather different from reading a book, despite the fact that literary models have usually been used to gauge reception processes. Broadcasting establishes modes of physicality, environment, and senses of being for audiences, what Scannell (1996) refers to as the "doubling of place." Moores (2004) goes on to argue that we might also apply this concept to all electronic media, including the Internet, accepting pluralizing, rather than marginalizing, multiple senses of place. While this also suggests a concern with media geographies, I want to hold the dimension of physicality in tension with its operation in time—that is, to render useful a sense of the dynamic propulsion of media processes as they come into contact with audiences.

Hence my methodology included research into *moments* of television that could capture the physical engagement of audiences with the broadcast text "in-action." To some extent, then, if I *do* want to deal with the mathematics of communication, then I propose the metaphor of "mechanics," which is a "branch of mathematics dealing with motion and tendencies to motion" (*OED*). In this way this research captures another dimension of watching television that reveals the workings of what it means to "take part" or, you might say, "to get it," to be implicated here in daytime talk shows as communicative *events*. The text is not entirely received as a set of encoded signs that are decoded, but rather a set of performative practices that meaningfully come alive. In mechanics, a "mechanism" refers to a "system of mutually adapted parts working together; a mode of operation of a process" (*OED*), a definition that resonates with Bakhtin's focus on the utterance (discussed in chapter 2) as being able to "determine others' responsive positions" (1986:76), like the workings of parts mutually producing a communicative exchange. Applying this principle to media audiences enables us to see meaningful engagements between text and audience as dynamic and in process. In this case we see a series of activities that revolve around ritually communicative forms of sociality and self-reflexivity. These are the key mediated mechanisms at work. Therefore, in the data in chapters 6 and 7 we see how in the women's interactions with television they move discursively through different topical positions in relation to the program and their own lives, through the close imbrication of textuality and subjectivity. In Volosinov's sense, we can see how meaning is multi-accentuated and thus not necessarily stable over time. Rather than being determined to fix positions at each end of the communicative process, as we might have wanted to in traditional audience research, we can instead adopt the more fluid metaphor of mechanics to capture the "drive belts" of mediated communication and the potential social changes they beget.

Gender Politics and Self-Reflexivity

But does that mean that the whole process is simply dependent upon individual audience members and individual programs? Yes and no. Individually these women all produce a rather unique series of interpretations in terms of the *content* of what they say about and to the program in relation to their individual experiences; but collectively the mechanical *performative* process produces a similar discursive pattern that results in a particular process of self-reflexivity. Chapter 7 argued that we can see this reflexivity as resonating with arguments around time-space distanciation, whereby social relations are experienced as lifted out of local contexts and re-embedded across time and space. In this sense, we might see how electronic media contribute to the proclamations about a self-reflexive culture in which the story of a life becomes increasingly significant.

Therefore, it is not only the *content* of media that allows us to understand the politics of the televised discourse, but also the mechanical and pragmatic process that can reveal something of the power at work in the communicative exchange. If, in this particular research, the dialogic engagements lead to very particular kinds of self-reflexivity, then mediated self-reflexivity is the performative dynamic that requires investigation. Chapter 7 suggested that the women's complex negotiations can be seen as transformed by contemporary ideas about self-reflexivity, rather than being entirely explained in terms of traditional ideas about women's genres producing referential modes of viewing. I will take this point further by taking into account the politics of self-reflexivity.

This book has constantly kept in tension arguments about the gendering of discursive strategies and their relative power relations, with contemporary theories about the mediation of interaction and experience. The former suggests that the women's interactive engagements with television are part of their womanly competences as speakers who are positioned closely to the personal and intimate world, while the latter might suggest that these processes are rather bound up in contemporary social arrangements through which we are *all* called to reflexively narrate our lives as processes of "individualization." Indeed, using Giddens's account of self-identity in the modern age, as in chapter 7, might seem to suggest that the gendering of the process is less significant than its production as a disembedded social relationship. Giddens argues that, "The transformation of time and space, coupled with the disembedded mechanisms, propels social life away from the hold of pre-established precepts or practices" (1991b:20). By this he means that the traditional structural categories of social life established through industrialization, such as gender and class relations for example, become wrenched out of their local contexts and become marginal concerns relative to the self-reflexive process of individualization that is characteristic of modernity.

This presents a curious dynamic, one that situates women as potentially ahead of the game if we accept Giddens's and Beck's descriptions of the individualization thesis as a process in which we are all equally implicated, where "people are being removed from the constraints of gender" (Beck, 1992:105). As we saw in chapter 1, the entry of talk show discourse into the media arena has been seen by some to represent a growing feminization of the public sphere. In this way there is leakage between masculine and feminine worlds that becomes open to reflexive refashioning. Lisa Adkins (2002) describes how this can be seen in contemporary ethnographies of the workplace, where traditionally womanly reflexive skills are becoming economically and publicly valued, just as the more recent registering of human-interest stories in the news is seen to be doing the same for the mediated public sphere.

However, while the individualization thesis posits a freeing of agency from structure, it is clear that in this case the women's self-reflexive engagements with the programs are not entirely liberated from their gendered roles. The mediation of the experience may make it a disembedded phenomenon, but that does not mean that it has wrestled free from a gendered process. In many of the cases the women's responses are framed very much within their traditional relational identities as mothers, caregivers, wives, partners, and so on. They are after all responding to a genre that usually reinforces relatively conservative norms in relation to gendered and hetero-normative expectations of domesticity and femininity. A growing body of work in sociology is questioning some of the basic tenets of the individualization thesis, even suggesting that modes of self-reflexivity actually often serve only to re-traditionalize and remake class and gender (Lury, 1998; Adkins, 2000; Skeggs, 2004). According to Skeggs, "Individualization cannot be anything but a cultural process involving differentiation from others and differential access to resources" (2004:53). In relation to the growing phenomenon of reality television, the emphasis upon self-representation is often seen as representative of neo-liberal effects of individualization (Dovey, 2000), but Wood and Skeggs (2004) argue that the ways in which the individual gets reproduced for the formats of television only re-route class and gender distinctions through a focus on morality.

Importantly, Lisa Adkins (2003) begins to question any essential link between self-reflexivity and individualization, suggesting that there are embodied aspects of identity that operate at a pre-reflexive level and therefore cannot easily be reflexively remade. In any case, Adkins points out that women are more immanently positioned in relation to reflexivity, which in her case study meant that it was difficult for women in the workforce to be seen to deploy reflexivity as a skill for promotion; rather it was seen that it is something that they should "naturally" be predisposed to undertake. Hochschild's (1983) analysis of flight attendants makes similar arguments about the unequal position of women employees when they are assumed to effortlessly carry out the labor of care. Adkins insists that a more grounded exploration of self-reflexivity would reveal how it is embodied within gendered action in actual life-world scenarios. Thus, reflexivity is often aligned more closely to habit rather than the freedom of gender: "Reflexivity does not concern a liberal freedom from gender, but may be tied into new arrangements of gender" (Adkins, 2003:26).

This book therefore describes how disembedded mechanisms of socia-bility and self-reflexivity routinely re-route gendered discursive practices. In the discussion of the discourse of the programs in chapter 3, and how the women associate with those discourses in chapter 5, these practices are experienced as an embedded set of routine and ubiquitous domestic habits. This is a type of "everyday" reflexivity that is at once transformed by, but is also in tune with, the mediated conditions of heightened modernity. In Rita Felski's (2000) analysis of the invention of everyday life she is critical of the way in which it has traditionally been associated either with mundane isolation or with resistance and subversion, which indeed seems to reflect the available positions with which we might want to force this conclusion. For Felski, the quotidian space of home has been seen as "existing outside the flux and change of an authentically modern life" while it is central to women's definitions of modernity. She continues, "A feminist theory of ev-eryday life might question the assumption that being modern requires an irrevocable surrendering from home, and might simultaneously explicate the modern dimensions of everyday experiences of home" (2000:26). Therefore, while Meyrowitz (1986) suggested that the private/public interface produced by modern media must at once begin to transform gender relations, here the mediation of home becomes a shared and *doubled* space, rather than a "non-space." The disembedded self-reflexive arrangements do not therefore "propel" the women out of their normative gender relations, but rather allow them to be experienced as multiplied and diffuse.

Through attempting to craft a picture of the socio-communicative sphere of daytime television in everyday life, this analysis has made visible the me-chanics of gendered forms of mediated sociality and self-reflexivity in the modern age. These are specific mediated social relationships that are ob-viously not the same as non-mediated forms, and are transformed by the process of broadcasting, but they are also re-embedded into daily routines in relatively traditional ways. This suggests that we need to explore how mediated communication can offer the potential to transform, relocate, or share social relationships, and begin to establish the power relationships at work in those relations as mechanics of communication. A focus upon the pragmatics of mediated communication, like this exploration of the gendering of talk on daytime television, might allow us insights into the varied, yet powerful ways in which we are dynamically implicated in the politics of mediated connectivity as it is embedded within the broader communicative web of everyday life.

Appendix:
Biographies of the Women

Here are details about the women involved in the study and information about their lives, backgrounds, and relationship to each other at the time of the empirical stage of the research. All of the women lived in or near "Chinnock," almost all attended the local Catholic Church, or were in some way connected to the community.

Polly

My mother. She is married to my father, an electrician, is in her early sixties and lives in her own home in a small village on the outskirts of "Chinnock." She has three adult children who at the time of the empirical phase of the study were thirty-four, thirty-two, and twenty-four. She has been a housewife since her children were born but used to work as a dinner lady at the local primary school. She is a committed member of the church Ladies Guild and until recently ran the Brownie Guide Pack with Eve, another member of the research group. She acted as the "gatekeeper" in my study, sounding out the Ladies Guild before my attendance, and helped in arranging interviews and providing the venue for the focus group. She knows all the women in the study, some of whom are her close friends and two of whom are her sisters— Sandra and Eve. Polly was involved in the focus group, but I chose not to interview my mother (unlike Hermes, 1995), because I felt that watching television with my mother presented another, too powerful, influence over the research findings.

Sandra

She is married, in her mid-fifties, with a nineteen-year-old son, and lives in her own home in a small village on the outskirts of "Chinnock." She and her husband, a self-employed driving instructor, are actively involved in the local Catholic Church. They are both "lay" ministers and regularly administer communion to the sick of the parish. Sandra is a key member of the Ladies Guild and takes a lead role in the organizing of their events. She is also a member of the Women's Royal Voluntary Service and delivers "meals-on-wheels" to elderly in the area. She also works part time as a school cleaner at the local high school. She is sister to Eve and Polly, and aunt to me. She is good friends with Patricia, Myra, Cathy, Alice, and Jana. She took part in an interview and a focus group.

Eve

Eve is married, in her late fifties, and lives in her now privately owned council house on an estate also in the same village as Sandra. Her husband is retired due to ill health, and she has two grown-up sons who have both left home but live close by. She is also actively involved in the local Catholic Church and is a member of the Ladies Guild. At the time of the interviews she was also "Tawny Owl" of the Brownie Guide Pack. She too is a member of the Women's Royal Voluntary Service and delivers "meals-on-wheels" as well as working part time as a cleaner at the local high school. She is the sister of Sandra and Polly, and aunt to me, and a close friend to Bette, Myra, Cathy, and Alice. She was interviewed for the study.

Jenny

Jenny is twenty-five years old, single, and living with her mother and brother in a small village outside "Chinnock." At the time of the study she was working part time at a local pub after giving up her job as a legal secretary to travel. She is a coach at the local gymnastics club. She is a friend of mine, Emma's, Jana's, Cathy's, and Angela's. She took part in an interview and focus group.

Alice

Alice is in her late forties and has four children between the ages of fifteen and twenty-three—two boys and two girls. She lives with her children and her husband, an engineer, in their privately owned home on an estate outside "Chinnock." She is actively involved in the local church and member of the Ladies Guild. Alice also works part time as a clerical assistant for the Child Protection Agency. She is a close friend to Polly, Eve, Sandra, Cathy, Myra, and Patricia. I went to school with her children. Alice took part in an interview.

Angela

Angela is thirty-two and married. Her husband runs his own business in car parts and they have two young daughters, ages two and five. She lives in a detached house on a more affluent new estate—an extension of "Chinnock." She is involved in the wider parish church and her children attend the local parish primary school. She works part time as a district nurse and is a close friend of Jana's and a friend of mine, Jenny's, and Emma's. She took part in an interview and focus group.

Cathy

In her late thirties, Cathy is divorced and lives with her two children, ages eleven and fifteen, in a village near "Chinnock" in a privately owned home. She is also involved in the local Catholic Church and a member of the Ladies Guild. Her eldest daughter attends the Catholic comprehensive school and her son attends a school for children with learning difficulties. She is a close friend of Sandra's and friends with Polly, Eve, Alice, Myra, Jana, and Cathy. Her daughter was a member of the church Brownie Pack. She took part in an interview and the focus group.

Myra

Myra is the oldest woman in the study. In her mid-seventies, she is originally from Ireland and lives with her also-retired husband in their own home in a village just outside "Chinnock." She has one son who has moved away from home. Myra lives very close to the church hall where the Ladies Guild meetings are held. Both she and her husband are very involved in church activities. She used to work as a support teacher at the local church primary school when I attended and is still a very active member of the Ladies Guild. She is good friends with Polly, Sandra, Eve, and Alice. She took part in an interview.

Bette

Bette is in her mid-sixties and lives in a council house in "Chinnock." She used to work in the theater and was an "aqua-belle" in the 1950s. Now retired, she lives near "Chinnock" town center with her lesbian partner in a rented council home. She is a good friend of Eve's and also knows Polly and Sandra, but is possibly the least integrated member of this group. Bette took part in an interview.

Patricia

Patricia is in her late fifties and lives in her privately owned detached home with her husband, a salesman, and one of their three daughters. The youngest daughter was eighteen at the time of the study and the other two were twenty-five and twenty-eight. She is actively involved in the Ladies Guild and church activities. Her husband is a minister at the church. She is very close friends with Sandra and also friends with Myra, Polly, and Eve. I also am good friends with one of her daughters. She took part in an interview and focus group, but unfortunately a recording fault meant that her interview was lost.

Emma

The youngest member of the study, she is twenty-one and a teacher training student at the local university. She lives with her family in "Chinnock" and attended the local Catholic secondary school. She is also a gym instructor at a local gymnastics club. She is close friends with me, Jenny, Jana, and Cathy. She took part in an interview.

Jana

Jana is thirty-two, divorced, and a part-time cardiac care nurse at a local hospital. She lives in her own home in "Chinnock" town center. She attends the Catholic Church, and her six-year-old son attends the local Catholic primary school. She is a close friend to Angela, Sandra, Jenny, and Emma. She took part in a focus group and an interview.

Notes

Introduction

1. For example, in the UK, Radio Four, the BBC's largely middle-brow non-music radio station, launched a series called *Word for Word*, in which one program, "Friends, Neighbours and Big Brothers" (Sept. 7, 2005), debated common anxieties about how contemporary television might influence, and damage, everyday vernacular. Contributions made to the program's discussion, most notably from a former chief inspector of schools, expressed the feeling that television was to blame for falling standards in young people's communication skills and for the gradual erosion of "standard" forms of English.

2. I take the phrase "drive belts" and adapt it deliberately from Bakhtin's essay on speech genres that helps to explain the social relevance of the dynamism of language: "Utterances and their types, that is speech genres, are the drive belts from the history of society to the history of language" (1986:65). I thank Shaun Moores for originally pointing out to me the importance of that sentence.

3. For the significance of particular time periods to the analysis of television's address, see Brunsdon et al. (2001), who discuss the changing space of the eight to nine o'clock slot on evening television as it adopts forms established in daytime television.

4. Sixty-six percent women, 25 percent men, and 8 percent children, *The Scotsman*, July 24, 1996.

Chapter 1: Talk Is Not So Cheap

1. Cited in Lumby (1997:122).

2. Carlton TV is an independent television franchise of ITV in the UK.

3. Cited in *The Scotsman*, July 24, 1996; originally quoted from the *Daily Mirror* in 1995.

4. In comparison, there has been little academic work that has engaged with the magazine program as a genre.

5. The presence of such a critical arena was seen by Habermas to exist in the coffee-houses and salons of seventeenth- and eighteenth-century France, where male members

of the bourgeoisie and intellectuals met to discuss works of literature. Here political discourse formed itself around rational debate and opened up a space that had previously been denied under the feudal system. Despite these meeting places having exclusionary criteria, Habermas was convinced of their critical capacity beyond the confines of the state as a space for public participatory discourse. However, he was less optimistic about political debate in the twentieth century, where the mass media can be thought of as constituting the public sphere. In this account, he suggests that the public sphere has undergone a process of "re-feudalization" that, he claims, has been secured by the mass media's obsession with "spectacle." The commodification of culture has transformed representative politics into "performance" removed from the lives of the populace. This account invokes the formation of the ideological category of the "public" as an uncritical mass disinterested in political participation. It is resonant in many evaluations that see a demise of conventional politics and a "crisis of public communication" (e.g., Blumler and Gurevitch, 1995).

6. Grindstaff (2002) in *The Money Shot* offers an interesting insight into the production of talk show styles through her ethnographic research of two production studios.

7. Pateman explains this historical formulation: "Humankind attempts to transcend a merely natural existence so that nature is always seen as of a lower order than culture. Culture becomes identified as the creation and the world of men because women's biology and bodies place them closer to nature than men, and because their child-rearing and domestic tasks, dealing with unsocialised infants and with raw materials, bring them into closer contact with nature. Women and the domestic sphere thus appear inferior to the cultural sphere and male activities, and women are seen as necessarily subordinate to men" (1989:124–25).

8. For example, in Kate Millet's profound reevaluation of the politics of power in *Sexual Politics:* "This essay does not define the political as that relatively narrow and exclusive world of meetings, chairman and parties. The term 'politics' shall refer to power-structured relationships, arrangements whereby one group of persons are controlled by another" (1970:124).

9. In the case of the representation of sex workers on the *Joan Rivers Show,* McLaughlin argues that, "Attention to sexual techniques and techniques of the body is prevalent in talk shows featuring sex work; in the talk show topics and issues are subsumed under spectacle, as the reasons for a woman's entering prostitution and its status as labor become buried under talk about techniques of oral sex and fingernail polish color" (1993:50).

10. For instance, among others, Peck cites Sampson, E. E (1981), 36. Also see Nicholas Rose, *Governing the Soul* (1984).

11. See also Deborah Cameron (1995a), *Verbal Hygiene.*

12. bell hooks (1990), "Talking Back."

13. She is referring to Austin's (1963) description of illocutionary speech acts, which will be explained in more detail in chapter 2.

Chapter 2: Making Talk *Talk* in Media Studies

1. Similar critiques of semiotics that develop the relational aspects of sign systems have developed in psychology (Gergen, 1991) although I focus here on the issues as they have related to media studies.

2. In the essay "Myth Today," Barthes develops Saussure's thesis. In Saussure, the division of the linguistic symbol into signifier and signified describes the arbitrary relationship of words and their meanings as a system of interrelated signs, a logic that Barthes takes further to apply to images and other cultural forms. He suggests that in a culturally produced image there is also a second order of meaning and thus a second level of division between a sign and its meaning. There is the *denotative* content of an image—what is actually to be seen—and the *connotative* content of an image—which refers to a more abstract, interpretative level of what is to be understood within the cultural climate. Barthes stresses that this is a structural analysis that rests on reading the relationship of signs to one another.

3. Television has largely been thought about as an aural medium associated with "distracted" viewing, a perspective that does not entirely account for the visual experience of television. While this book cannot adequately account for the relationship between the aural and the visual, see Caldwell (1995) and Wheatley (2004) for examples of how this assumption should be revisited.

4. Quoted in Weedon, Tolson, and Mort (1980a), from Hoggart (1959).

5. Volosinov's work enjoyed rather short-lived attention at the CCCS in Britain in 1976; see Woolfson (1976) and Tolson (1976).

6. Much of this argument is characterized by the dualistic "synchrony" versus "diachrony" debate. Abstract objectivists understand language as synchronic, stable over time, while Volosinov and others who stress the social character of language understand it as diachronic in nature, that is dynamic and subject to historical and social change.

7. Charles Woolfson (1976) in "The Semiotics of Working Class Speech," did take his direction from Volosinov. He suggested that a genuinely Marxist approach to semiotics would take the verbal sign as the key to social consciousness. What is important about Woolfson's essay is that he does actually address some of the methodological issues of conducting research into speech genres and provides us with transcripts of recordings of primary conversational data. There is potential here for cultural analysts to take a new direction in researching informal everyday communication (through transcripts of speech) as a form of "behavioral ideology." He describes social interaction as the battleground where ideological tensions are constantly being contested. This concurs with Volosinov's assertions that ideological signs are never fixed but are *multi-accentuated*, dynamic in lived experience. It is here in actual speech forms that the complexity of social consciousness can be convincingly explored. However, Woolfson's article, while it provided a beginning, lacks an analysis of the coded and rule-bound nature of social interaction (see Tolson, 1976). This criticism is not a call for a reinvestment in a structuralist approach to language; rather it suggests Woolfson's failure to consider the discourse in terms of its *genre*.

8. The term "face" in interaction derives from Goffman (1967) and is based upon everyday usages such as "losing face" and "saving face." Utterances therefore are potentially threatening to someone's face and thus every person has *face needs*. It is particularly pertinent to the rituals of politeness whereby speakers would normally avoid face-threatening acts (Brown and Levinson, 1987).

9. Little wonder that for so long in British broadcasting, masculine modes of address dominated (see Corner, 1993).

10. Langer documents television's "personality system," which allows such a relationship to form, in contrast to the star system of the film industry: "Whereas the star system

operates from the realms of the spectacular, the inaccessible, the imaginary, presenting the cinematic universe as 'larger than life,' the personality system is cultivated . . . as 'part of life'; whereas the star system always has the ability to place distance between itself and its audiences through its insistence on 'the exceptional,' the personality system works directly to construct and foreground intimacy and immediacy; whereas contact with stars is unrelentingly sporadic and uncertain, contact with television personalities has regularity and predictability; whereas stars are always playing 'parts' emphasizing their identity as 'stars' as much—perhaps even more than—the characters they play, television personalities 'play themselves'" (Langer, 1981:354–55).

11. Munson tells us that "*House Party* offered the simulated sociality of a 'party' by bringing the housewife into the studio—and the advertised products into her home. The borders between home, stage and marketplace—between spectacle and dialogue—seemed to have collapsed. The co-presence of the spectator's and the host's body and vocality, the performance space, and the media apparatus were all redefining 'spectatorship' by inscribing aspects of folk culture and interpersonal rituals, 'people are funny' storytelling, and anecdotal personal experience" (1993:53–54).

12. The presenters' lives are also some of the common matter regularly found in the British tabloid press. Richard Madeley's (presenter of *This Morning*) shoplifting charge and Ann Diamond's (presenter of *Good Morning*) cot death campaign after the death of her own son, as well as her divorce from her producer husband, all received extensive coverage in British tabloid press.

13. John Searle's (1969) *Speech Acts* outlines five basic types of action that one can perform while speaking: representatives (e.g., asserting), directives (e.g., requesting), commissives (e.g., promising), expressives (e.g., thanking), and declaratives (e.g., appointing).

14. See, for example, Scannell (1991b) and Tolson (2006).

15. Cited in Marriott (1997).

16. The "third turn receipt" is used in everyday question-and-answer sequences in face-to-face conversations.

17. Cited in Tolson (1991:179).

18. "Register" is a term provided by Halliday (1978) that is used in stylistics to refer to a "socially defined variety of language, such as scientific or legal English" (Crystal, 1995:457).

Chapter 3: Daytime Talking

1. Robert Kilroy-Silk hosted his own talk show for seventeen years until January 2004, when he quit the show after being suspended by the BBC for alleged racist comments he made in his column in the *Sunday Express*.

2. While many of the current talk shows may now also emphasize alternative sexual relationships, Gamson's (1998) book describes how the "freak" factor is brought about by a hetero-normative framework. Similarly, those who write about Oprah discuss "the family" as one of the structuring devices of the discourse.

3. A different version of some of the following arguments, containing a longer discussion of the hosts' management strategies in *Kilroy,* appears in Wood (2001).

4. This is a description that is usually applied to male hosts—Donahue for example—in the more "public issue" oriented versions of the genre. Female hosts—Oprah, Ricki Lake,

Sally Jesse Raphael, and Vanessa—are usually characterized as "therapists" rather then "heroines" in the therapy sub-genre.

5. I am referring to interruptions that are power related and marked by aggressive inter-jections rather than interruptions that can be understood as neutral or rapport orientated (Goldberg, 1990).

6. Greatbatch (1992) describes the way in which interviewees maintain their institutional footing by directing their talk not to the co-interviewee but to the interviewer. Disagreement is strengthened if the interviewee breaks with this expectation to direct their talk to the co-interviewee.

7. The BBC axed *Good Morning* after what the press described as the "sofa wars." *This Morning* has consistently high ratings and is still on the air, now running for over twenty years.

8. This distinction between primary addressee and overhearer becomes crucial at later stages in this book.

9. Montgomery (1986a) notes that traditional research in the field of language and ideology has been more concerned with third-person discourse and not with discourse that has been primarily concerned with its interaction with its audience.

10. This program received a good deal of press attention when complaints were made by the Impotence Association and the drug manufacturers (*The Guardian,* Sept. 18, 1998).

11. This process is enhanced by the extra-textual resources that accompany much television. For example, on *This Morning's* accompanying website (http://www.itv-thismorning .co.uk/) there is a link to "backstage" that offers links to "meet the presenters," "meet the experts," and "meet the crew." These links offer personal biographies as well as information about life on the show.

12. The couple's personal relationship is often subject matter for the tabloid press. After some photographs of Judy in a bikini on holiday were featured in the tabloid press with cruel commentary, Richard was interviewed for the front page of the *Scottish Mirror* (May 2, 1996), with the headline, "THE TRUTH ABOUT OUR MARRIAGE, Judy gives me a tremendous sexual charge."

13. See Ervin-Tripp (1964).

Chapter 4: Method

1. Uses and gratifications studies into "para-social interaction" often analyze psycho-metric correlations (e.g., Rubin and Perse, 1987; Rubin and McHugh, 1987; Perse, 1990; Alperstein, 1991; Auter, 1993).

2. This follows Umberto Eco's work, which discussed the viewer's reading of a TV message as being dependant upon his/her "general framework of cultural references . . . his ideological, ethical religious standpoints . . . his tastes, his value systems, etc." (1972:115).

3. This work is thought to bridge some territory with uses and gratifications research. Although it is ethnographic, it does not engage directly with the same questions of power that inform the CCCS work. For instance, Lull does not interpret his findings about family hierarchies in terms of the wider political system of patriarchy, as does Hobson.

4. For instance, Lyn Thomas's (1995) research on *Inspector Morse* is presented in two parts; an analysis of the text in terms of its gender representation, quality, and English-ness, and an analysis of a focus group discussion about the program in terms of how the

discourses identified in the textual analysis are mobilized in the discussion about the text. However, while Thomas's study does to some extent bring together the *findings* of the textual analysis with those from the audience readings of the text, it does not entirely bring together "ethnographic" practice with textual form. The audience research still takes place in the educational institution and textual analysis and audience research are analytically treated as separate entities.

5. It is important to note that Walkerdine's central argument in this essay is about her place as observer of the situation. Her subsequent interpretation of the experience involves inserting herself in the text and engaging with her own subjective experience.

6. She criticizes Willis et al. (1990), who suggest that there is no difference between high and popular culture with regard to processes of meaning production: "Although laudable in its intention to reassert the value of low-valued popular culture, there are dire consequences to such an approach: general, everyday media use is identified with attentive and meaningful reading of specific texts, and that is precisely what it is not. . . . Media use is not always meaningful or at least a secondary activity" (Hermes, 1995:15).

7. Indeed, Spigel (2006) discusses the way in which television's introduction into the United States was accompanied by fears of noise pollution.

8. For Butler, gender becomes a set of ritual acts of repetition, a concept she bases on Derrida's theory of iterability: "Performativity cannot be understood outside of a process of iterability, a regularized and constrained repetition of norms. And this repetition is not performed *by* a subject; this repetition is what enables a subject and constitutes the temporal condition for the subject. This iterability implies that performance is not a singular "act" or event, but a ritualized production, a ritual reiterated under and through constraint, under and through the force of prohibition and taboo, with the threat of ostracism and even death controlling and compelling the shape of the production, but not, I will insist, determining it fully in advance" (1993:95).

9. I have changed the name of the town.

Chapter 5: Talking about Daytime Talk

1. Although one woman said that her husband bought her a television for the kitchen to solve the problem of arguing over program choice.

2. There had recently been public discontent over a news story about young offenders going on government-funded sailing holidays, which may have provided the background for this discussion.

3. The power at work in conversational interaction between doctor-patient interviews is an area many conversational analysts have researched.

4. Unlike the para-social indicator of attractiveness in the "Para Social Interaction" scale used in uses and gratifications research.

Chapter 6: Talking Back

1. Sacks et al.'s (1974) work on turn-taking assumes a system for interaction in which the "model" implies a desired mode of ordered conversation in which there would be no gaps and no overlaps present in the exchanges. This has been generally recognized as

a normative model in English-speaking communities. The presence of gaps or overlaps is usually considered as signifying conversational malfunction (Zimmerman and West, 1975), and Coates (1994) comments that even from an early age we are made aware of such an organizing principle as we are told to wait our turn and not to interrupt.

2. However, it is important here to recall accounts of gendered patterns of conversational interaction. While some authors see the cooperatively constructed floor as a specifically "feminine" competence, Cameron (1998) shows how this can also be employed by males in certain contexts. Therefore, we must be reminded that traditionally culturally constructed "masculine" and "feminine" modes of speaking are "performances" (Butler 1990) that are brought into play in particular *contextual* encounters.

3. Goffman also points to the weakness in this rule. He suggests that it is usual to assume that to sustain involvement participants often ensure that there is no prolonged period of time where no one takes the floor, "but equally there can be no talk occurring yet the participants can still be in a state of talk" (1981:130).

4. This is not always the case in all of the utterances in the data, as no doubt the methodological necessity of my presence does make me part of the interactive framework. It might be argued that it is my presence in the first place that instigates these responses, but equally one might argue that they would be mentally thought through, if not verbally and audibly evoked, as a characteristic of "inner speech" (Volosinov, 1973).

5. Originally in Labov (1972), *Language and the Inner City;* reprinted in Jaworski (1999), *The Discourse Reader.*

Chapter 7: Texts, Subjects, and Modern Self-Reflexivity

1. That is not to say that older structures such as class *are* disappearing, but that a sense of collective consciousness of them *is*, in favor of making more individual differentiations between self and others on the basis of issues such as taste, consumption practices, and lifestyle (Savage, 2000).

2. For Giddens (1991a) these are social-scientific knowledge and techniques of self-therapy, and for Beck (1992) they involve the dissemination of lay knowledge on science and the environment.

3. See Jason Jacobs (2001) for a discussion of why the aesthetic production values of *ER* mean that it deserves to be considered as "quality" television.

4. See chapter 2 for a discussion of how the text-reader model of audience reception, derived from a literary structuralist emphasis in media and cultural studies, led scholars away from understanding broadcasting as communication.

Conclusion

1. See Ian Hutchby's (2001) book *Conversation and Technology* for a conversational analytical approach to the relations between conversation and media technologies.

Bibliography

Adkins, Lisa. (2000) "Objects of Innovation: Post-occupational Reflexivity and Re-traditionalisation of Gender." In S. Ahmed, J. Kilby, C. Lury, M. McNeil, and B. Skeggs (eds.), *Transformations: Thinking through Feminism*. London: Routledge, pp. 259–73.

———. (2002) *Revisions: Gender and Sexuality in Late Modernity*. Buckingham: Open University Press.

———. (2003) "Reflexivity: Freedom or Habit of Gender." *Theory, Culture & Society* 20 (6), pp. 21–42.

Allen, Robert C. (1985) *Speaking of Soap Operas*. Chapel Hill: University of North Carolina Press.

Alperstein, Neil M. (1991) "Imaginary Social Relationships with Celebrities Appearing in Television Commercials." *Journal of Broadcasting and Electronic Media* 35, pp. 43–58.

Althusser, Louis. (1971) "Ideology and Ideological State Apparatuses." In *Lenin and Philosophy and Other Essays*. Ben Brewster (trans). London: New Left Books, pp. 127–88.

Ang, Ien. (1985) *Watching Dallas: Soap Opera and the Melodramatic Imagination*. London: Methuen.

Ang, Ien, and Joke Hermes. (1996) "Gender and/in Media Consumption." In James Curran and Michael Gurevitch (eds.), *Mass Media and Society*. 2d ed. London: Arnold, pp. 307–29.

Austin, John L. (1963) *How To Do Things with Words*. Cambridge, Mass.: Harvard University Press.

Auter, P. J. (1993) "TV that Talks Back: An Experimental Validation of a Para-social Interaction Scale." *Journal of Broadcasting and Electronic Media* 36, pp. 173–81.

Bakhtin, Mikhail Mikhailovich. (1986) *Speech Genres and Other Essays*. Austin: University of Texas Press.

Barthes, Roland. (1973) *Mythologies*. London: Paladin.

Baudrillard, Jean. (1988) *Selected Writings*. Cambridge: Polity Press.

Bausinger, Herman. (1984) "Media, Technology, and Daily Life." *Media, Culture & Society* 6, pp. 343–51.

Beck, Ulrich. (1992) *The Risk Society: Towards a New Modernity.* London: Sage.

Benhabib, Seyla. (1992) *Situating the Self: Gender, Community, and Postmodernism in Contemporary Ethics.* Cambridge: Polity Press.

Bennett, Tony. (1996) "Figuring Audiences and Readers." In James Hay, Lawrence Grossberg, and Ellen Wartella (eds.), *The Audience and Its Landscape.* Colorado: Westview Press, pp. 145–59.

Blumler, Jay, and Michael Gurevitch. (1995) *The Crisis of Public Communication.* London: Routledge.

Boden, Deirdre, and Don H. Zimmerman. (1991) *Talk as Social Structure.* Cambridge: Polity Press.

Bolter, Jay David, and Richard Grusin. (2000) *Re-mediation: Understanding New Media.* Cambridge: MIT Press.

Boyle, Karen. (2005) *Media and Violence.* London: Sage.

Brand, Graham, and Paddy Scannell. (1991) "Talk, Identity, and Performance: The Tony Blackburn Show." In Paddy Scannell (ed.), *Broadcast Talk.* London: Sage, pp. 201–26.

Brown, Mary Ellen. (1990) *Television and Women's Culture.* London: Sage.

———. (1994) *Soap Opera and Women's Talk.* London: Sage.

Brown, Penelope, and Stephen Levinson. (1987) *Politeness: Some Universals in Language Usage.* Cambridge: Cambridge University Press.

Brunsdon, Charlotte. (1981) "Crossroads: Notes on Soap Opera." *Screen* 22 (4), pp. 32–47.

———. (1992) "Text and Audience." In Ellen Seiter et al. (eds.), *Remote Control.* London: Routledge, pp. 116–29.

———. (1993) "Identity in Feminist Television Criticism." *Media, Culture & Society* 15 (2), pp. 309–20.

———. (2000) *The Feminist, the Housewife, and the Soap Opera.* Oxford: Oxford University Press.

Brunsdon, Charlotte, Catherine Johnson, Rachel Moseley, and Helen Wheatley. (2001) "Factual Entertainment on British Television: The Midlands TV Research Group's '8–9 Project.'" *European Journal of Cultural Studies* 4 (1), pp. 29–62.

Buckingham, David. (1991) "What Are Words Worth? Interpreting Children's Talk about Television." *Cultural Studies* 5 (2), pp. 228–45.

Butler, Judith. (1990) *Gender Trouble: Feminism and the Subversion of Identity.* London: Routledge.

———. (1993) *Bodies That Matter: On the Discursive Limits of Sex.* New York: Routledge.

Caldwell, John T. (1995) *Televisuality: Style, Crisis, and Authority in American Television.* New Brunswick, N.J.: Rutgers University Press.

Cameron, Deborah. (1992a) "Not Gender Difference but the Difference Gender Makes—Explanation in Research on Sex and Language." International Journal of the Sociology of Language 94, pp. 13–26.

———. (1992b) Review of Deborah Tannen's *You Just Don't Understand. Feminism and Psychology* 2 (3), pp. 465–89.

———. (1995a) *Verbal Hygiene.* London: Routledge.

———. (1995b) "Rethinking Language and Gender Studies: Some Issues for the 1990s."

In Sara Mills (ed.), *Language and Gender*. Milton Keynes, UK: Open University Press, pp. 31–44.

———. (1998) "Performing Gender Identity: Young Men's Talk and the Construction of Heterosexual Masculinity." In Jennifer Coates (ed.), *Language and Gender: A Reader*. Oxford: Blackwell, pp. 270–83.

———. (2000). *Good to Talk? Living and Working in a Communication Culture*. London: Sage.

Carbaugh, Donal. (1988) *Talking American: Cultural Discourses on Donahue*. Norwood, N.J.: Ablex.

Cardiff, David. (1988) "Mass-Middlebrow Laughter: The Origins of BBC Comedy." *Media, Culture & Society* 10 (1), pp. 41–60.

Carey, James. (1989) *Communication as Culture*. New York: Unwin Hyman.

Carpignano, Paulo, et al. (1990) "Chatter in the Age of Electronic Reproduction: Talk Television and the Public Mind." *Social Text* 25 (26), pp. 33–55.

Cassell, Joan. (1977) *A Group Called Women: Sisterhood and Symbolism in the Feminist Movement*. New York: Davis Mackay.

Caughie, John, L. (1986) "Social Relations with Media Figures." In Gary Gumpert and Robert Cathcart (eds.), *Inter/Media: Interpersonal Communication in a Media World*. Oxford: Oxford University Press.

Clayman, Stephen. (1991) "News Interview Openings: Aspects of Sequential Organisation." In Paddy Scannell (ed.), *Broadcast Talk*. London: Sage, pp. 48–75.

———. (1992) "Footing in the Achievement of Neutrality: The Case of News-Interview Discourse." In Paul Drew and John Heritage (eds.), *Talk at Work*. Cambridge: Cambridge University Press, pp. 163–98.

Coates, Jennifer. (1989) "Gossip Revisited: Language in All-Female Groups." In Jennifer Coates and Deborah Cameron (eds.), *Women in Their Speech Communities*. London: Longman, pp. 94–122.

———. (1993) *Women, Men, and Language*. London: Longman.

———. (1994) "No Gaps, Lots of Overlap: Turn-Taking Patterns in the Talk of Women Friends." In David Graddol, Janet Maybin, and Barry Stierer (eds.), *Researching Language and Literacy in Social Context*. Clevedon, Avon: Multilingual Matters, pp. 177–92.

———. (1996) *Women Talk: Conversation between Women Friends*. Oxford: Blackwell.

———, (ed.). (1998) *Language and Gender: A Reader*. Oxford: Blackwell.

Coates, Jennifer, and Deborah Cameron (eds.). (1989) *Women in Their Speech Communities*. London: Longman.

Collins, Louise. (1994) "Gossip: A Feminist Defence." In Robert F. Goodman and Aaron Ben Ze'ev (eds.), *Good Gossip*. Lawrence: University Press of Kansas.

Corner, John. (1993) "General Introduction: Television and British Society in the 1950s." In John Corner (ed.), *Popular Television in Britain*. London: Routledge, pp. 1–21.

———. (1999) *Critical Ideas in Television Studies*. Oxford: Oxford University Press.

Corner, John, Kay Richardson, and Natalie Fenton. (1990) *Nuclear Reactions: Form and Response in "Public Issue" Television*. London: John Libbey.

Crystal, David. (1985) *A Dictionary of Linguistics and Phonetics*. London: Basil Blackwell.

———. (1995) *Cambridge Encyclopedia of the English Language*. Cambridge: Cambridge University Press.

Dahlgren, Peter. (1995) *Television and the Public Sphere.* London: Sage.

Daly, Mary. (1978) *Gyn/Ecology: The Metaethics of Radical Feminism.* Boston: Beacon Press.

Dayan, Daniel, and Elihu Katz. (1992) *Media Events: The Live Broadcasting of History.* Cambridge, Mass.: Harvard University Press.

Dovey, Jon. (2000) *Freakshow: First-Person Media and Factual Television.* London: Pluto Press.

Dugdale and Saymore. (1992). "I'm a British Doodle Dandy." *The Guardian,* Dec. 7.

Durham Peters, John. (1993) "Distrust of Representation: Habermas on the Public Sphere." *Media, Culture & Society* (15), pp. 541–71.

———. (2006) "Media as Conversation, Conversation as Media." In James Curran and David Morley (eds), *Media and Cultural Theory.* London: Routledge, pp.115–28.

Eco, Umberto. (1972) "Towards a Semiotic Enquiry into the Television Message." *Working Papers in Cultural Studies,* Center for Contemporary Cultural Studies. University of Birmingham, vol. 3, pp. 103–21.

Edelsky, Carole. (1981) "Who's Got the Floor?" *Language in Society* 10, pp. 383–421.

Ellis, John. (1982) *Visible Fictions: Cinema, Television, and Video.* London: Routledge.

———. (2002) *Seeing Things: Television in the Age of Uncertainty.* London: I. B. Taurus.

Emler, Nicholas. (1994) "Gossip, Reputation, and Social Adaptation." In Robert F. Goodman and Aaron Ben Ze'ev (eds.), *Good Gossip.* Lawrence: University Press of Kansas, pp. 117–38.

Engel Manga, Julie. (2003) *Talking Trash: The Cultural Politics of Daytime TV Talk Shows.* New York: New York University Press.

Ervin-Tripp, Susan. (1964) "An Analysis of the Interaction of Language, Topic and Listener." *American Anthropologist* 66 (6), pp. 86–102.

Fairclough, Norman. (1984) "The Conversationalisation of Public Discourse and the Authority of the Consumer." In Russell Keat, Nigel Whiteley, and Nicholas Abercrombie (eds.), *The Authority of the Consumer.* London: Routledge, pp. 253–68.

———. (1992) *Discourse and Social Change.* Cambridge: Polity Press.

———. (1995) *Media Discourse.* London: Edward Arnold.

Featherstone, Mike. (1991) *Consumer Culture and Postmodernism.* London: Sage.

Felski, Rita. (2000) "The Invention of Everyday Life." *New Formations* 39, pp. 15–31.

Fishman, Pamela. (1980) "Interactional Shitwork." *Heresies* 2, pp. 99–101.

Fiske, John. (1992) "Moments of Television: Neither the Text Nor the Audience." In Ellen Seiter et al. (eds.), *Remote Control: Television Audiences and Cultural Power.* London: Routledge, pp. 56–78.

Fraser, Nancy. (1989) *Unruly Practices: Power, Discourse, and Gender in Contemporary Social Theory.* Cambridge: Polity Press.

Freedman, Des. (2006) "Internet Transformations: Old Media Resiliences in the 'New Media' Revolution." In James Curran and David Morley (eds.), *Media and Cultural Theory.* London: Routledge, pp. 275–90.

Gamson, Joshua. (1998) *Freaks Talk Back: Tabloid Talk Shows and Sexual Non-Conformity.* Chicago: University of Chicago Press.

Gauntlett, David, and Annette Hill. (1999) *Living Television: Television, Culture, and Everyday Life.* London: Routledge.

Geertz, Clifford. (1973) *The Interpretation of Cultures: Selected Essays*. New York: Basic Books.

Gergen, Kenneth. (1991). *The Saturated Self*. New York: Basic Books.

Giddens, Anthony. (1991a) *The Consequences of Modernity*. Cambridge: Polity Press.

———. (1991b) *Modernity and Self Identity*. Cambridge: Polity Press.

Gillespie, Marie. (1995) *Television, Ethnicity, and Cultural Change*. London: Routledge.

Gilligan, Carol. (1982) *In a Different Voice: Psychological Theory and Women's Development*. Cambridge, Mass.: Harvard University Press.

Gluckman, Max. (1963) "Gossip and Scandal." *Current Anthropology* 4, pp. 307–16.

Goffman, Ervin. (1967) *Interaction Ritual: Essays on Face-to-Face Behavior*. New York: Anchor Books.

———. (1969) *The Presentation of Self in Everyday Life*. Harmondsworth: Penguin Books.

———. (1981) *Forms of Talk*. Oxford: Basil Blackwell.

Goldberg, J. A. (1990) "Interrupting the Discourse on Interruptions: An Analysis in Terms of Relationally Neutral, Power- and Rapport-Oriented Acts." *Journal of Pragmatics* 14, pp. 883–903.

Goodwin, Marjorie. (1990) *He-Said, She-Said: Talk as Social Organization Among Black Children*. Bloomington: Indiana Press.

Gramsci, Antonio. (1971) *Selections from the Prison Notebooks*. New York: International Publishers.

Gray, Ann. (1992) *Video Playtime: The Gendering of a Leisure Technology*. London: Routledge.

Greatbatch, David. (1992) "On the Management of Disagreement between News Interviewees." In Paul Drew and John Heritage (eds.), *Talk at Work*. Cambridge: Cambridge University Press, pp. 93–137.

Grice, Herbert Paul. (1957) "Meaning." *Philosophical Review* 67, pp. 377–88.

———. (1975) "Logic and Conversation." In Peter Cole and Jerry Morgan (eds.), *Syntax and Semantics: Speech Acts, vol. 3*. New York: Academic Press, pp. 41–58.

Grindstaff, Laura. (2002) *The Money Shot: Trash, Class, and the Making of TV Talk Shows*. Chicago: University of Chicago Press.

Haarman, Louann. (1999) "Performing Talk." In Louann Haarman (ed.), *Talk about Shows: La parola e lo spettacolo*. Bologna: Cooperativa Libraria Universitaria Editrice.

Habermas, Jürgen. (1989) *The Structural Transformation of the Public Sphere: An Inquiry into a Category of Bourgeois Society*. Cambridge: MIT Press.

Hall, Stuart. (1980) "Encoding/Decoding." In Stuart Hall, Dorothy Hobson, Andrew Lowe, and Paul Willis (eds.), *Culture, Media, Language: Working Papers in Cultural Studies*. London: Hutchinson, pp.128–38.

Hall, Stuart, Dorothy Hobson, Andrew Lowe, and Paul Willis (eds.). (1980) *Culture, Media, Language: Working Papers in Cultural Studies*. London: Hutchinson.

Halliday, Michael. (1978) *Language as Social Semiotic*. London: Edward Arnold.

Hanks, W. F. (1989) "The Indexical Ground of Deictic Reference." In *Papers from the 25th Annual Regional Meeting of the Chicago Linguistic Society*, pp. 104–22.

Heritage, John. (1985) "Analyzing News: Aspects of Talk for the Overhearing Audience." In T. Van Dijk (ed.), *Handbook of Discourse Analysis, vol. 3: Genres of Discourse*. New York: Academic Press, pp. 95–117.

Heritage, John, and David Greatbatch. (1991) "On the Institutional Character of Institutional Talk: The Case of News Interviews." In Deirdre Boden and Don Zimmerman (eds.), *Talk and Social Structure*. Cambridge: Polity Press, pp. 93–137.

Hermes, Joke. (1995) *Reading Women's Magazines: An Analysis of Everyday Media Use.* Cambridge: Polity Press.

Hobson, Dorothy. (1980) "Housewives and the Mass Media." In Stuart Hall et al. (eds.), *Culture, Media, Language.* London: Hutchinson, pp. 105–14.

———. (1982) *Crossroads—The Drama of a Soap Opera.* London: Methuen.

———. (1991) "Soap Operas at Work." In Ellen Seiter et al. (eds.), *Remote Control: Television, Audiences and Cultural Power.* London: Routledge, pp. 150–67.

Hochschild, Arlie. (1983) *The Managed Heart: The Commercialization of Human Feeling.* Los Angeles: University of California Press.

Hoggart, Richard. (1959) *The Uses of Literacy.* London: Chatto and Windus.

hooks, bell. (1991) "Talking Back." In Russell Ferguson et al. (eds), *Out There: Marginalization and Contemporary Culture.* Cambridge: MIT Press, pp. 337–44.

Horton, Donald, and Richard Wohl. (1956) "Mass Communication and Para-Social Interaction: Observations on Intimacy at a Distance." *Psychiatry* 19 (3), pp. 215–29.

Hudson, Richard. A. (1996) *Sociolinguistics.* 2d ed. Cambridge: Cambridge University Press.

Hutchby, Ian. (1996) *Confrontation Talk: Arguments, Asymmetries, and Power on Talk Radio.* Mahwah, N.J.: Lawrence Erlbaum.

———. (2001) *Conversation and Technology.* Cambridge: Polity Press.

Hutchy, Ian, and Robin Wooffitt. (1998) *Conversation Analysis.* Cambridge: Polity Press.

Huyssen, Andreas. (1986). "Mass Culture as Woman: Modernism's Other." In Tania Modleski and Kathleen Woodward (eds.), *Studies in Entertainment.* Bloomington: Indiana University Press, pp. 188–207.

Hymes, Dell. (1971) "Competence and Performance in Linguistic Theory." In Renira Huxley and Elisabeth Ingram (eds.), *Language Acquisition: Models and Methods.* London: Academic Press.

———. (1974) *Foundations in Sociolinguistics: An Ethnographic Approach.* Philadelphia: University of Pennsylvania Press.

———. (1981). *In Vain I Tried To Tell You.* Philadelphia: University of Pennsylvania Press.

Illouz, Eva. (2003) *Oprah Winfrey and the Glamour of Misery: An Essay on Popular Culture.* New York: Columbia University Press.

Jacobs, Jason. (2001) "Issues of Judgement and Value in Television Studies." *International Journal of Cultural Studies* 4 (4), pp. 427–47.

Jaworski, Adam, and Nicholas Coupland. (1991) *The Discourse Reader.* London: Routledge.

Jhally, Sut, and Justin Lewis. (1992) *Enlightened Racism: "The Cosby Show," Audiences, and the Myth of the American Dream.* Boulder, Colo.: Westview Press.

Johnson, Leslie (1988) *The Unseen Voice: A Cultural History of Early Australian Radio.* London: Routledge.

Jones, Deborah. (1980) "Gossip: Notes on Women's Oral Culture." *Women's Studies International Quarterly* 3, pp. 193–98.

Joyner-Priest, Patricia. (1995) *Public Intimacies, Talk Show Participants, and Tell-all TV.* Cresskill, N.J.: Hampton Press.

Kapor, Mitchell. (1993) "Where is the Digital Highway Really Heading? The Case for a Jeffersonian Information Policy." *Wired* 1 (3).

Katz, Elihu, Jay Blumler, and Michael Gurevitch. (1974) "Utilisation of Mass Communications by the Individual." In Jay Blumler and Elihu Katz (eds.), *The Uses of Mass Communication.* London: Sage, pp. 19–32.

Kramer, Cheris. (1977) "Perceptions of Female and Male Speech." *Language and Speech* 20 (2), pp. 151–61.

Kristeva, Julia. (1984) *Revolution in Poetic Language.* P. Waller (trans.). New York: Columbia University Press.

Kurtz, Howard. (1996) *Hot Air: All Talk All the Time.* New York: Basic Books.

Labov, William. (1972) *Language in the Inner City: Studies in Black English Vernacular.* Philadelphia: University of Pennsylvania Press.

Lakoff, Robin. (1975) *Language and Women's Place.* New York: Harper and Row.

Landes, Joan. B. (1998) "Introduction." In Joan Landes (ed.), *Feminism: The Public and the Private.* Oxford: Oxford University Press, pp. 1–20.

Landman, Jane. (1995) "The Discursive Space of Identity: *The Oprah Winfrey Show.*" *Metro* 103, pp. 37–44.

Langer, John. (1981) "Television's Personality System." *Media, Culture & Society* 4, pp. 351–65.

Lash, Scott. (2002) *Critique of Information.* London: Sage.

Lash, Scott, and John Urry. (1994) *Economies of Signs and Space.* London: Sage.

Lawson, Mark. (1995) "Inside Story: One Too Many Ands and Buts." *The Guardian,* May 5.

Leech, Geoffrey. (1983) *The Principles of Pragmatics.* London: Longman.

Levin, Jack, and Arnold Arluke. (1987) *Gossip: The Inside Scoop.* New York: Plenum Press.

Levinson, Steven. (1983) *Pragmatics.* Cambridge: Cambridge University Press.

Liebes, Tamar, and Elihu Katz. (1990) *The Export of Meaning.* Oxford: Oxford University Press.

Livingstone, Sonia. (1994) "Watching Talk: Gender and Engagement in the Viewing of Audience Discussion Programmes." *Media, Culture & Society* 16, pp. 429–47.

———. (2002) *Young People and New Media.* London: Sage.

Livingstone, Sonia, and Peter Lunt. (1994) *Talk on Television.* London: Routledge.

Lull, James. (1980) "The Social Uses of Television." *Human Communication Research* 6 (3), pp. 197–209.

———. (1990) *Inside Family Viewing.* London: Routledge.

Lumby, Caroline. (1997) *Bad Girls: The Media, Sex, and Feminism in the 90s.* New South Wales: Allen and Unwin.

Lury, Celia. (1998) *Prosthetic Culture: Photography, Memory, and Identity.* London: Routledge.

Matelski, Marilyn. (1991) *Daytime Television Programming.* Netcong, N.J.: Butterworth-Heinemann.

Matheson, Hilda. (1933) *Broadcasting.* London: Thornton Butterworth.

Marriott, Stephanie. (1996) "Time and Again: 'Live' Television Commentary and the Construction of Replay Talk." *Media, Culture & Society* 18, pp. 69–86.

———. (1997) "The Emergence of Live Television Talk." *Text* 17 (2), pp. 181–98.

Masciarotte, Gloria-Jean. (1991) "C'mon, Girl: Oprah Winfrey and the Discourse of Feminine Talk." *Genders* 11, pp. 81–110.

McLaughlin, Lisa. (1993) "Chastity Criminals in the Age of Electronic Reproduction: Re-viewing Talk Television and the Public Sphere." *Journal of Communication Inquiry* 17 (1), pp. 41–55.

McRobbie, Angela. (1982/1991) "The Politics of Feminist Research: Between Talk, Text, and Action." *Feminist Review* 12 (1982), reprinted in Angela McRobbie, *Feminism and Youth Culture*. London: Macmillan.

Mellencamp, Patricia. (1990) *High Anxiety: Catastrophe, Scandal, Age, and Comedy.* Bloomington: Indiana University Press.

Meyrowitz, Joshua. (1985) *No Sense of Place: The Impact of Electronic Media on Social Behavior.* Oxford: Oxford University Press.

Millett, Kate. (1970) *Sexual Politics.* New York: Doubleday.

Mills, Sara (ed.). (1995) *Language and Gender.* London: Longman.

Milroy, Lesley. (1980) *Language and Social Networks.* Oxford: Blackwell.

Modleski, Tania. (1983) "The Rhythms of Reception: Daytime Television and Women's Work." In E. Ann Kaplan (ed.), *Regarding Television: Critical Approaches—An Anthology*. Los Angeles: American Film Institute, pp. 67–75.

Moerman, Michael. (1988) *Talking Culture: Ethnography and Conversational Analysis.* Philadelphia: University of Pennsylvania Press.

Moi, Toril. (1985) "Marginality and Subversion: Julia Kristeva." In Toril Moi, *Sexual Textual Politics: Feminist Literary Theory.* London: Routledge, pp. 150–73.

Montgomery, Martin. (1986a) "Language and Power: A Critical Review of *Studies in the Theory of Ideology* by John B. Thompson." *Media, Culture & Society* 8, pp. 41–64.

———. (1986b) "DJ Talk." *Media, Culture & Society* 8, pp. 421–40.

———. (1999) "Talk as Entertainment: The Case of *The Mrs. Merton Show*." In Louann Haarman (ed.), *Talk about Shows: La Parola e lo Spettacolo*. Bologna: Cooperativa Libraria Universitaria Editrice.

Moores, Shaun. (1990) "Texts, Readers, and Contexts of Reading: Developments in the Study of Media Audiences." *Media, Culture & Society* 12, pp. 9–29.

———. (1993) *Interpreting Audiences: The Ethnography of Media Consumption.* London: Sage.

———. (1995) "Media, Modernity, and Lived Experience." *Journal of Communication Inquiry* 19 (1), pp. 5–19.

———. (1997a) "The Mediated Interaction Order." Paper presented at the British Sociological Association Conference, Edinburgh, UK.

———. (1997b) "Broadcasting and Its Audiences." In Hugh Mackay (ed.), *Consumption and Everyday Life*. London: Sage/Open University, pp. 213–58.

———. (2000) *Media and Everyday Life in Modern Society.* Edinburgh: Edinburgh University Press.

———. (2004) "The Doubling of Place: Electronic Media, Time-Space Arrangements and Social Relationships." In Nick Couldry and Anna McCarthy (eds.), *Media Space: Place, Scale, and Culture in a Media Age*. London: Routledge, pp. 21–36.

Morley, David. (1980) *The Nationwide Audience.* London: BFI.

———. (1986) *Family Television: Cultural Power and Domestic Consumption*. London: Comedia, Routledge.

Morley, David, and Charlotte Brunsdon. (1999) *The Nationwide Television Studies*. London: Routledge.

Morley, David, and Roger Silverstone. (1990) "Domestic Communication—Technologies and Meanings." *Media, Culture & Society* 12 (1), pp. 31–55.

Moseley, Rachel. (2002) *Growing Up with Audrey Hepburn: Text, Audience, Resonance*. Manchester: Manchester University Press.

Munson, Wayne. (1993) *All Talk: The Talk Show in Media Culture*. Philadelphia: Temple University Press.

Neale, Steve. (1980) *Genre*. London: British Film Institute.

Oakley, Ann. (1974a) *The Sociology of Housework*. London: Martin Robertson.

———. (1974b) *Housewife*. London: Allen Lane.

———. (1975) *Sex, Gender & Society*. London: Temple Smith.

Ochs, Elinor. (1979/1999) "Transcription As Theory." Reprinted in Adam Jaworski and Nicholas Coupland (eds.), *The Discourse Reader*. London: Routledge, pp. 167–82.

Pateman, Carole (1989) *The Disorder of Women*. Oxford: Polity Press/Basil Blackwell.

Peck, Janice. (1995) "TV Talk Shows as Therapeutic Discourse: The Ideological Labour of the Talking Cure." *Communication Theory* 5 (1), pp. 58–81.

Perse, Elizabeth M. (1990) "Media Investment and Local News Effects." *Journal of Broadcasting and Electronic Media* 34 (1), pp. 17–36.

Plummer, Ken. (2001) *Documents of Life 2: An Invitation to Critical Humanism*. London: Sage.

Poster, Mark. (1995) *The Second Media Age*. Cambridge: Polity Press.

Press, Andrea. (1991) *Women Watching Television*. Philadelphia: University of Pennsylvania Press.

Radway, Janice. (1984) *Reading the Romance: Women, Patriarchy, and Popular Literature*. Chapel Hill: University of North Carolina Press.

Rakow, Lana. (1986) "Rethinking Gender Research in Communication." *Journal of Communication* 36 (4), pp. 11–26.

———. (1992) "The Field Reconsidered." In Lana Rakow (ed.), *Women Making Meaning: New Feminist Directions in Communication*. New York: Routledge.

Rath, Claus-Dieter. (1985) "The Invisible Network: Television as an Institution in Everyday Life." In Philip Drummond and Richard Paterson (eds.), *Television in Transition: Papers from the First International Television Studies Conference*. London: BFI, pp. 199–204.

Rose, Nicholas. (1989) *Governing the Soul: The Shaping of the Private Self*. London: Routledge.

Rosengren, Karl Erik, and Sven Windahl. (1972) "Mass Media Consumption as a Functional Alternative." In Dan McQuail (ed.), *Sociology of Mass Communications*. Middlesex: Penguin, pp.166–94.

Rubin, A. M., and M. P. McHugh. (1987) "Development of Parasocial Interaction Relationships." *Journal of Broadcasting and Electronic Media* 31, pp. 279–92.

Rubin, A.M., and E. M. Perse. (1987) "Audience Activity and Soap Opera Involvement: A Uses and Effects Investigation." *Human Communication Research* 14, pp. 246–68.

Sacks, Harvey. (1978) "Some Technical Considerations of a Dirty Joke." In J. Schenken (ed.), *Studies in the Organization of Conversational Interaction.* New York: Academic Press, pp. 249–70.

———. (1992) *Lectures on Conversation.* Oxford: Blackwell.

Sacks, Harvey, Emanuel Scheggloff, and Gail Jefferson. (1974) "A Simplest Systematics for the Organisation of Turn-Taking in Conversation." *Language* 50 (4), pp. 696–735.

Sampson, E. E. (1981) "Cognitive Psychology as Ideology." *American Psychologist* 36 (7), pp. 730–43.

Saussure, Ferdinand de. (1988 [1916]) *Course in General Linguistics.* Chicago: Open Court Press.

Savage, Micheal (2000) *Class Analysis and Social Transformation.* Buckingham: Open University Press.

Scannell, Paddy. (1991a) "Introduction: The Relevance of Talk." In Paddy Scannell (ed.), *Broadcast Talk.* London: Sage, pp.1–13.

———. (ed.). (1991b) *Broadcast Talk.* London: Sage.

———. (1992) "Public Service Broadcasting and Modern Public Life." In Paddy Scannell, Philip Schlesinger, and Colin Sparkes (eds.), *Culture and Power.* London: Sage, pp. 317–48.

———. (1996) *Radio, Television, and Modern Public Life.* Oxford: Blackwell.

———. (2000) "For Anyone-as-someone Structures." *Media, Culture & Society* 22, pp. 5–24.

Schiffrin, Deborah. (1994) *Approaches to Discourse.* Oxford: Blackwell.

Schlesinger, Philip, et. al. (1992) *Women Viewing Violence.* London: BFI.

Searle, John. (1969) *Speech Acts.* Cambridge: Cambridge University Press.

Seiter, Ellen. (1999) *Television and New Media Audiences.* Oxford: Clarendon Press.

Shattuc, Jane. (1997) *The Talking Cure.* London: Routledge.

Silverstone, Roger. (1994) *Television and Everyday Life.* London: Routledge.

———. (1999) "What's New about New Media?" *New Media and Society* 1 (1), pp. 110–12.

Silverstone, Roger, Eric Hirsch, and Davie Morley. (1992) "Information and Communication Technologies and the Moral Economy of the Household." In Roger Silverstone and Eric Hirsch (eds.), *Consuming Technologies.* London: Routledge, pp. 15–31.

Simmel, Georg. (1950) *The Sociology of Georg Simmel.* Glencoe, Ill.: Free Press.

Skeggs, Beverley. (2004) *Class, Self, Culture.* London: Routledge.

Spacks, Patricia. (1985) *Gossip.* New York: Alfred Knopf.

Spigel, Lynn. (1992) *Make Room for TV: Television and the Family Ideal in Post-War America.* Chicago: University of Chicago Press.

———. (2006) "Silent TV." Paper presented to the Society for Cinema and Media Studies Conference, Vancouver, Canada, March.

Spender, Dale. ([1980]1994) *Man Made Language.* 2d ed. London: Pandora Press.

Squire, Corinne. (1994) "Empowering Women? The Oprah Winfrey Show." *Feminism and Psychology* 4 (1), pp. 63–79.

Stanley, Liz, and Sue Wise. (1983) *Breaking Out: Feminist Consciousness and Feminist Research.* London: Routledge.

Stephen, Jaci. (1996) "A Couple of Swells." *Media Guardian,* May 6.

Talbot, Mary. (1995) "A Synthetic Sisterhood: False Friends in a Teenage Magazine." In

K. Hall and M. Bucholtz (eds.), *Gender Articulated: Language and the Socially Constructed Self.* London: Routledge, pp. 143–65.

Terranova, Titziana. (2004) "Communication beyond Meaning: On the Cultural Politics of Information." *Social Text* 22 (3), pp. 51–73.

Thomas, Lynn. (1995) "In Love with Inspector Morse: Feminist Subculture and Quality Television." *Feminist Review* 51, pp. 1–25.

Thompson, John. (1994) "Social Theory and the Media." In David Crowley and David Mitchell (eds.), *Communication Theory Today.* Cambridge: Polity Press.

Thomson, John. (1995) *The Media and Modernity.* Cambridge: Polity Press.

Thornborrow, Joanna. (1997) "Having Their Say: The Functions of Stories in Talk Show Discourse." *Text* 17 (2), pp. 241–62.

Thorne, Barry, Cheris Kramarae, and Nancy Henley (eds.). (1983) *Language, Gender, and Society.* Rowley, Mass.: Newbury House.

Tolson, Andrew. (1976) "On the Semiotics of Working-Class Speech." *Working Papers in Cultural Studies,* Center for Contemporary Cultural Studies, University of Birmingham, vol. 9, pp. 199–204.

———. (1991) "Televised Chat and Synthetic Personality." In Paddy Scannell (ed.), *Broadcast Talk.* London: Sage, pp. 178–200.

———. (2001) "Talking about Talk: The Academic Debates." In Andrew Tolson (ed.), *Television Talk Shows: Discourse, Performance, Spectacle.* Mahwah, N.J.: Lawrence Erlbaum, pp. 7–30.

———. (2006) *Media Talk: Spoken Discourse on TV and Radio.* Edinburgh: Edinburgh University Press.

Toynbee, Polly. (1996) "This Week Column," *Radio Times,* May 11–17.

Van Zoonen, Lisbet. (1994) *Feminist Media Studies.* London: Sage.

Volosinov, Valentin. (1973) *Marxism and the Philosophy of Language.* New York: Seminar Press.

Walkerdine, Valerie. (1986) "Video Replay: Families, Films and Fantasy." In Victor Burgin, James Donald, and Cora Kaplan (eds.), *Formations of Fantasy.* London: Methuen, pp. 167–99.

Weedon, Chris, Andrew Tolson, and Frank Mort. (1980a) "Introduction to Language Studies at the Centre." In Stuart Hall et al. (eds.), *Culture, Media, Language.* London: Routledge, pp. 177–85.

———. (1980b) "Theories of Language and Subjectivity." In Stuart Hall et al. (eds.), *Culture, Media, Language.* London: Routledge, pp. 195–216.

Wheatley, Helen. (2004) "The Limits of Television? Natural History Programming and the Transformation of Public Service Broadcasting." *European Journal of Cultural Studies* 7 (3), pp. 325–39.

———. (2006) *Gothic Television.* Manchester: Manchester University Press.

White, Mimi. (1992) *Tele-advising: Therapeutic Discourse in American Television.* Chapel Hill: University of North Carolina Press.

Williams, Raymond. (1974) *Television, Technology, and Cultural Form.* London: Fontana.

———. (1979) *Politics and Letters, Interviews with* New Left *Review.* London: New Left Books.

Willis, Paul et al. (1990) *Common Culture: Symbolic Work at Play in Everyday Cultures of the Young.* Milton Keynes, UK: Open University Press.

Wilson, Sherryl. (2003*) Oprah, Celebrity, and Formations of Self.* Basingstoke, UK: Palgrave.

Wood, Helen. (2001a) "'No, YOU rioted': The Pursuit of Conflict in Management Strategies on *Kilroy.*" In Andrew Tolson (ed.), *Television Talk Shows: Discourse, Performance, Spectacle.* Mahwah, N.J.: Lawrence Erlbaum, pp. 65–88.

———. (2001b) "Interacting with TV." PhD diss., Open University, UK.

———. (2005) "Texting the Subject: Women, Television, and Modern Self-Reflexivity." *Communication Review* 8 (2), pp. 115–35.

———. (2007) "The Mediated Conversational Floor: An Interactive Approach to Audience Reception." *Media, Culture & Society* 29 (1), pp. 75–103.

Wood, Helen, and Beverly Skeggs. (2004) "Notes on Ethical Scenarios of Self on British Reality TV." *Feminist Media Studies* 4 (2), pp. 205–8.

Woolfson, Charles. (1976) "The Semiotics of Working-Class Speech." In *Working Papers in Cultural Studies,* Center for Contemporary Cultural Studies, University of Birmingham, vol. 9, pp. 163–97.

Zimmerman, Don H., and Candace West. (1975) "Sex-roles, Interruptions, and Silences in Conversation." In Barry Thorne and Nancy Henley (eds.), *Language and Sex: Difference and Dominance.* Rowley, Mass.: Newbury House, pp. 105–29.

Index

HELEN WOOD is principal lecturer in media studies at De Monfort University, Leicester, England. She has recently coedited the working papers of the Birmingham Center for Contemporary Cultural Studies for Routledge and has also published a number of articles and book chapters on popular television and television reception.

Feminist Studies and Media Culture

University of Illinois Press
1325 South Oak Street
Champaign, IL 61820-6903
www.press.uillinois.edu